A HUNDRED MILLION DOLLARS A DAY

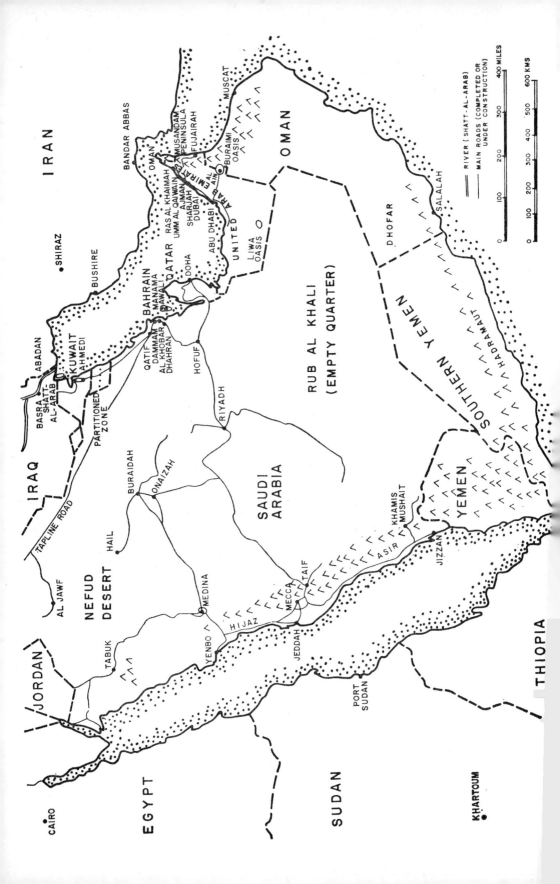

A
Hundred Million
Dollars a Day

$

MICHAEL FIELD

SIDGWICK & JACKSON
LONDON

First published in Great Britain by
Sidgwick and Jackson Limited in 1975

Copyright © 1975 Michael Field

ISBN 0 283 98210 1

Printed in Great Britain by
John Sherratt and Son, Park Road, Timperley, Altrincham,
Cheshire WA14 5QQ
for Sidgwick and Jackson Limited
1 Tavistock Chambers, Bloomsbury Way
London WC1A 2SG

Contents

List of Illustrations

Preface and Acknowledgements

This book is not about OPEC oil, but about OPEC money – petrodollars. In particular it is concerned with the money of four Arabian Peninsula oil producers, Saudi Arabia, Kuwait, Abu Dhabi and Qatar, which are now receiving far more revenues than they can spend and are commonly regarded as the 'surplus' OPEC states.

The surpluses of these four Arab countries in 1974 were not necessarily the biggest earned by OPEC members. In that year Iran generated a bigger surplus than any country bar Saudi Arabia, and Venezuela ran a bigger surplus than Abu Dhabi and Qatar. What puts the main Arabian Peninsula oil producers in a category on their own is the fact that they seem likely to continue to generate a surplus beyond 1980, when Iran and Venezuela and most of the other OPEC members will have returned to a position of equilibrium or deficit. So while the non-surplus states, with immediate development potential, can regard their present oil income solely as a source of capital for internal investment, which will enable them to live off their own industrial and agricultural output by the time their oil runs out, the surplus states are forced to regard a large part of their income as a 'national pension fund', which, once their oil is exhausted, will yield a cash income (or will be liquidated) to enable their incomplete development process to be continued.

It is this difference in attitude towards current income, as much as anything else, which distinguishes the two categories of OPEC states, and makes foreign investment one of the most important and conspicuous features of the Arabian Peninsula countries' economies.

The purpose of the analysis in this book of both private and government surplus capital in Saudi Arabia, Kuwait, Abu Dhabi and Qatar is to provide facts. The intention is to describe both the institutions which handle this money and the foreign investments of these states, in order that this 'evidence' can be used to make accurate

7

generalisations of a sort which were not always a feature of the comment on Arab investment current in 1974. It is also hoped that the material here will help to remove some of the suspicion of Arab money which has been so apparent in the West over the past fifteen months. To some degree at least the Europeans and Americans are now going to have to accept Arab investment institutions as part of their financial world. This book is designed to make this acceptance easier.

The period during which this book was being researched and written – from the autumn of 1972 to the end of 1974 – saw the most dramatic changes in Middle East oil and finance. These resulted in major pieces of research and even bits of text being scrapped or revised. The sheer speed of the changes also meant that it became impossible to bring all parts of the text up to date simultaneously when the book was finished in December 1974, and consequently there are considerable variations in the cut-off dates of different chapters.

The monetary chapters at the end of the book run up to Christmas 1974, and the early chapters on oil to October 1974; but most of the middle chapters are revised versions of text written at the end of 1973 or the first half of 1974, and parts of these chapters have remained virtually unchanged since the late summer of 1973. There have also been odd updates made in the first few months of 1975.

Given these difficulties, and the fact that I have tried to make this book as comprehensive and as wide-ranging as possible, there are bound to be mistakes and passages of incomplete and misleading material. For these I apologise – and I hope especially that they do not cause embarrassment either to any of the institutions concerned or to those personally involved with Arab money.

My thanks are due to some two hundred people, some of them mentioned in the text, who have given up their time to talk to me in the past two years or so. In particular I am most grateful to my agent, Patrick Seale, who thought of the original idea for this book – back in 1971; to Fuad Itayim, who allowed me to use the library of Middle East Economic Survey and backnumbers of his invaluable magazine; to five members of the staff of the *Financial Times*, Richard Johns, Adrian Hamilton, Anthony Harris, C. Gordon Tether and David Housego, whose articles provided an important source of ideas and enabled me to keep up to date with the subject; and, finally, to Sandy Johnstone Smith, the former Night Editor of the *Daily Sketch* and present landlord of the Blackboys Inn, who, over a pint of his excellent bitter one evening, thought up the title of this book.

1st April 1975.

Introduction

TWELVE DAYS
THAT CHANGED THE WORLD

The events which led up to the oil crisis in the winter of 1973/4 began to unfold during the weekend of 6 and 7 October. A few minutes after 2 p.m. on Saturday, the 6th, four divisions of the Egyptian second and third armies stormed across the Suez Canal, while on Israel's northern border seven hundred Syrian tanks, in parade ground formation, broke through the barbed wire of the cease-fire strip and advanced towards Kuneitra and Rafid.

Both attacks achieved almost total surprise, and within half an hour the east bank of Suez was festooned with the Egyptian flag – each unit having been issued with its own flag before the assault began.

But despite the show the Egyptians made of liberating their territory, President Sadat's purpose in launching the Fourth War was not to achieve a total military victory in Sinai, but to provoke an international crisis which would force the super powers to make Israel withdraw from all the territories occupied in 1967. A major part of this strategy involved the threat of the 'oil weapon' – and only three days after the outbreak of fighting the possibility of a cutback began to look very real. Following a long session of the Kuwait Council of Ministers on Tuesday came the ominous announcement that the Minister of Finance and Oil, Mr Abdel-Rahman Atiqi, had been instructed to contact his colleagues among the Arab producing states with a view to holding an emergency meeting to 'discuss the role of oil in the light of the Middle East conflict'.

*　　*　　*

By pure coincidence it happened that Saturday 6 October was also the day on which a group of oil company delegates, led by George

9

Piercy of Esso, began to assemble in Vienna for talks on new oil prices with OPEC – the Organization of Petroleum Exporting Countries. The states immediately concerned with the negotiations were just the six Gulf members of the Organization – Iran, Iraq, Kuwait, Saudi Arabia, Qatar and Abu Dhabi – but according to normal OPEC practice the changes agreed for this region would automatically be reflected in adjustments in other OPEC states in South America, Africa and South East Asia. The price issue was therefore a non-political matter, and was not confined to the Arabs.

The company delegates in Vienna were certainly aware that the increase to be demanded was substantial – and given the buoyant state of the free market for oil in Europe, they knew that their bargaining position would not be strong. However, when the two sides met in the OPEC offices, at number 10 Doktor Karl Lueger Ring, on Monday the 8th, the companies found that the producers' demands were far beyond anything which they could accept. Neither OPEC nor the companies released any figures, but it was believed that the Arabs and Iranians were thinking of a price increase per barrel (35 imperial gallons or 42 US gallons) of anything from fifty to a hundred per cent, while the companies were initially prepared to concede only twenty per cent.

On the evening of the next day, Tuesday, the company delegates submitted a revised offer – which was rejected as not reflecting true market conditions. It was intended that after an adjournment, during which both sides would reappraise their positions, there should be a third meeting at the end of the week – but at 1 a.m. on Friday morning George Piercy telephoned Shaikh Ahmed Zaki Yamani, the Saudi Minister of Petroleum and Mineral Resources, to say that the companies needed an extra fortnight. This short conversation marked the last time that OPEC and the western oil industry were to hold formal negotiations on prices.

Throughout the week the producers had been confident that it would not take long to reach agreement, and they were clearly disappointed not to have settled the new prices at the first attempt. Later on Friday after a further round of discussions among themselves, the six Gulf states announced that they were going to hold a meeting four days later 'to decide on a course of collective action to determine the true value of the crude oil they produce'.

*   *   *

So on 16 and 17 October both the price and political weapon issues came to a head in Kuwait. First the six Gulf members of OPEC met. As Yamani had suggested when he left Vienna, they quickly abandoned the idea of holding any more consultations with the companies, and at one o'clock in the morning of the 17th they announced that they were raising the price of their crude oil by some seventy per cent. Both the size of this increase, and the fact that it was made unilaterally were unprecedented. Saudi Arabian Light, the major Gulf export crude which is used as a 'marker' for all crudes in the area, rose from $3.01 per barrel to $5.11.

Immediately after this announcement, the Iranian delegation, anxious to disassociate itself from any politically motivated cutbacks which the Arabs might declare within the next twenty-four hours, boarded a flight back to Tehran.

A few hours later, at 11 a.m., representatives of ten Arab oil exporters (including several states which were not members of OPEC) went into session at the Kuwait Sheraton – a few yards from the Ministry of Finance and Oil. The political weapon issue being discussed was, of course, totally separate from pricing policy – but throughout the day a good deal of confusion reigned among the journalists reporting the meeting, and when, at 9.30 p.m., a communiqué was produced, there followed a further period of anxiety as the press tried to discover the details of the Arabs' decision.*

Only one copy of the statement was issued, and this was handwritten in Arabic – reflecting the somewhat militant mood of the delegates that day. At several points various important phrases had been lightly crossed out and others pencilled in, and after the communiqué had been put through the hotel copying machine for distribution to those few journalists who could read Arabic, the alterations did not show up clearly. Nor was it possible to obtain clarification from any of the ministers. In fact Shaikh Ahmed Zaki Yamani, who had been the main influence at the meeting, was on his way to Riyadh, the Saudi capital, in his private jet even before the communiqué was issued.

But although a number of mistakes found their way into Western newspapers the next day, the communiqué still emerged as an essentially moderate document. It began by pointing out that 'for the sake of world co-operation' and in the interests of the consumers, the Arab states were already making a sacrifice in producing more oil than was justified by their own economic requirements; and it went on

*This description of the meetings in Kuwait has been taken from *Insight on the Middle East War*, written by the Insight team of the *Sunday Times*, and published by André Deutsch.

to contrast this policy with the United States' support for Israel and its occupation of Arab territories. Then, towards the end of the communiqué, the ministers set down their decision: 'Because of all this, the Arab oil ministers . . . decided to start immediately reducing oil production by not less than five per cent per month from September levels. The same percentage will be applied in each month compared with the previous one until the Israeli withdrawal is completed from the whole Arab territories occupied in June 1967, and the legal rights of the Palestinian people are restored.'

The idea underlying the cutbacks was fairly simple. The Arabs recognized that their capacity for hurting the United States directly was limited – because at that time the U.S. depended on the Arabs for little more than ten per cent of its total requirements. So the theory was that if America's allies in Europe and Japan (which depended on Arab oil for roughly seventy-five per cent of their requirements) could be squeezed, they in turn would bring pressure to bear on Washington.

But in the days that followed the oil weapon became rather more sophisticated. One by one the Arab producers announced that they were placing a total embargo on shipments to the United States and the Netherlands, and, with reference to part of the original communiqué which stated that countries assisting the Arabs would receive oil as normal, they defined Britain and France as favoured nations. In addition to these measures the Arabs introduced three unspoken destination rules. They implied that they would not object to favoured nations sharing their Arab supplies with 'neutral' nations – like Germany and Italy; and that they would not retaliate if they found that the embargoed states were receiving additional supplies of Iranian or Nigerian crude at the expense of the favoured or neutral states. On the other hand they made it clear that any consumer country supplying Arab oil to the Netherlands or the United States would itself be embargoed.

The burden of implementing the embargoes and the favoured nation treatment was thus placed firmly on the shoulders of the consumer governments and the oil companies. Combined with the fact that neutral nations were invited to redefine their position with regard to the Arab-Israeli conflict, and be elected to the favoured status (as happened later to Belgium and Japan), this inevitably had a strongly divisive effect on the industrialized countries. Britain and France were understandably reluctant to share their supplies even within the confines of the destination rules (let alone make any attempt to defy the embargoes by instituting a formal oil sharing scheme); and when the companies adopted a policy of sharing Iranian and Nigerian crude in order to 'spread the misery' they received nearly as much public criticism in the favoured nations as was being heaped on the Arabs.

These divisions in the ranks of the consumers were only accentuated when the cuts turned out to be considerably bigger than the minimum agreed in Kuwait. Saudi Arabia reduced its production by an immediate ten per cent, and then by additional amounts in respect of its exports to the Netherlands and the United States; and, with the exception of Iraq, which agreed to the embargo policy but did not make any official reduction in its output, the other Arab states followed the Saudis' example. By the middle of November the exports of the two biggest Arab producers, Saudi Arabia and Kuwait, were down by between thirty and forty per cent.

The reaction among the consumer nations varied. In different countries Sunday motoring was banned, speed limits were lowered, oil companies were ordered to reduce deliveries to their customers, and campaigns were put in hand to encourage households to save electricity. No country remained unscathed, and all became very nervous when they contemplated the prospect of successive five per cent cuts continuing into 1975. At the same time, as a result of the price rise, virtually every western nation realized that it would be running an enormous balance of payments deficit, for the rest of the 1970s or longer.

*   *   *

The twelve days from 6 to 17 October 1973 not only marked the end of the era of cheap and plentiful energy, which the affluent consumers of Europe, America and Japan had come to take for granted in the years of unprecedented growth and prosperity which had followed the end of the Second World War: they changed the world.

Neither the price rise nor the production cuts should have been unexpected. OPEC had been saying that new market conditions justified a major rise in the price of crude oil since the end of the Organization's previous negotiations with the companies at the beginning of June. Similarly, King Faisal of Saudi Arabia (without whose co-operation the oil weapon could never have worked) had for several months been telling the world that he was reconsidering his old opinion that oil and politics did not mix, and had hinted that whether or not war broke out, he was thinking either of freezing production or imposing some limits on the growth of output.

The statements of both King Faisal and the OPEC ministers were widely reported in the Western press, but relatively few people took the warnings seriously, and even fewer bothered to work out their long term significance. Everyone was assuming that the domination of the world by the industrial powers of the northern hemisphere would continue indefinitely – and neither governments nor corporations took into account in their economic planning, the likelihood of a radical change in the oil situation.

So when the producers exploited their latent power the West was taken by surprise. The cutbacks and embargoes turned out to be relatively short-lived, but the rise in the price of oil was followed on 23 December by another massive increase. In response to the upsurge in free-market prices caused by the cutbacks, the Gulf members met in Tehran and raised their prices by a further 120 per cent. This took the Saudi Arabian Light 'marker' crude from $5.11 to $11.65.

The price increases were (or in late 1974 appeared to be) permanent, and, because of the horrifying disequilibrium they caused in the world's payments system, they brought with them the possibility of a worldwide recession and unemployment on a scale not seen since the 1930s. This alarming outlook was accompanied in 1974 by further causes for anxiety, including: the universal collapse of stock exchange prices; the dramatic fall in the price of base metals and the equally dramatic explosion in the price of soft commodities like wheat, maize and sugar; the succession of huge exchange losses and failures in the banking sector – which gave rise to speculation about a world-wide financial collapse such as that triggered off by the failure of Austria's Creditanstalt Bank in 1931; and the prospect of inflation getting completely out of hand and culminating in a 'Global Weimar'.

It was with reference to these problems that the United Nations Secretary General, Dr Kurt Waldheim, in his address to the General Assembly in August 1974, spoke of the 'note of helplessness and fatalism' creeping into world affairs.

To a considerable extent the problems are inter-related, and they are especially bound up with the oil price issue – either as causes or effects (or both). Together they have forced the industrial powers, and the rest of the world, to begin a fundamental reappraisal of such crucial matters as: the future of economic growth and the prospects for a continued rise in standards of living; the necessity for conservation and diversification of energy sources; the future distribution of economic power and the location of the world's new industrial capacity; and the reform of the international payments system.

But if it is possible to isolate two of the problems, and to classify them as being more serious than the rest, then they are those of inflation and the chaotic state of the payments system caused by the oil price increases. Both of these could lead to an appalling international depression.

Whether or not the second problem will lead to a depression will depend in large measure on the way in which the vast surpluses of the oil producers are used. They have the capacity to wreck the monetary and banking systems, or to bring about a regeneration of the world economy by stimulating faster economic growth in countries which have so far remained underdeveloped. It is the biggest of these surpluses – those belonging to the countries of the Arabian Peninsula – which form the subject of this book.

1

THE ARRIVAL OF OPEC

The two massive price increases in 1973 were the culmination of a dramatic shift of bargaining power from the consumers to the producers of oil which had begun three years earlier in the summer of 1970. During this short period, which was marked by a succession of price adjustments and a string of takeovers of the local operations of western companies, the old order in the Middle Eastern oil industry had been swept away. In the West this revolution was seen, naturally, as an outright disaster, and in the OPEC states it was viewed as the triumphant conclusion of a twenty-year struggle for a fair return on a diminishing natural resource. To understand how this revolution came about, and to appreciate the producers' attitude towards the change, it is necessary to go back to the beginning.

The first concession in the Gulf area was granted in 1901 by the Iranian government to a wealthy Australian prospector named William Knox D'Arcy. After a number of dry holes and an acute financial crisis, oil was finally discovered in 1908 at Masjid-i-Sulaiman, and in 1912 the Anglo-Persian Oil Company,* which had been formed under British-government sponsorship to operate the concession, began to export the oil through the port of Abadan.

During the years between the two World Wars further concessions were granted in Iraq and in the states of the Arabian Peninsula – and the operating groups in every case were made up chiefly by members of the seven major oil companies which have dominated the world oil business throughout this century. In approximate order

---

*The Anglo-Persian Oil Company was renamed the Anglo-Iranian Oil Company in 1935, and British Petroleum in 1954.

B

of size these are Standard Oil of New Jersey,* Royal Dutch-Shell, Texaco, Standard Oil of California (Socal), Mobil, Gulf and British Petroleum. The only other company to participate in these early days was Compagnie Française des Pétroles (CFP or Total), which is considerably smaller than the big seven, but is often regarded as an eighth major because of the world-wide spread of its operations.

In Iraq the concessionaire was the Iraq Petroleum Company group, which was composed of IPC itself, the Mosul Petroleum Company in the north of the country, and the Basrah Petroleum Company in the south. These companies were owned five per cent by Calouste Gulbenkian, and in 23¾ per cent blocks by British Petroleum, Shell, CFP and a partnership of Mobil and Standard Oil of New Jersey. Subsequently the IPC group obtained two on-shore concessions in the south of the Gulf, which it operated through the Qatar Petroleum Company and the Abu Dhabi Petroleum Company.

In Kuwait the onshore acreage went to a fifty-fifty partnership of British Petroleum and Gulf, who formed the Kuwait Oil Company; and in Saudi Arabia the Eastern Province and large areas offshore were awarded to the Arabian American Oil Company (Aramco), owned by Standard Oil of New Jersey, Standard Oil of California, and Texaco with thirty per cent each, and by Mobil with ten per cent.

These three groups, IPC, KOC and Aramco, together with two offshore operators – Shell Qatar and Abu Dhabi Marine Areas (two-thirds British Petroleum and one-third CFP) – retained control of the main concessions in all the bigger Arab states of the Gulf area until the early 1970s.

Under the original terms of their concessions the companies were given exclusive rights for drilling, extraction, and the building of pipelines, the ownership of all oil produced from the time it reached the well-head, and immunity from taxes and customs dues. The host governments had no control over the amount of drilling carried out nor the volume of exports, and in the concession areas the companies appropriated for themselves a quasi-colonial authority. The governments' receipts, apart from an initial down payment and a rental, came in the form of a fixed royalty of about twenty cents a barrel. The price of crude in those days was a purely company matter and had no bearing on government revenues.

*Standard Oil of New Jersey changed its name to the Exxon Corporation in 1972. Its products are marketed under a variety of names, the most common of which is Esso.

Except in Iran, payments made to Middle Eastern governments during the 1930s were negligible. In 1938 exports from the Gulf area averaged only 320,000 barrels a day – of which 200,000 b/d came from Iran, rather under 100,000 b/d from Iraq, 20,000 b/d from Bahrain (where Texaco and Socal held a concession through the Bahrain Petroleum Company), and the rest, a minute quantity, from Saudi Arabia. In contrast to these small figures the United States in the same year produced about 3.5 million b/d, or just over sixty per cent of total world output, while Venezuela produced about 600,000 b/d.

In the years after the Second World War, however, the United States rapidly swung round from being a major exporter to being a small net importer, and, to meet European demand, the companies undertook a big expansion of their Middle Eastern production. Compared with U.S. operations the cost of bringing Gulf crude on stream was very low, and in order that this oil should compete with Texan and Venezuelan crude in Europe and on the United States east coast, the companies, under pressure from Washington, gradually lowered the f.o.b. prices quoted in the Gulf from a level of parity with Texas at the beginning of 1948 (when Saudi Arabian Light stood at $2.68) to $1.75 in June 1949. At this figure the landed cost of Gulf crude in New York – composed of $1.75 f.o.b. price, $1.11 freight and $0.11 import duty – was more or less equal to the landed costs of Texan crude ($2.68 f.o.b. price and $0.24 freight) and Venezuelan crude ($2.55 f.o.b. price, $0.24 freight and $0.11 import duty).*

These developments were of only academic interest to the Middle Eastern governments until 1950, when the Venezuelans, who have traditionally been ahead of the Arabs and Iranians with innovations in company/government relations, sent a delegation to the Gulf to explain the advantages of the fifty-fifty profit split they had legislated into being in 1948. Under the new system, introduced in Saudi Arabia at the end of 1950 and in Iraq and Kuwait a few months later, the producers took a posted or tax reference price (which at that time was the normal f.o.b. price – $1.75 – at which the operating company would sell to third parties at the loading terminal), deducted the production cost (which in the Gulf comes to about ten

*The details of oil prices in the 1940s and 1950s in these paragraphs have been taken from *A History of OPEC* written by Fuad Rouhani and published by Praeger. Other information in this chapter has been drawn from *The Community of Oil Exporting Countries* written by Zuhayr Mikdashi and published by George Allen and Unwin.

cents, and represents salaries and supplies for the operator), and taxed the remainder (representing the company's profit) at fifty per cent. Assuming that no special discounts off the posted price were given, this arrangement increased the producers' revenue or 'take' per barrel from about $0.20 to $0.82.

At this point, therefore, the producer governments became price conscious, and in retrospect they did not fail to notice that the adjustments of the late 1940s had been to their considerable disadvantage.

In one state, however, the change in concession terms did not proceed amicably. A long series of disputes between Iran and its concessionnaire culminated in 1951, when the government, under the effective leadership of Dr Mossadeq, nationalized the Anglo-Iranian Oil Company. Together the major companies immediately organized an embargo of Iranian production, and during the next two years only two small tankers (one Italian and one Japanese) loaded at Abadan. Iran was virtually bankrupted. In 1953 Mossadeq was overthrown, and the government was forced to back down and grant a lease (which was a concession in all but name) to a new multi-national group of companies – Iranian Oil Participants. This group, generally known as the Consortium, was composed of British Petroleum (forty per cent), Shell (fourteen per cent), the five American majors (seven per cent each), CFP (six per cent) and a number of smaller American 'independent' companies (five per cent).

The Mossadeq débâcle provided a reminder of the strength of the majors, and although in 1961 the revolutionary Iraqi government of General Kassem expropriated more than $99\frac{1}{2}$ per cent of the IPC group's concession, on the grounds that this area was not being exploited by the companies, no government in Iran nor any Arab state again nationalized a productive operation until 1971.

This did not mean that the companies were entirely popular in the Arab states. Apart from resentment of the almost sovereign power they enjoyed, the main complaints were that the concessions were too large in area and their duration too long, that they were run almost entirely by foreign nationals, and that despite the obligation of the concessionnaires to act in the interests of the host country, it had generally been found that when a conflict of interest had arisen between the concessionnaire's host and its parent state, the company had sided with the latter.

Furthermore, while this resentment was gathering force in the early 1950s, it was found that the fifty-fifty profit split was not quite as good as it seemed. When computing their tax liability the companies were always able to press the producers into giving them discounts off the posted price – like the marketing allowance (which was hardly justified when almost all production was sold to affiliates of the operator or to third parties under long-term contracts) and volume discounts. In fact Abdullah Tariki, the radical Saudi Oil Minister during the 1950s, calculated soon after fifty-fifty came into force that the effective split of profits was 32/68 in favour of the companies.

Worse still, the price discrepancy between Texan, Venezuelan and Gulf crudes in the 1950s continued to expand. In 1953 twenty-five cents was added to the price of Texan and Venezuelan crudes, while Gulf crudes went up by only twenty-two cents, and two years later the Venezuelan price was reduced by twenty-five cents. These adjustments destroyed the principle of equalization at New York, and ushered in a new era in which the price of Gulf crudes was to be determined by the supply and demand position in Europe rather than in America – which directly or indirectly had been the basis for all quotations for Gulf crudes since 1929.

In these new circumstances the growing availability of production capacity in the Middle East, and increasing competition in the European market, led the companies to start giving their own discounts off the posted price for sales to third parties. It was at this stage that posted (or tax reference) prices, and the f.o.b. (or market) prices in the Gulf began to part company. Given that the fifty-fifty profit split was still worked out on the basis of the posting, this meant that the producer governments' effective share of profits began to climb back towards the fifty per cent it was always supposed to have been.

Then in 1957, after the closure of the Suez Canal, all prices were put up – and although in the Middle East the increase was smaller than in Texas and Venezuela, the new price of $2.12 represented the highest posting for Saudi Arabian Light since 1948. These levels were maintained until February 1959, when there was a general reduction in which Gulf crudes fell more than the others. Two months later the Venezuelan price was lowered again, and in August 1960 the Gulf price was reduced without any parallel reduction being made elsewhere. Thus the discrepancy between Gulf and Texan crude had expanded from zero in 1948 (when both crudes were priced at $2.68) to $1.16 in 1960 – when Texan crude stood at $3.00 and the Saudi Arabian Light posting at $1.84.

From the point of view of the producers the posted price cuts of 1959 and 1960 were very damaging. The governments in the Middle Eastern capitals and Caracas were never consulted about the changes, and they were angered by a system where the size of their budgets, their domestic prosperity (and, indirectly, political stability), their development prospects – in fact the whole future of their nations – could be determined by decisions taken in oil company headquarters thousands of miles away in Europe and America.

Inevitably it was a major part of producer government policy to change this situation. For ten years there had been regular but informal exchanges of information and ideas among the exporters – the obvious example being the Venezuelans' decision to send a delegation to the Gulf to explain the fifty-fifty profit split. At the same time the Arab League, ever since its creation in 1945, had entertained the idea of creating a petroleum association of Arab countries – but to be effective it was realized that the association would have to include non-Arab members.

It was the general reduction of prices in 1959 that brought these ideas to fruition, when, in April, the First Arab Petroleum Congress met in Cairo, and invited Iranian and Venezuelan representatives as observers. In the conference room itself only matters affecting Arab countries (the formation of national oil companies, for instance) were discussed. The more important business took place in the lobby where the Saudi and Venezuelan Ministers, Abdullah Tariki and Perez Alfonso, sponsored the formation of an Oil Consultation Commission.

Then in September 1960, a month after the further reduction of Middle Eastern prices, the oil ministers of Iran, Iraq, Saudi Arabia, Kuwait and Venezuela met in an atmosphere of crisis in Baghdad. The Oil Consultation Commission was already defunct, having run into opposition from Iran and Iraq who objected to the inclusion of Egypt, and the ministers decided to create a permanent and stronger institution. The body that emerged was OPEC – the Organization of Petroleum Exporting Countries. Since OPEC's formation the original five members have been joined by Qatar in 1961, Libya and Indonesia in 1962, Abu Dhabi in 1967, Algeria in 1969, Nigeria in 1971, Ecuador in 1973 and Gabon (as an associate member) in 1974.

*   *   *

At first the majors ignored OPEC. As required by a resolution passed at the Organization's fourth conference in June 1962 the members addressed protests to the companies against the price reduction of August 1960, and demanded that prices be restored to their previous level. The companies refused to enter into any collective negotiations, on the grounds that such action would be likely to breach the U.S. anti-trust laws, but, when each operating group replied to its host individually, their answers were identical. They argued that the development of prices did not depend on their own will, but was determined by economic factors over which they had no control; and they added that these factors had in fact necessitated a reduction greater than that effected in 1960. In support of their case they pointed out that even at the new reduced prices they were still obliged to give discounts to independent purchasers because market prices were still lower than the postings.

OPEC realized that the only way to achieve a restoration of posted prices would be to force up market prices, and this the producers decided would best be done by limiting the annual growth in their output. So over two years (from mid-1965 to mid-1967) the members, who now included Qatar, Indonesia and Libya among their number, worked out a joint production programme. In both years they over-estimated the overall growth in demand for OPEC oil, which meant that the actual growth in production turned out to be lower than the planned increments, and at the same time certain members, notably Libya and Saudi Arabia, and, to a lesser extent, Iran, made no effort to keep within their quotas. The obvious conclusion was that in a period when prices were low enough to cause a tight budgetry condition in some states, those countries which were either new exporters and/or had big oil reserves and expensive development programmes, would not be willing to make a temporary sacrifice and await an improvement in the value of their production, but would be tempted to increase revenues by maximizing the volume of their output.

However, OPEC did manage to increase its members' effective share of profits during the 1960s, and this it achieved in two ways. First in 1963 the companies accepted a big cut in the marketing allowance, which they were able to deduct as an expense before making the fifty-fifty split, and, secondly, and much more important, the Organization negotiated two agreements on the expensing of royalties.

These agreements the Middle Eastern members saw as removing an anomaly in their fiscal arrangements, and as bringing their taxes into line with the system prevailing in Venezuela. Although the producers' revenues had always nominally been made up of a royalty of $12\frac{1}{2}$ per cent of the posted price (as payment for the oil itself), and income tax (representing the fifty per cent tax on the profits from the sale of this oil), payments made under the heading of royalties had, since the introduction of fifty-fifty, been totally deducted from income tax, and, the Arabs and Iranians claimed, might just as well never have existed. The producers, referring to the normal internationally accepted arrangements, under which the royalty payer was entitled to deduct the royalty only from his gross income when computing his tax liability, wanted royalties to be treated as an expense in their own countries also – and in 1964 this was what was agreed.

As part of a package deal the companies received various further discounts off the posted price. These discounts were set to be reduced each year (this process being considerably accelerated by the second round of negotiations in 1968), but in essence the new system worked as follows: the companies would deduct the production cost, the $12\frac{1}{2}$ per cent royalty, and whatever discount was applicable, from the posted price, then split the remainder fifty-fifty, and then add the royalty on to the governments' share.

The agreements on royalty expensing and the marketing allowance raised the producer governments' take per barrel by about eight cents – in the case of Saudi Arabian Light from $0.84 at the end of 1960 to about $0.92 in 1968. This represented a fairly significant improvement in financial terms, and it proved the advantages of being able to negotiate on a collective basis through OPEC.

But during the 1960s as a whole developments were taking place in the oil industry which were to be of much greater significance to the producer governments than the royalty expensing agreements.

In 1957 oil had been found in Libya. Unlike the big producing areas in the Gulf, not all Libyan acreage had originally been awarded to just one group; and as the concessions were evaluated and brought on stream during the 1960s, it became clear that although Esso, Shell, Texaco, Socal, Mobil and British Petroleum all held productive reservoirs, some of the largest oil fields lay beneath acreage held by 'independent' American companies. These were Occidental, which held a concession on its own, and Amerada Hess, Continental (Conoco) and Marathon, which were combined in the Oasis group with Shell. Compared with the majors the independents were small companies (though by any normal standards they would rank as giants) – and they were new to the oil business outside north America.

Throughout the 1960s Libyan crude remained relatively cheap. Until December 1965 the companies made their profit split on the basis of realized (market) prices, and not posted prices, and although both of these prices were slightly higher (on account of Libya's geographical position) than those obtaining for similar crudes in the Gulf, the short haul Libyan production could still be landed in Europe at a price significantly below that of Gulf crude.

This led to a very rapid expansion of output. Between 1962 and 1970 Libyan production grew from 20,000 barrels a day to 3.3 million b/d, while output in all the Middle Eastern states combined grew from 5.6 million b/d to 13.8 million b/d.* With access to these large volumes of cheap crude, the independents were able to break into the European market (as Conoco, for instance, entered Britain through a chain of cheap petrol stations called Jet) and initiate a price cutting war which was to last until the end of the decade.

The new competition led to a further erosion of market prices in the Gulf, and because the existence of OPEC prevented a lowering of postings, the major companies' margins were squeezed. In fact the net earnings per barrel on the seven majors' eastern hemisphere operations dropped from sixty cents in 1958 to thirty-three cents in 1970. Meanwhile the effective profit split in the Gulf by the end of the decade had climbed to something in the region of 70/30 in favour of the producer governments.

Although it was not particularly apparent at the time, in retrospect it is evident that during the 1960s there was a weakening of the majors, and a loosening of the oil industry's control over prices – while the appearance of the independents in Libya introduced a weak link into the companies' ranks which was shortly to have momentous consequences.

* * *

The collapse of the established order in the Middle Eastern oil industry came very suddenly. It began on 3 May 1970 when a Syrian bulldozer engaged in a cable-laying project broke Tapline, the pipe carrying Saudi crude from Dhahran, the Aramco town in the Eastern Province, to Sidon on the Mediterranean coast. Repairs could have been completed in twelve hours, but the Syrians, demanding higher transit dues, refused to allow work to begin, and so deprived the oil industry of half a million barrels a day of short haul crude. Tapline was to stay closed for nine months, until a coup d'état in Damascus brought to power President Assad, whose government quickly negotiated a big increase in dues plus a lump sum of $9 million for damage caused by the oil spill.

At the time Tapline was broken the new revolutionary Libyan regime of Colonel Qadhafi, who had ousted King Idris in September

*To put these figures into perspective the oil consumption of the big industrial powers in 1970 was: U.S.A. 14.3 million b/d, Canada 1.5 m b/d, Japan 4.0 m b/d, Britain 2.1 m b/d, France 1.9 m b/d, Germany 2.7 m b/d, Italy 1.7 m b/d.

1969, had for four months been negotiating for higher prices to take account of the full freight advantage its concessionnaires enjoyed, and to bring the price of its crude in Europe into line with the European price of Gulf crudes. In June and August the Revolutionary Command Council stepped up its pressure on the companies by enforcing production cut-backs – beginning, in what became the classic Libyan style, with the most vulnerable independent, Occidental, which derived nearly a third of its earnings from its Libyan venture.

By the beginning of September the oil industry had lost a total of one and a quarter million barrels a day of short haul crude – and because making up Mediterranean losses with crude brought round the Cape from the Gulf required six tankers for every one used before, freight rates soared. The Worldscale in which these rates are expressed went from W95 at the beginning of May to W261 at the beginning of September; in money terms this meant that the cost of transporting a barrel of crude from the Gulf to Europe rose from $1.10 to $3.00.

Winter was drawing close, demand in Europe was higher than expected, and one by one the companies in Libya surrendered – led, naturally, by Occidental, and followed by the other independents in the Oasis group, Amerada Hess, Conoco and Marathon. The majors held out a bit longer, but eventually the Socal/Texaco partnership, Amoseas, broke ranks, and then Esso and Mobil and, finally, Shell gave in too. The Libyans got a price rise of thirty cents a barrel, and their tax rates raised from fifty per cent to amounts varying from fifty-four to fifty-eight per cent in lieu of the government's demand for retroactive payments.

These changes did rather more than take account of the Libyan crudes' freight advantage, and so the Gulf members of OPEC immediately demanded better prices themselves, and the companies promptly agreed to pay nine cents more on heavy crudes* and a higher tax rate of fifty-five per cent. Venezuela characteristically wasted no time in discussions and by legislation raised its tax rate to sixty per cent.

Then in December 1970, at OPEC's twenty-first conference in

---

*The posted prices of different crudes vary according to the oil's specific gravity, which is normally expressed in degrees API (American Petroleum Institute). Higher API numbers denote lighter crudes which yield a higher proportion of light products – gasoline and kerosene – and fetch a higher price. The more important Gulf crudes vary from 27° API for Arabian Heavy to 40° API for Qatar Dukan. Arabian Light, the 'marker', is 34° API. North African crudes are very light – mostly 40° API in Libya, and up to 44° API in Algeria.

Caracas, it was decided that the Gulf members should seek a further round of increases. The companies and governments of the West reacted forcefully. Several times in January ministers of the main oil consuming states met in Washington and Paris; and the oil industry, benefiting from the United States Justice Department opinion that the American companies in binding together to face OPEC would not violate the anti-trust laws, formed itself into a united front combining majors, independents and European national companies, like Petrofina of Belgium and ERAP of France.

On 12 January 1971 an oil company delegation led by Lord Strathalmond of British Petroleum met Jamshid Amuzegar, then the Iranian Finance Minister, Saadoun Hammadi, the Iraqi Minister of Oil and Minerals, and Shaikh Ahmed Zaki Yamani, the Saudi Minister of Petroleum and Mineral Resources, in Tehran. The negotiations that followed were dramatic – with scores of journalists in Tehran keeping the talks in the western newspaper headlines and prominent in the television news programmes for week after week.

On 16 January the company delegation presented proposals agreeing in principle to an upwards revision of prices, but insisting that the negotiations should cover all OPEC members so as to avoid the leap-frogging of the past few months. The companies lost this point, and on 19 January the OPEC negotiators produced their demands – a price increase for Gulf crudes of forty-five cents on a barrel of 40° API crude, and larger amounts for heavier oils. The companies countered with an offer of nine cents, and then came up with sixteen cents, while the OPEC negotiators on 2 February quoted thirty cents as their rock bottom demand.

The next day OPEC held an extraordinary conference in Tehran, and all members resolved to stop their concessionnaires' exports if the companies did not respond to their minimum demands by 15 February. With one day to go before the deadline the companies gave in, and, in addition to the immediate rise of thirty-three to forty cents (depending on the type of crude) and the removal of all remaining discounts and allowances, it was agreed that postings would increase by five cents in respect of escalation (rising demand for oil) and by two and a half per cent in respect of inflation on 1 June 1971, and by the same amount on 1 January 1973, 1974 and 1975. The price of Saudi Arabian Light rose to $2.18 in February 1971, compared with $1.84 after the August 1960 reduction, and the government take increased from $0.93 at the beginning of 1970 to $1.26. The new take was about thirty per cent above the take prevailing in 1958 – when at $2.12 the posting was higher than at any other time during the 1950s or 1960s. But, if allowance is made for inflation, the take resulting from Tehran cannot have been much more than five per cent higher than that obtaining thirteen years earlier.

For their part the six Gulf countries represented at Tehran guaranteed that there would be no further claims until after 31 December 1975, no embargoes, and no leap-frogging should the Mediterranean producers conclude better terms.

As it turned out the Libyans, and later the Iraqis and Saudis, who negotiated separately for that part of their production which was shipped from Mediterranean terminals, improved considerably on the Tehran increases. On 2 April an agreement signed in Tripoli gave a posted price rise of ninety cents, and stabilized the Libyan tax rate at fifty-five per cent.

2

A SELLERS' PARADISE

In the weeks that followed the Tehran and Tripoli Agreements the morale of the companies and the consumer governments underwent a revival. It was clear to everybody that the oil industry was not going to return to the conditions of the 1960s, but at least it was felt that a new equilibrium had been established between the companies and the producers, and that a few years of stability could be expected. The extra taxes were promptly passed on to the European motorist, freight rates fell to an all-time low, the *Financial Times* oil share index rose forty points in only two months, and the city pages of the newspapers predicted the companies' return to prosperity. The popular theme was that although the price had been high, it had been worth paying.

But everybody was disastrously wrong. The years 1970 and 1971 saw a fundamental shift from a buyers' to a sellers' market in oil, and in these conditions the producers were able to see that nothing stood in the way of their making further demands. Some of the demands represented old ambitions formulated by OPEC in the 1960s, and others arose in response to specific or general developments in world economic conditions during the period 1971–74. But, whatever the origins of the ensuing upheaval, the hoped-for stability lasted for exactly 136 days after the Tripoli Agreement – and then for three years not a day passed when there was not some major issue pending or being negotiated, either by all the producers acting under the OPEC umbrella, or by individual states or regional groups.

After Tehran and Tripoli the first two price increases, which together amounted to some twenty per cent, resulted from the devaluations of the dollar in December 1971 and February 1973. With the exception of Saudi Arabia, which was paid twenty per cent

29

in sterling and eighty per cent in dollars, the Gulf producers received all of their revenues in sterling. On the basis of dollar posted price calculations this meant that the devaluations were liable to lead to a substantial cut in the size of their revenue cheques – although in practice, in the weeks between the devaluations and the subsequent compensation agreements, the companies continued to make the dollar/sterling conversion at the old rate.

Both of these increases were regarded by the producers as minor modifications of Tehran to deal with circumstances which had not been foreseen in February 1971; but as early as the second dollar agreement, signed in Geneva on 1 June 1973, members of the OPEC delegations were beginning to talk of a wholesale revision of the Tehran settlement.

It was being pointed out that the two and a half per cent inflation increment built into the Tehran Agreement was not keeping pace with the increasing cost of OPEC members' imports from the industrialized countries; and, more fundamentally, the producers were beginning to argue that the bids being made for the small amounts of crude that they were selling on the open market themselves, and the buoyant state of the oil market in Rotterdam, showed that the whole set of prices negotiated at Tehran had become out of date. They suggested that because the cost of their oil to their concessionnaires, and their own taxes and royalties were still based on modified 1971 prices, the companies were making excessive profits on any crude resold on the free market, while they themselves were largely excluded from sharing in the boom. Indeed their percentage share of profits was lower than it had been before Tehran. A few weeks later these arguments were summed up in public, when Yamani announced: 'The Tehran Agreement is dead or dying, and is in need of extensive revision.'

Yamani's comments were followed by the unsuccessful negotiations in Vienna at the beginning of October (described in the Introduction), and these led to the oil ministers of the Gulf members of OPEC meeting in Kuwait on 16 October and raising the Saudi Arabian Light marker crude posting from $3.01 to $5.11. This increase represented a much more fundamental break with the past than the Tehran Agreement. It established the principle of the producers setting their prices unilaterally (as the companies used to do before the formation of OPEC), and to some extent it enabled them to determine their own profit share. As such the October 1973 price increase can be seen as the logical conclusion of all the producers' efforts over the previous twenty years.

At the same time as the ministers announced their decision in Kuwait they stated that in future their posted prices would be set at about forty per cent above prevailing market prices (which should have given them a profit share of eighty-five per cent) – but in the months that followed it became clear that the difficulties involved in determining what was the true market price would make this formula impracticable. The inevitable result of the Arab production cutbacks, announced the day after the price rise, was that market prices soared – to a point in December when a batch of crude sold by the Iranian government was auctioned for the staggering sum of $17.40 a barrel. In these conditions the OPEC Economic Commission's search for a figure which it could recommend to its ministers when they met in December for the agreed quarterly revision of prices became impossible; and the views of a company delegation, which suggested that no change should be made until the market had become more stable, were brushed aside.

So when the OPEC ministers reassembled on 22 December at Tehran (which was chosen specifically so that the price issue could be disassociated from the Arab production cuts) there were major differences in policy. At one extreme Yamani, acting on the instructions of King Faisal, argued for a relatively modest rise which would have increased the marker crude posting from $5.11 to $7.50; and at the other extreme the Shah of Iran, taking advantage of the chaos caused by the cutbacks, suggested a price of $14. According to reports on the meeting which emerged during the following weeks, the Shah was able to steamroller the conference into accepting his views, and the Saudis were forced to agree to an unfavourable compromise of $11.65. This increase brought the government take up to exactly $7 a barrel – compared with $0.93 in 1970, $1.26 after the Tehran Agreement, $1.76 in September 1973, and $3.04 in October. In a speech on 23 December, just after the new price had been announced, the Shah stated that a $7 take corresponded to the minimum cost of extracting oil from shale or coal, which, he claimed, represented the only realistic long-term basis on which to price Gulf crude. In view of the fact that the Iranians had earlier been arguing for a take of $10, this claim must be regarded as something of an *ex post facto* justification.

*   *   *

The arrival of the seven dollar a barrel revenue did not mark the end of the growth in government take. In 1974 there were no formal price increases – in fact throughout the year Saudi Arabia was exerting pressure for a reduction. But there was a steady increase in take (which with the production cost makes up the cost of crude to the consumer) as a result of changes in the ownership of production operations.

These began with an issue called 'Participation' which involved the producer governments buying a share in their concessionnaire companies, and gaining a direct say in such matters as the relinquishment of concession acreage, the employment of nationals, production rates, and investment in new capacity. Apart from being satisfactory on nationalist grounds – because no state enjoys having foreign companies controlling its major source of income – the idea behind participation was that it would give the producers a foothold in the oil industry, which would later enable them to mount their own crude-oil sales operations, or expand their national companies downstream into the tankering, refining and marketing business.

These ideas had first been put by Saudi Arabia to Aramco in 1964, and they had been endorsed by OPEC's Declaratory Statement of Petroleum Policy in 1968; but the producers did not feel strong enough to call the companies to discuss the issue until after the Tehran Agreement, when they met for OPEC's twenty-fourth conference in Vienna in July 1971. Six months later negotiations on participation got under way with Yamani representing Saudi Arabia, Kuwait, Abu Dhabi, Qatar and (in the early stages) Iraq. In March 1972 the companies accepted the idea in principle, and in October, after more detailed discussions on compensation formulas and the disposal of the governments' production share, the General Agreement on Participation was announced in New York. This gave the producers a twenty-five per cent share of operations from 1 January 1973, and contained provisions for the shareholding to increase in stages to fifty-one per cent at the beginning of 1982. Under a more complex arrangement the producers agreed to sell back to the companies most of their production share at a price roughly mid-way between the tax paid cost (i.e. the take plus the production cost) and the posting, while the remainder they were to sell on the open market for whatever price they could get. This share of crude was very small – only two and a half per cent of total output in 1973 rising to seven and a half per cent in 1976.

Like a number of other agreements concluded by the producers and the companies in the three years after 1971, the General Agreement on Participation was no sooner signed than it began to become obsolete.

In February 1971 Algeria had seized fifty-one per cent of its French concessionnaires, CFP and ERAP, and although the two companies had immediately sponsored a highly effective embargo of their nationalized production, the takeover had eventually been accepted. In December that year Libya had nationalized all British Petroleum's operations on its territory; and at the beginning of June 1972 Iraq had nationalized IPC. In Libya's case an embargo was still in force in 1974, but with the Iraqi takeover IPC had decided to take no action pending a settlement of its dispute through the mediation of Nadim Pachachi, who was retiring from the post of OPEC Secretary General at the end of that year.

The success of these measures prompted the Kuwait National Assembly (which held a well established reputation as an obstructor of government oil policy) to reject the Participation agreement, and demand that all the Kuwait Oil Company's assets be nationalized. This sentiment was only reinforced by the Iranian takeover of the Consortium's operations in May 1973, and by Libya's seizure of fifty-one per cent of all the bigger operators on its territory in August and September; and so the Kuwait government was forced to reopen negotiations with KOC with a view to obtaining a majority stake. This it got in May 1974, when British Petroleum and Gulf agreed to the state share being raised to sixty per cent.

The fact that Kuwait was renegotiating made it politically impossible for Saudi Arabia and the lower Gulf states not to follow suit. During the summer of 1974 sixty per cent takeovers were announced in Qatar, Abu Dhabi and Bahrain, while Saudi Arabia took the same stake only as an interim measure, in the meantime negotiating a radically new arrangement which would give it a hundred per cent of production operations, and would leave Aramco as a contractor and major buyer. By October 1974 the Saudi-Aramco deal had not yet been finalized, but it seemed inevitable that the new arrangement would be copied in all the other Gulf producers.

The mushrooming growth of 'Participation' in 1971–74 was serious in itself for the majors, because it undermined one of the foundations of their power – namely their ownership or control of huge assets at all stages of the industry: production, tankering, refining and marketing. But participation, in giving the Middle-Eastern countries their own share of production, also had a direct effect on the level of government take, and therefore on the cost of oil to the consumers.

In 1973, when the amount of crude in government hands was fairly small, this effect was not noticeable, but in the summer of

C

1974, as the government share expanded to sixty per cent, the increase in state revenues per barrel (illustrated below, using the Saudi marker crude) was quite dramatic. While receipts remained at $7 a barrel on the forty per cent of production still owned by the companies (known as equity crude), the sixty per cent of production classed as participation crude was sold back to the companies at about $11 (only just below the posting) – and when one took a weighted average of these prices the take worked out at roughly $9.35.

In fact the situation was a little more complicated than this because the governments retained a proportion of their sixty per cent share of participation crude for sale on the open market at the posted price, and when in successive auctions bids failed to come up to this level, rather than sell it back to their former concessionnaires, they kept it in the ground. This meant that the true proportion of equity to participation crude in the hands of the major companies was nearer fifty-fifty, and that the weighted average price was nearer $9; but more important was the fact that the majors, with $9 crude, could sell to smaller companies at, say, $10 – undercutting the government sales and causing the failure of the auctions, while still making a handsome profit of one dollar a barrel.

This the producer governments found intensely annoying, and during the summer of 1974 they took steps to try to cream off some of the 'excess' profit. They raised the royalty rate on equity crude (in two stages) from twelve and a half to sixteen and a half per cent, and they increased the tax rate on equity crude from fifty-five to sixty-five per cent. This increased the weighted average price as applied to the marker crude (assuming a theoretical 40/60 equity/participation crude ratio) by almost forty cents to $9.74. At this level it was reasoned that the majors would either have to take a cut in profits on crude sales, or become less competitive by raising their resale prices to a point nearer the posting – while the posted price itself, which small companies were invited to pay at state auctions, remained unchanged.

Although OPEC continued to use the Saudi Arabian Light marker crude as the most convenient basis for its calculations, at the time that the tax and royalty adjustments were made, at OPEC meetings in Quito in June and Vienna in September, Saudi Arabia refused to associate itself with the collective decision. It claimed, rightly, that the major companies' profits could have been squeezed more effectively if the increase in the charges on equity crude had been coupled with a reduction of the posted price. Later, in October, the Saudis reversed this policy and called on Aramco for backpayments.

The members of OPEC made a great play of the fact that the increased taxes and royalties were not supposed to be passed on to the consumer – while knowing full well that this was by far the most likely outcome of their decisions. This idea of using taxes at the producing end of the industry to cut back company profits while not affecting the consumer was unrealistic. OPEC's action could certainly reduce the company profits on sales of crude – but sales of crude, outside long-term contacts between those majors with a surplus (like British Petroleum and Gulf) and those with a deficit (like Shell and Mobil), are small compared with the companies' sales of refined products, and so most of the extra charges were bound to end up in increased prices in petrol, kerosene, heating and diesel oils and industrial fuels.

The implied argument in OPEC's statements was that, because the majors were making vast profits on their crude sales and adequate profits on their other sales, it would have been possible for them to reduce their profit at every stage of their operations and to absorb all of the increased taxes and royalties themselves. But here again the OPEC arguement was invalid – for two reasons.

First, because the producers were simultaneously taking steps to reduce the companies' liftings of equity crude, and thus move the proportion of equity to participation crude back towards the official 40/60 ratio, the extra charges worked out at considerably more than the forty cents they appeared to be – and at this higher level their absorption by the companies would have been impossible. Secondly, even if the extra charges had been small enough to be absorbed, the majors, like any other companies, would not have surrendered profits unless forced to do so. The only way in which the companies could have been deprived of a large slice of their overall profits would have been by concerted producer and consumer government action, and in a period when the industrialized countries were extremely anxious that the industry should discover new sources of oil outside OPEC areas, the consumer governments were, perhaps, reluctant to take such steps.

* * *

The outcome of the developments in 1974 was that OPEC and the oil industry began to talk in terms of *one* price – the $9.74 weighted average price. Strictly speaking this terminology was premature, but with the complete Saudi takeover of Aramco pending, and the likelihood of this move being accompanied by the disappearance of equity crude and the whole posted price system, it seemed inevitable that by mid-1975 the distinction between 'price' and 'government take' would have ceased to exist. This means that the expression 'price' as used later in this book will be synonymous with 'revenue per barrel'.

Putting a figure on future price levels, however, is a more difficult matter. During the autumn of 1974 both Saudi Arabia and Iran were speaking of using the Aramco deal to build a new stable price structure, and of the possibility of there being a modest lowering of prices at the beginning of 1975. But whether this talk of a reduction referred to the future single price being below the $9.74 weighted average price, or below the $11.65 posting (which was of course the price which the OPEC national oil companies asked at state auctions) was left unclear. In view of the Saudis' apparent inability to force a reduction on the other more militant OPEC members earlier in the year, and their reversal of policy on implementing the tax and royalty adjustments, the latter interpretation – possibly involving a small real increase for the consumers – seemed more plausible.

For the longer term, in 1974 there was a major divergence of views in the industrialized countries on future levels of oil consumption, on the volumes of OPEC exports that would be required to meet this demand, and, consequently, on OPEC's ability to maintain high prices. The basic differences existed between the United States and the Organization for Economic Co-operation and Development (OECD) on one hand, and the European and Japanese governments on the other.

Washington's opinion was that prices had already passed their peak, that the power of the producers was waning, and that the West should therefore try to break the OPEC cartel and allow normal market forces to take over. It seems that the Americans' optimism was influenced by the surplus of OPEC production capacity that appeared during the summer of 1974, and by the belief that if the industrialized countries could make a further cut in their consumption (on top of that already caused by the price rises) and push ahead with the development of indigenous oil reserves and alternative energy sources, then those OPEC states with the biggest reserves (like Saudi Arabia) would begin to fear that their oil might one day be left in the ground, while those producers with smaller levels of output and ambitious development programmes (like Algeria) would fear that their exports might fall so low that their spending plans would be affected. In these circumstances the Americans hoped that both groups of producers might deem it wisest to cut oil prices before it was too late.

The Europeans and Japanese, who had most to lose in the event of a confrontation policy backfiring, were deeply sceptical about the American assessment. They naturally supported the principle of developing alternative sources of energy, for balance of payments reasons, but they did not see this policy having much effect on OPEC's attitude towards prices until the end of the decade at the earliest, and they were afraid that any Western retaliation or non-cooperation, designed to break the cartel, would only provoke OPEC members. So the emphasis in European and Japanese thinking was on trying to evolve a *modus vivendi* with the producers, and on working out new international arrangements for trade, development and surplus revenues recycling which would enable the high oil prices to be accommodated with a minimum of disruption. The French in particular wished to see all these issues made the subject of an international conference, which would include representatives of the industrial nations, the oil producers and the Third World.

The question of which of these two radically different interpretations of the price situation was correct was of fundamental importance to the consumers. It affected not only their balance of payments prospects, but also their assessment of whether they would have to encourage the OPEC members to raise their output in future – in which case the consumers were going to have to help the producers with their internal industrialization and with the protection of their monetary assets; or whether OPEC was in too weak a position to demand such help – in which case the consumers could expect to see the producers' monetary assets eaten away by inflation, and find the real transfer of wealth which they would be obliged to make to the producers considerably reduced.

The cautious soft-line European and Japanese attitude to the price issue and related problems was probably more realistic than the United States view. The statements by American leaders contained a certain amount of sabre rattling – designed partly for internal consumption and partly to scare the producers – as was admitted by Mr John Sawhill, the chief of the Federal Energy

Administration who told Senator Henry Jackson's permanent investigations committee in September that the U.S. had no concrete
policy capable of dealing with the situation.

There is no doubt that the growth in Western oil imports from
OPEC states during the 1970s will be much lower than that predicted before the crisis. The bigger consumer states are already
taking steps to develop alternative sources of energy – coal, nuclear
power and synthetic crude from shales and tar sands – and to diversify
their sources of conventional crude away from OPEC – which means
finding indigenous oil reserves, because any Third World country
which begins exports on a major scale is bound to see its interests
being best served by becoming an OPEC member. But it is very
unlikely that this self-sufficiency policy will lead to a real decline in
OPEC exports on a scale sufficient to undermine the price level.
For this to happen there would have to be a massive contribution
from the alternatives – and although it may be possible to produce
coal, nuclear power and syncrude at a price lower than that of
conventional crude, it will be physically impossible until the middle
1980s to make these fuels available on a scale large enough to effect
a major reduction in oil's share of the total energy market.

So, with the consumers slightly increasing the volume of their oil
imports from OPEC states in the short to medium term (while
lessening their proportional dependence on OPEC members) it
seems that up to 1980 at least the producers will still be able to set
whatever price they like by regulating the level of their output. In
these circumstances the theoretical ceiling for prices will be determined by the amount of money which the producers will be able to
extract from the consumers without causing an economic collapse,
or, more realistically, without forfeiting the friendship and goodwill
of the rest of the world. But in practice it is not expected that in real
terms prices will rise much beyond the $11.65 posting of 1974.

There will probably be periodic increases to keep pace with the
rate of inflation in the industrialized countries. This was part of the
justification OPEC advanced for the increase in tax and royalty rates
in 1974; with reference to the longer term, the Shah of Iran, speaking
in Canberra during a visit to Australia in September, suggested that
a future stable price system might be linked to an index of twenty or
thirty major commodities. So in money dollar terms the price of
crude in 1980 might have reached almost any level. But in terms of
constant 1974 dollars (which is the only index it is possible to use in
the present circumstances) it seems that after a slight drop in 1975
and 1976, in the later 1970s, as the industrial countries move out of

recession, the price will recover and rise slightly to about $12 in the Gulf in 1980 and $13 elsewhere.*

*   *   *

There remains the question of why it is that in the space of only four years the oil producers have been able to establish themselves in such an extraordinarily powerful position. Why did the price negotiations of 1970/71 not follow the pattern of the long drawn-out discussions on royalty expensing in the 1960s, and why did the various takeovers not result in the same ignominious surrender as that forced on Dr Mossadeq in 1953?

There is certainly no point in the consumers turning on the major companies and suggesting that if they had behaved in a less high-handed manner during the 1950s the producers would not have hit back so hard in the 1970s. From the consumers' own point of view the majors have performed extremely effectively since the Second World War. For twenty-five years they provided Europe and Japan with an uninterrupted supply of oil at a stable price. There was, admittedly, a temporary reduction of supplies when the Suez Canal was closed in 1956, but in 1967 the consumers were completely unaffected by the embargoes and production stoppages which followed the Six Day War, and in 1973 there is no doubt that the world-wide scope and flexibility of the majors' operations enabled them to spread the burden of the cutbacks among the industrialized countries very much more fairly than would have been possible had the job been left to the consumer governments. At the same time, from the producers' point of view, the companies have made an important social and economic contribution to the regions in which they operate, through training local employees (an area where IPC was particularly successful in Iraq) and through stimulating the growth of local contracting and trading enterprises.

Nor is it possible to attribute the course of events to any corporate strength of OPEC itself. Although one speaks of 'OPEC demands' or 'OPEC decisions', any initiative the Organization takes is purely the result of individual members' wishes – and more often than not this has meant the wishes of the Shah or King Faisal. Members have been anxious to prevent OPEC from evolving any sort of supra-

*The projections for the price of oil, OPEC production levels, revenues, and cumulative surpluses in 1980, given in this chapter and in Chapters 3, 4 and 13, are based on a very simplified version of the figures being used by a major oil company in late 1974.

national power which might bring pressure to bear on their own oil policies, and all of the schemes which might have given the Organization some authority – like plans to unify members' petroleum laws and to set up an OPEC High Court – have been failures.

The producers' initial successes in 1970 and 1971 were caused by the unexpectedly sharp rise in demand that winter and by the fortuitous closure of Tapline. Both these events were short term phenomena (although the sudden jump in European demand was followed by a steep, but more consistent, increase over the next two years) – and, in retrospect, one can see that there might have been a chance for the companies and the consumers to defeat the producers at that time. All the OPEC members, including Kuwait and Saudi Arabia, were feeling a budget squeeze, and their ability to hold out in a confrontation was limited.

The fact that the consumers were roundly defeated at Tehran and Tripoli is attributed by M. A. Adelman, Professor of Economics at the Massachusetts Institute of Technology, to the United States government capitulating in advance of the negotiations.* In January 1971 the American Secretary of State, John Irwin, warned the Shah of the damage which would follow in Europe and Japan if supplies were cut off, and stated publicly that the U.S. was interested in 'stable and predictable' prices – which, Adelman says, could only have meant higher prices. Furthermore, Adelman suggests: 'It is hard to imagine a more effective incitement to extreme action than to hear that it will do one's opponents great damage' – and in this context it is not surprising that shortly after his meeting with Irwin the Shah made his first threat to cut off production. So the suspicion exists that Washington never really wanted to put up a fight, and that its motive was a desire to slow down the Japanese economy (which is overwhelmingly dependent on oil from the Gulf) and to make Japanese industrial exports less competitive.

Yet even if the consumers had won the confrontation of 1971 their victory would not have lasted long. Something much more fundamental than the Tapline closure or America's adverse trade balance with Japan was changing the oil industry at the time of Tehran.

During the 1950s and 1960s there was a big surplus of production capacity – caused originally by the huge postwar expansion of Middle-Eastern operations, and then added to by the rapid development of Libya. Every major oil-producing country, including the United States, was running its output below full potential, and every

*The information in this paragraph has been drawn from 'The Phoney Oil Crisis', an *Economist* survey written by Dan Smith and published on 7 July 1973.

country was able to increase its output each year. The Middle-Eastern states, and Iran especially, were competing to secure for themselves as big a share of the annual production increment as possible.

Meanwhile the economies of the Western industrial countries were becoming more and more dependent on Middle-Eastern oil – which at that time enjoyed a considerable competitive advantage over other fuels. The consumer governments were doing little to encourage the companies to explore for higher cost reserves outside OPEC areas; and, because margins were being squeezed by the surplus of production capacity and by the entry of the independents into eastern-hemisphere operations, the companies themselves had neither the incentive, nor (to some extent) the capital to diversify their upstream operations.

But in the early 1970s several factors combined to reverse this situation. First, the industrial world entered a two-year period of boom, accompanied by a steep rise in oil consumption. Secondly, Venezuela and a number of medium sized producers began to reach their maximum production potential, while in Algeria, Libya, Iraq and Kuwait nationalization disputes and conservation measures caused varying amounts of capacity to be shut in at different times. And, thirdly, the USA also reached its production ceiling and began supplementing its traditional imports from Canada and Venezuela with supplies from the Middle East and Africa. United States' imports from the Arab countries and Iran grew from 0.6 million barrels a day in 1971, to 1.0 million b/d in 1972, and, despite the Arab embargo, to 1.7 million b/d in 1973.

The combined effects of these developments were to remove the surplus of production capacity and to throw on to the eastern hemisphere crude oil market a country which accounted for about thirty per cent of the world's oil demand, and which was increasing its consumption every year by about the same amount as the whole of western Europe.

Before the price rises of 1973 it appeared that the Middle East would have to look after virtually all the increase in world demand for the next fifteen years. OPEC found itself in a sellers' paradise – with a few of its members holding a monopoly of expandable production capacity.

3

THE WORLD'S OIL RESERVES

Three major questions arise from the discussion at the end of the last chapter of the shortage of spare production capacity. First, is there a real danger that the world's oil reserves will actually run dry during the next ten or twenty years? Secondly, if there is not an absolute shortage, to exactly what extent will the Western world be able to diversify its sources of oil between 1974 and the middle 1980s, when the increase in demand should be taken up by the alternatives – coal, shales, tar sands and nuclear power? And, thirdly, what are the production levels of the different Middle-Eastern states expected to be by the end of this decade?

To begin this analysis one must look at the projected growth in demand for oil in the non-communist world over the next ten years or so. In 1974 demand in the major consumer states fell about ten per cent below the pre cut-back crisis level of September 1973 – but during the second half of the decade and the early 1980s it is expected to start growing again, though only at a very slow rate. A likely increase would be from 47.6 million barrels a day in 1973, to 52.2 million b/d in 1980 and 57.5 million b/d in 1985. Assuming that this projection will turn out to be correct, in the three main industrial areas oil consumption might increase as follows:

million b/d	*1973*	*1980*	*1985*
United States	16.8	18.0	19.5
Europe	15.2	15.4	18.0
Japan	5.4	6.6	7.9

These projections are considerably lower than the estimates current before the crisis of late 1973 – when it was thought that world demand might run to 74 million barrels a day in 1980 and as much as 100 million barrels a day in 1985, and when Japanese demand alone was expected to reach about 11 million barrels a day in 1980 and 15 million barrels a day in 1985. The downwards revision of the figures is accounted for partly by an anticipated slow down in the growth rate of the industrial countries (which in 1974 and 1975 is expected to be near zero); and partly by the assumption that those countries which are most dependant on imported oil (like Japan) will launch a crash programme of diversification designed to replace at least part of the projected increase in their oil imports with alternative energy sources – notably nuclear power.

*   *   *

On the basis of the revised consumption figures it can be calculated that extractions from the Free World's oil reservoirs (which at the end of 1973 contained 530 billion barrels) in the period from 1974 to 1985 inclusive will total 220 billion barrels). If at the same time additions to reserves* were to be made at a rate of 20 billion barrels a year (gross) – which would be less than two-thirds of the rate current between 1955 and 1973, when there was a gigantic upwards revision of estimates for Middle-Eastern fields – then by 1985 the Free World's reserves would still be 550 billion barrels. At the rate of production predicted for 1985 this would leave enough oil for twenty-six years (assuming that there were no further additions to reserves), compared with a reserves/production ratio at the end of 1973 of thirty years. So, if these assumptions on additions in the 1974–1985 period turn out to be correct, the Free World's oil reserves are not in imminent danger of running dry, and there will be enough oil left in 1985 to allow for a smooth change-over to the alternatives.

Of course the crucial question is whether new reserves *will* be added at the rate of 20 billion barrels a year – and this is very much a matter for guesswork. Many of the world's sedimentary basins (particularly those offshore) have not yet been surveyed at all, and even where there has been some seismic work and promising structures have been located, it will not be possible to tell whether oil is present until exploratory wells have been drilled. In some

---

*The oil industry's expression is 'proven *commercially recoverable* reserves' – in other words, the amount of oil which 'geological and engineering information indicate with reasonable certainty to be recoverable under existing economic and operating conditions'. The industry's figures are only estimates, and may be subject to quite wide margins of error.

sedimentary basins oil may never have been formed, or cracks or
tilting in the structures may have allowed it to drain away millions
of years ago.

There will inevitably be some relatively small additions to reserves
as a result of the price rises of 1971/74, which have made a commercial proposition of such North Sea fields as Auk, Montrose and
Argyll. There is also hope that the price rises will stimulate the
development of improved secondary recovery techniques which will
enable the industry to extract some of the two-thirds of a reservoir
which are now left behind. And there is the further possibility that a
more thorough appraisal of some of the newer fields will lead to a big
upwards revision of reserves estimates.

But the major part of additions to reserves will have to come from
new discoveries. To add, say, 15 billion barrels a year (gross) to reserves
between 1974 and 1985, the drillers will have to find the equivalent
of seven new fields a year the size of Statfjord, Ekofisk, Forties, Brent
and Ninian, the five giants of the North Sea – and, except in the
Middle East, fields of this size are rare.

Among the established non-communist producing countries, the
onshore regions of the United States (south of the forty-ninth parallel)
have already been very thoroughly explored, and the same applies
to Trinidad and to Venezeula, where output has fallen since 1970.
Canada has only 9 billion barrels of proven reserves, in Alberta,
but there is considerable potential off the coast of Nova Scotia, and
in the Mackenzie River delta and Arctic islands. Of the other two
significant producers outside the Middle East and North Africa (which
are discussed at the end of this chapter), Indonesia, with reserves of
10 billion barrels, has been carrying out extensive offshore drilling
with moderate success; and Nigeria, where large-scale production
only got under way in 1969, is new to the oil business, and may
eventually see its reserves double or even treble the 15 billion barrels
reported at the end of 1973.

There are, of course, several completely new areas only just being
opened up, and by far the most exciting of these are the Alaskan
North Slope and the North Sea. In Alaska uncertainties over the
future of the pipeline to the south coast brought exploratory drilling
to a halt from 1970 (the year after the famous $900 million auction)
to 1974. Throughout this period the vast structure around Prudhoe
Bay, which contains about a quarter of total United States reserves,
remained the only proven commercial discovery. Activity in the
North Sea has been more intense, and between 1970 and 1974
some thirty fields were discovered in the Norwegian and British

sectors – though none were as big as the Alaskan structure. In mid-1974 proven reserves in both Alaska and the North Sea were estimated at 10 billion barrels – and it was thought that possible reserves might be 40 billion barrels in the North Sea and roughly the same amount in Alaska.

There is nothing new elsewhere to compare with these two areas, either in size or in proximity to the major industrial consumers, but there have been some important discoveries relatively near to the markets in Mexico, and, on a smaller scale, in Australia, in the northern Aegean near Thassos, and off the Mediterranean coast of Spain. In rather more remote areas Texaco and Gulf began exporting oil from Ecuador in 1972 – by pipeline across the Andes from the Amazon basin; and further south there has been a major revival of interest in Bolivia, and a string of discoveries in Peru. There have also been small finds in some of the equatorial African countries, including Gabon and Congo-Brazzaville.

Encouraging as these new discoveries are, they will not by themselves be sufficient if the Free World is to make additions to its reserves at a rate of 20 billion barrels a year. Towards the beginning of the 1980s some totally new areas will have to be opened up – and the best prospects lie offshore. It is thought that the world's continental shelves may contain several hundred billion barrels of oil, but at present drilling can only be carried out in the relatively shallow parts of these waters – in the Gulf of Mexico, the Persian Gulf, and, near the limit of a semi-submersible rig's capacity*, at about 470 feet, east of the Shetland Islands.

At far greater depths than these there are some interesting possibilities, such as the Barents Sea, south-east of Spitzbergen, and the Hatton-Rockall area – a sedimentary basin of about the same size as the northern North Sea, which was quietly incorporated into Scotland in 1971. Here the water depth is 3,000 feet, and the weather conditions are even worse than the hundred mile an hour winds and the seventy-five foot waves encountered in the North Sea.

In the long term it may be technically possible to drill in these

*The two types of unit most commonly used in offshore drilling are: (1) the jack-up rig – operating in depths of 150/200 feet, and carrying retractable legs which are lowered to the sea bed and then used to 'jack-up' the work deck; and (2) the semi-submersible – a much larger self-propelled vessel, with a hull floating 100 feet below the surface and held in place by anchors. These vessels are used in water depths of 200/550 feet. Still at an experimental stage commercially there are some highly sophisticated deep-water drilling ships, held in position by a series of propellers, which, in response to instructions from a computer, balance the forces of currents, winds and waves.

waters. The United States National Science Foundation has carried out drillings at the remarkable depth of 15,000 feet, and some of the majors have started experiments with ships capable of operating at around the depths of Rockall and the Barents Sea. But for commercial purposes, none of the companies have even begun to carry out seismic surveys in areas of this sort.

*   *   *

With a major investment effort and a steady improvement in drilling and recovery technology it seems possible that the Free World's reserves will receive additions of some 20 billion barrels a year between 1974 and 1985. But to what extent the West will be able to lessen its dependence on OPEC is a very different matter.

Beyond the end of the present decade predictions become impossible, because nobody knows where the major discoveries of the later 1970s are going to be made. But in the period up to the end of 1980 the non-communist world will have to rely on fields which were already producing or being developed in 1974, and on fields which will be discovered in 1975 and 1976 onshore, or in shallow waters offshore, close to the major markets. So any breakdown of the sources of the 52.2 million barrels a day of oil that are likely to be consumed in 1980 must be based mainly on known producing areas – and for the purpose of the analysis in this chapter these areas will be divided into three blocks: countries that are not *at present* members of OPEC (other than the smaller Persian Gulf states), non-Middle East OPEC countries, and the Middle East.

Because of the impetus given to oil exploration by the price rises of 1973 it may be possible to raise production in the non-OPEC countries by 1980 to over 20 million b/d. This is quite a high figure – it compares with production in 1973 of 16.2 million b/d – but it is based on three sets of very plausible calculations. First, it is assumed that Alaska will be producing nearly 2 million b/d, and that the United States production south of the forty-ninth parallel will be maintained near the 1973 level of 11 million b/d. This should be possible if the Federal government opens up one or more of the four reservoirs formerly set aside for the requirements of the U.S. navy in war time, and if, as a result of big new leases of Federal acreage, some discoveries are made off the coasts of California and Louisiana. There may also be a few discoveries onshore – such as Socal's important strike at McKittrick, California, in September 1973.

Secondly, it is assumed that the U.K. sector of the North Sea will be producing some 2/3 million barrels a day (making Britain more or less self-sufficient), and that the strict conservationist policy being formulated by Norway in the early 1970s will be partially relaxed to allow exports of, say, 0.5 million barrels a day. And, thirdly, it is assumed that there will be no decrease in Canada's output (which was running at 2.1 million barrels a day in 1973), and that there will be a contribution of about 2 million barrels a day from some of the new areas opened up in 1974 – like Peru and Malaysia.

Moving now to the OPEC areas, it seems likely that in 1980 the non-Middle Eastern countries – Venezuela, Ecuador, Nigeria, Indonesia, Libya and Algeria – will be producing about 9 million barrels a day, which would be roughly the same as their output in 1973 and slightly below their projected capacity. This will leave the Middle East to raise its output from 21 million barrels a day in 1973 to slightly under 23 million barrels a day.

The Middle East would have no difficulty in maintaining this level of production. At the end of 1973 the proven reserves of the countries around the Persian Gulf stood at 350 billion barrels (almost exactly two-thirds of the Free World total) and this was divided between Saudi Arabia 148 billion barrels (twenty-eight per cent of the Free World total), Kuwait and Iran 65 billion barrels each, Iraq 30 billion barrels, Abu Dhabi 19 billion barrels, the Kuwait/Saudi Arabia Partitioned Zone 10 billion barrels, Qatar 7 billion barrels, and in Oman, Dubai, Sharjah and Bahrain combined 6 billion barrels. On top of this the North African states – Libya, Algeria, Egypt and Tunisia contain a further 50 billion barrels – and when Syria's 7 billion barrels are added in as well one comes up with the Arab states and Iran holding seventy-seven per cent of the non-communist countries' reserves and sixty-four per cent of the world's total reserves.

Nor are these figures likely to mark the limit of the Arab and Iranian reserves, because, by the standards of the United States and Venezuela, the Persian Gulf and North Africa have not been very extensively explored – and the discrepancy between proven and probable reserves is considerable. In Iran, which has been more thoroughly drilled than most of its neighbours, the Shah has suggested that there may be as much as 96 billion barrels; and in Saudi Arabia, where several new fields were discovered in the early 1970s, probable reserves amount to 220 billion barrels at the minimum. In Kuwait and Qatar what fields there are onshore have most likely already been discovered, but offshore prospects are more encouraging – especially in Kuwaiti waters, where drilling in the 'Golden Triangle' was halted in the early 1960s by a boundary dispute with Iran and

Saudi Arabia. Similarly, in Abu Dhabi, which is the newest of the big Gulf producers, there is bound to be a major expansion of reserves both onshore and offshore, particularly in the Liwa Oasis area, where development of the huge Zarrara field has been held up by a Saudi territorial claim. At the end of July 1974 the two states announced that they had reached agreement in principle (pending King Faisal's assent) on a compromise settlement in this area, but they did not release details.*

Of all the Middle Eastern producers the best prospects for future discoveries lie in Iraq. During the thirty-six years following its arrival in 1935 the IPC group developed only a very minor part of its concession acreage, but since the expropriation measures of General Kassem in 1961 the Iraq National Oil Company has brought on stream the northern half of the Rumaila field, discovered originally by the Basrah Petroleum Company, and has begun development work on a number of other structures. Although the northern areas of Iraq, including Kirkuk and Mosul, are not expected to contain much more oil, on the basis of an IPC survey which the Iraqis had analysed by American consultants, the probable reserves of southern Iraq are thought to be over 80 billion barrels – which, with 15 billion barrels already proven in the north, would make the Iraqi reserves second only to those of Saudi Arabia.

Apart from the volume of its reserves and the colossal size of the individual fields (al Ghawar in Saudi Arabia is as big as the proven reserves of the U.S.A. and Alaska rolled together), the Middle East is also unique in being extraordinarily cheap to develop. During the 1960s the cost of finding new reserves amounted to one and a half cents a barrel – against $1.40 in the U.S.A., $1 in Canada, fifteen cents in Venezuela and thirteen cents in Africa. Then the average Middle Eastern well produces 10,000 barrels a day, compared with only 15 b/d in the U.S.A., and this makes for a low investment per

*Saudi Arabia's ambitions on Abu Dhabi territory date back to the 1930s. The two specific claims, made in 1935 and 1945, varied greatly in size – but both included the Liwa Oasis and the surrounding sand sea in the south of the Emirate, and the second extended up to the Buraimi Oasis on the Omani border, which the Saudis occupied for a time in the early 1950s. In 1971 Saudi Arabia recognized Oman, and relinquished its claim to the eastern half of the Buraimi Oasis, and since then it appears to have tacitly dropped its claim to the western half – known in Abu Dhabi as Al Ain. It is thought that the more recent agreement over the Liwa will lead to Saudi Arabia granting diplomatic recognition to the federation of the United Arab Emirates, which was formed when Britain withdrew from the Gulf in December 1971. The U.A.E. members are the seven former Trucial States: Abu Dhabi, Dubai, Sharjah, Ras al Khaimah, Ajman, Umm al Qaiwain, and Fujairah.

barrel a day of capacity – only $100 onshore in the Gulf, against $600 in Nigeria and $2,500 off the Scottish mainland. Finally the cost of production varies from six cents in Kuwait to thirty-five cents offshore Dubai, while elsewhere it averages fifty-one cents in Venezuela, eighty cents in the U.S.S.R., eighty-two cents in Indonesia, and $1.31 in the U.S.A. – where some of the more recent finds have worked out at $3.00.

With these enormous low cost reserves the Middle Eastern producers would have no difficulty in installing at least 42 million b/d of capacity by 1980. Shaikh Ahmed Zaki Yamani has spoken on a number of occasions of Saudi Arabia producing 20 million b/d, and Aramco has budgeted for the installation of 13.2 million b/d by 1977. The Iraqis are planning to install 4.5 million b/d by 1978 and 6 million b/d by 1980 – though, given their intention of continuing to export the bulk of their output via Mediterranean terminals, there is some doubt as to whether they will be able to install more than 4.5/5 million b/d. In Abu Dhabi, assuming that reserves continue to expand as anticipated, it would be possible to raise capacity to 5 million b/d by 1980, and in Iran there would be no difficulty in installing enough capacity for the country to reach its official production limit of 8 million b/d. In Kuwait it would be feasible to install 4 million b/d of capacity, but it is most unlikely that the official limit of 3 million b/d will be exceeded.

The limit on Kuwaiti production was originally imposed in 1972, after two deputies, Salim al Marzoukh and Badr al 'Ujail, claimed in the National Assembly that the state's reserves were not 65 billion barrels but only 26 billion barrels. The two men calculated that if production were allowed to grow by six per cent a year Kuwait's oil would be exhausted by 1985, while with a freeze it would last until 1996. Although no official figures have ever been published, a survey later showed that the accepted 65 billion barrels was in fact correct – but given the rather limited prospects for future discoveries, and the desire to spin out production over as long a period as possible while maintaining high prices, the government decided to keep the limit in force.

As the example of Kuwait shows, it is one thing to be able to produce and quite another to be willing to produce. Some of the Middle Eastern countries, notably Saudi Arabia, feel that in the 'right political circumstances' they have a certain moral responsibility to raise their output to meet the industrial countries' growing demand; and others, Iraq, Oman and the smaller shaikhdoms, will need to produce as much as they can – but in general the producers'

D

decision may depend largely on calculations of financial self-interest.

Up to mid-1974 the figures worked out very much on the side of keeping the oil in the ground. A quick glance at the performance of oil versus paper money between the middle of 1970 and September 1974 shows that over roughly four years Gulf crude appreciated in terms of government take by more than 900 per cent; while, given the drop in the parity of the two main investment currencies, and the high rate of inflation in the West, reserve funds invested in deposits or fixed interest securities cannot have done very much better than keep their value no matter what rate of interest they received.

But in the later 1970s the situation may be less one-sided. If, as suggested in the previous chapter, the governments' revenues per barrel in constant dollar terms are unlikely to rise much more than $2 above the weighted average price of $9.74 in September 1974, then oil in the ground will become more or less a constant value asset. In this case the assets which the producers receive in return for their oil will no longer be required to appreciate in real terms if they are to compare with oil as an investment. They will have to do no more than maintain their value in the face of inflation. To some extent the producers will be able to guard against inflation themselves, by putting their money into real assets (like property), but to protect the bulk of their reserves they will ask for some sort of co-operation from the consumer governments.

If they get this co-operation it ought to be worthwhile for the producers to export as much oil as the consumers require, and on this assumption it is possible to give a tentative breakdown of the Middle Eastern countries' production levels in 1980, as follows:

million barrels a day	1973	1974	1980
Bahrain	0.06	0.06	0.06
Sharjah	nil	0.1	0.2
Oman	0.3	0.3	0.4
Dubai	0.3	0.3	0.3
Qatar	0.6	0.5	0.5
Partitioned Zone	0.5	0.5	0.5
Kuwait	2.8	2.3	1.7
Abu Dhabi	1.3	1.3	1.5
Iraq	2.0	1.9	2.3
Iran	5.9	6.1	5.8
Saudi Arabia	7.3	8.2	9.5
TOTAL	21.06	21.56	22.76

4

THE PROBLEMS OF WEALTH

If the increase in Middle East oil production during the second half of the 1970s is not likely to be very dramatic in comparison with pre-crisis expectations, the revenues received by the producing states are going to be running at a level which would have seemed inconceivable a few years ago. In 1970, the year of the Tehran Agreement, the combined oil income of the Gulf exporters ran to just over $4 billion. By 1980 it could be $100 billion. So while production will rise by little more than fifty per cent over the decade as a whole, revenues may multiply twenty-five times.

By 1980 it seems that a reasonable prediction for the price of a barrel of crude would be $12 in the Gulf and $13 elsewhere. If it is assumed that the bulk of Iraqi crude and half a million barrels a day of Saudi crude will still be pumped to the Mediterranean where it will fetch $13, it is possible to combine these price assumptions with the production forecasts listed at the end of the last chapter to give a state by state breakdown of revenues in 1980 as shown on page 52.

The bald figures themselves convey little impression of just how much these revenues will be worth; but to give some idea of what the Saudi revenues of $43 billion would be able to buy, they can be compared with a few projects that are well known to have been expensive. They would allow the Kingdom to finance the Apollo moon programme in about seven months, the research and development costs of the Concorde or the construction cost of the Channel Tunnel in some three to four weeks, and the building of the Sydney Opera House in fifteen hours. To give a more realistic comparison though, the Saudi income in 1980 would not be very much greater than the taxes raised by the United Kingdom Treasury in the year

$ million	1973	1974	1980
Bahrain	not available	not available	260
Sharjah	,,	,,	880
Oman	,,	,,	1,750
Dubai	,,	,,	1,310
Qatar	600	1,650	2,190
Kuwait (inc. half PZ income)	2,800	8,000	8,540
Abu Dhabi	1,200	4,300	6,570
Iraq	1,900	6,000	10,620
Iran	5,600	22,000	25,400
Saudi Arabia (inc. half PZ income)	7,200	29,000	42,890
TOTAL	19,300	70,950	100,410
TOTAL OPEC	28,900	106,300	143,110

ending in April 1973. These totalled £17 billion – or about $40 billion.

Cumulatively, during the whole of the present decade the oil revenues (in constant dollars) will probably add up to around $170/190 billion for Iran, $60/70 billion for Iraq, and $320/360 billion for the Arabian Peninsula – which gives a total of $550/620 billion. For the sake of comparison, the revenues received in the Gulf from 1901, when D'Arcy was granted his concession to prospect for oil in Iran, up to the Tehran Agreement at the beginning of 1971 were only $33.6 billion – and, whatever the legends surrounding the oil states in terms of Western economies this figure is relatively small – substantially less than the exports of Germany in 1971 alone. So just as the Tehran Agreement represented the beginning of a new era in the oil industry, it also marked the beginnings of a move by the producers into a totally new league of wealth; and this raises a whole series of questions on how much of the money can be spent, what will happen to the surplus, and what will be its effect on both the producers themselves and on the rest of the world.

The standard approach to these problems is to divide the producers into two groups. First, there are those states which have balanced economies and large populations, and will therefore go on putting their revenues into development as they have done before. This category embraces five of the OPEC states outside the Middle East – Nigeria, Algeria and Indonesia (all of which may continue to run a deficit) and Venezuela and Ecuador; but in the Gulf it includes only Iran and Iraq. Perhaps one might also incorporate Bahrain and Oman in this category – more as a measure of the very small size of Bahrain's revenues and Oman's extreme backwardness than of any vast economic potential. But otherwise Libya and all the states of the Arabian Peninsula fall into the second group – producers who will be unable to spend their income as fast as it comes in, and will therefore amass huge cash surpluses.

But this is not to say that all of these states are already very rich by Western standards, or highly developed. In fact, quite apart from the idea of their moving on to a new scale of wealth, for most of them it will be a novelty to have any large and permanent surplus at all.

Probably there is only one state in the Gulf, Kuwait, which matches up to the popular Western image of an oil shaikhdom – and even there any visitor expecting to see an Arab Los Angeles would be sadly disillusioned. In the pre-Tehran era Kuwait got $10 billion of the $33 billion paid to the Gulf producers. During the 1950s and 1960s this turned the country into the world's most comprehensive welfare state and biggest per capita giver of aid, and saw at various times the Kuwaiti government stand as the largest single source of capital on the London money market. But all this only happened because Kuwait had exactly the right surplus money combination – very large revenues for a long period, a small population (which is still under a million) and a small geographical area. Only one other OPEC state, Libya, which received $5.6 billion between 1962 and 1970 for a population of two million, built up a huge surplus in this period – and here there was nothing comparable to the Kuwaiti welfare state.

In contrast to Kuwait, Saudia Arabia is a quarter the size of the United States. It has a population of five million, which is bigger than Kuwait's but still minute for such a large country, and although it also received $10 billion before Tehran, it never generated much of a surplus. In the late 1950s it found itself overspending at a time when its revenues were levelling off, and in 1958, when its debts reached $400 million the riyal was devalued by forty per cent, and the government called for assistance from the International Monetary Fund.

Then in Abu Dhabi's case the oil only came on stream in 1962, and up to 1971 it received just $780 million – which was rather less than the cumulative revenues of Qatar, where production began at the same time as it did in Kuwait. It is true that after 1967, when a new ruler first started spending the money, Abu Dhabi town changed from a bush village to a frontier settlement to something approaching a city faster than anywhere else in the world, but in the process the state overspent so badly that rival shaikhdoms delighted in claiming, with unfair exaggeration, that by 1970 there was not even enough money left to repair the air conditioners in the government offices. Even now Abu Dhabi is still in the early stages of development, and it has proved itself extremely vulnerable to demands from other Arab countries and institutions for hand-outs. Officially it is obliged to put only ten per cent of its income into the United Arab Emirates budget, but in practice it foots the development bill for all the other states bar Dubai. Given that these states occupy a considerably larger and more rugged area than Kuwait, and also have rather more development potential, Abu Dhabi only began to have a significant surplus in 1974.

So it is clearly wrong to think of all the Arabian Peninsula states as being in exactly the same position at present. Any visitor to the area will notice immediately that for states so close together their character, appearance and stage of development are remarkably different. But even in the less advanced states which have a long way to go before they reach the Kuwaiti level of development, a surplus is now beginning to accumulate, simply because there are limits to the speed with which revenues can be spent. There are what might be called development bottlenecks. Obviously it is impossible to set up inland industries until roads have been built, and in the same way Saudi Arabia's mineral wealth, which includes a promising copper discovery at Jebel Sayid, north east of Jeddah, large amounts of iron ore and phosphates, and a very high grade magnesium deposit, cannot be exploited until it has been properly surveyed.

To make matters worse there is a human bottleneck too. In Saudi Arabia during the 1972/3 fiscal year, when the budget totalled a mere $3,500 million, the ministries managed to disburse only sixty or seventy per cent of their allocations. Although some Arabs resent one noticing it, this growing shortfall of expenditure, which has also been seen in Libya and Iraq, is not only the result of the allocations being over-optimistic to start with. Part of the blame also falls on bureaucracies which are enormously overstaffed, slow and incompetent. A good number of the junior and middle rank officials in Arab countries (and throughout the developing world as a whole) are reluctant to take responsibility, and not notably energetic either – which is why the merchants in the Gulf employ Indians and Pakistanis. As a result even the most trivial decisions may be shunted up the ministries to land on the desk of a minister. In Saudi Arabia it is not unheard of for the King himself to have to deal with remote provincial land claims.

But behind all these short-term obstacles to spending, the basic range of conventional development opportunities offered by the Arabian Peninsula, and especially by the small featureless deserts of Kuwait and Qatar, is itself restricted. First there is the infrastructure to be built. This includes roads, ports, hospitals, sea-water desalination plants, power stations, schools and airports. These last projects are being put up on a truly grand scale – particularly in the U.A.E. where Dubai has facilities capable of handling three jumbo-jets at once, to serve a population of under 70,000. Then there are a few obvious outlets for productive investment – refineries, petro-chemical and fertilizer plants, cement factories, light industries, shrimp fisheries, and, in Ras al Khaimah, Fujairah and the Asir region of south-western Saudi Arabia (all of which benefit from winter rainfall), there is some agricultural potential. In the Saudi Eastern Province there are also big reserves of ground water, but, like oil, this is irreplaceable, and as the Saudis have been using it without stint, estimates of how long it will last vary from a hundred to only thirty years. In any event it will probably be extremely difficult to expand cultivation beyond one per cent of the Saudi Arabia's total area.

It goes without saying that the infrastructure can only be built once, and in some states – Kuwait, Bahrain and Dubai, which was a thriving entrepot some time before oil came on stream in 1969 – it is now almost complete. This in turn means that the market is quickly saturated with heavy construction equipment – lorries especially. And with the very small populations of the Gulf states*, it is not long before most middle-class citizens also have their cars, air-conditioning units, deep freezes and stereo sets. Admittedly in Saudi Arabia, where the oil wealth has had to be spread a lot more thinly so far, there is still scope for higher consumer spending, and a rise in government salaries is always accompanied by a surge in demand for air conditioners. But, as an example of what happens in the Gulf, while Kuwait's oil revenues doubled from 1968 to 1972 imports went up by only seven per cent.

Over the six years from 1975 to 1980 the Arabian Peninsula states' spending on industrial and infrastructural projects, and on defence – which is now probably absorbing as much money as is going into development – cannot possibly exceed $120 billion (in

*Kuwait 850,000; Bahrain 220,000; Qatar 110,000; Abu Dhabi 60,000; Dubai 65,000; other U.A.E. 60,000 and Oman 750,000. In contrast, Iran has a population of 31 million and Iraq 9 million.

constant dollar terms), even if allowances are made for accelerated spending under the special development arrangements discussed later in this chapter. So, temporarily disregarding the likelihood of further large sums being given away – as Saudi Arabia agreed to meet much of the Egyptian bill for the fourth Arab-Israeli war – by 1980 their accumulated surplus (assuming a real rate of interest of zero) could amount to between $200 and $240 billion – which would be more than the monetary reserves of the entire world in January 1974. Qatar and Abu Dhabi will probably account for a relatively small part of this, while Kuwait, having less spare spending capacity to start with, will accumulate rather more; but the vast bulk of this money will belong to one state – Saudi Arabia. Even at a time when revenues were running at comparatively tiny levels in the two years following the Tehran Agreement, Saudi reserves grew by 368 per cent – which, broken down during 1972, works out at $90 million a month.

*   *   *

Now one might think from this analysis – dividing the producers into surplus and non-surplus groups – that the rest of the oil money story lies simply in taking a more detailed look at development prospects, and discovering how the remaining surplus will be invested. But a large part of the intelligentsia in the producing states – the civil servants, businessmen, bankers and journalists – have for some time been convinced that there is much more to the subject than this.

Compared with their contemporaries in the West, whose attention is focused overwhelmingly on domestic matters, the better educated Arabs and Iranians have had to evolve a distinctly international outlook. They are more concerned with economic and political relations between states, and more sensitive to changes in these affairs. And the reasons are obvious enough. Many of them have been educated in the West and travel there frequently; most of their countries have been occupied or protected by a colonial power; the size of their governments' oil revenues and budgets have been determined largely by whether the industrial world is enjoying a boom or not; the safety of their investments depends on the strength or weakness of other peoples' currencies; and, among the Arabs, the outcome of their paramount political obsession – Palestine – is felt to rest with the sympathies and interests of America. In short, their lives are heavily influenced by what is happening in the world outside, and naturally enough international politics and economics are far more frequently discussed than they are in the West. This is not to say that the conclusions reached are always the right ones – there is, or was, for example, an understandable but exaggerated tendency to see Middle East politics too much in terms of big power conspiracies. But in this instance of the energy crisis/oil revenues equation, it does at least mean that people began to think about the situation in some considerable depth, long before the subject began to be discussed in Europe and America.

The problem is, of course, a new one, too new and still too confused in 1974 for any definite consensus to have emerged, but one of the preliminary and more obvious conclusions seems to be that the countries with the bigger economies, like Iran, can look forward to something better than being just more-successful-than-average developing states, while the Arabian Peninsula producers will not simply become larger or smaller versions of Kuwait (which is by no means universally admired anyway). Beyond this there is little positive agreement – in the sense of views on what the producers will become as opposed to what they will not become – but there is in the background a somewhat ill-defined and nebulous feeling with a good deal of wishful thinking and philosophy mixed in with the hard predictions, that the answer will involve a dramatic, unprecedented and permanent shift in the balance of world economic power.

To follow the train of reasoning which leads to this conclusion it is best to start by looking at how the Arabs and Iranians, and other developing nations, have seen the economic position of themselves, as suppliers of primary commodities, vis-à-vis the industrialized world so far. First the oil producers obviously do not view themselves as being fabulously rich – and nor are they, for in the non-surplus states which make up the majority of their number, per capita incomes are still way below those applying in the West. One might assume that surely the surplus states, like Kuwait, are an exception here. But if the idea of wealth is taken not as meaning bank accounts full of paper money, but as being real assets, as found in the developed nations, and implying a store of industrial capacity, and a supply of trained manpower and inventive ability, it is clear that the Arabian Peninsula states are even worse off than the Iran/Venezuela group.

The West meanwhile has waxed prosperous, and Jahangir Amuzegar, the chief of the Iranian economic mission in Washington, explained how in a paper published by *Petroleum Intelligence Weekly* in July 1973: 'Without doubt,' he claimed, 'the rapid post-war exploitation of Mideast and North African oil resources, and their export at bargain-basement prices to West Europe, America and Japan helped provide the basic underpinnings of fast economic growth and unprecedented material prosperity in the industrial world.' And he adds that the irony of this economic miracle lay in the way it was achieved – 'by subsidies from the oil producing countries, mostly poor and struggling countries, at the expense of their limited and irreplaceable assets'.

Thus the pattern of trade as seen from the Third World end has meant that the producers of commodities, whether mineral or agricultural, have had to sell their exports cheap, and then watch the industrial world help itself to a big slice of profit (in the form of wages and salaries) for turning these commodities into manufactured goods, before it sells them back to the original producers at a higher price. The oil states have not suffered as badly as some, because between 1958 and September 1973 their revenues per barrel rose slightly, but only slightly, more than the cost of their manufactured imports. But most of the developing world has been starved of capital, and during the 1960s the gap between it and the industrial world was widened, not closed.

So there has been what the Third World commodity exporters consider to be a totally unfair sense of values, and this point was ringed round very neatly by a short conversation which took place in Geneva on the evening of the second 'dollar compensation' agreement. A member of one of the OPEC delegations had just been bought a whisky by the Middle East correspondent of *The Financial Times* at the punitive price of 15 Swiss francs (rather over £2), and looking at the small quantity in the bottom of his glass he observed: 'This cost you the equivalent of over two barrels – seventy gallons – of crude.' And he went on to reflect on the absurdity of this, when the whisky was made of renewable ingredients, barley and water, while his crude oil, once burned, was irreplaceable.

But now, the producers believe, things are changing, and Amuzegar argues that the Western world has only itself to blame: 'The rich industrial nations', he says, 'favoured the cheap oil policy because of a false sense of security, as if the world had an inexhaustible supply of energy – as though no end were in sight. By an economic myopia of incomprehensible dimensions millions upon millions of energy-gobbling products – from impractically big and fast cars to profligately trivial household gadgets – were allowed to flood the market, only to be replaced soon by bigger, faster, and more power-thirsty models.' Thus he suggests that the consumers have perpetrated a hoax on themselves, and on their 'still unborn generations', not only by polluting 'planet earth' directly through fumes and smoke, and indirectly by all the other waste of fast industrial growth, but by squandering an invaluable raw material, and by making it uneconomic for other sources of energy to be developed.

If the consumers had not underpriced oil in the past, demand in the early 1970s would have been lower, there would have been no shortage of production capacity, and prices would not have risen so fast. As it is the consumers must now pay a penalty for their shortsightedness.

Writing in *The Financial Times* Lombard column on this 'long needed redressing of the balance between the "haves" and the "have nots"', C. Gordon Tether spelt out the dramatic nature of this development: 'The way in which the oil producing states are now pushing the affluent countries around in such a blatantly offhand manner represents a new phenomenon in world affairs – a clear-cut reversal of an order of things that, almost from the time men first became internationally minded has enabled the manufacturing countries of the northern hemisphere to lord it over the rest with almost complete impunity.'

Only a few weeks after these words had been written the 'offhand manner' was graphically illustrated by the Shah of Iran, who warned the industrial countries that the days were over when they could afford to pay people for not working, and suggested that in future the children of rich parents who took to terrorism, or led hippy lives, would have to rethink their attitudes towards industrial civilization and settle down to work.

*   *   *

This reversal of the old order has so shaken the basis of the producer/consumer relationship that a whole range of previously fundamental assumptions on the producers' economic interests and behaviour have now gone by the board. Up to 1971 it was taken for granted that the producers would always need to sell as much oil as they could – and the failure of the mid 1960s production programme proved the point. But now that they have got a price which they consider reflects the true scarcity value of their oil, they have the power to ask the unprecedented question of whether they really want to raise their output to meet the industrial countries' demand or not.

Given some inducements from the consumer, it can be assumed that in the end the producers will raise their output to the level suggested at the end of the last chapter. But they are still likely to be producing more than they need to produce; and this leads on to another unprecedented question – what will they want in return?

For the non-surplus countries the answer is obvious – cash. There are no restrictions on Iran and Iraq and the producers outside the Middle East turning their revenues into industrial assets. The Iranians have been talking since about 1970 or 1971 of moving towards the 'Great Civilization', and of building their country up into a second Japan. Although it is easy to be cynical at how the Iranian economy in its present state matches up to these predictions,* in theory the long-term potential does exist.

But for the Arabian Peninsula states, cash on its own is not enough. However big their bank balances become, as already explained money alone does not bring real, Western-style wealth, and it is precisely this, with all its benefits of balanced economies, a high standard of living for their people, something to rely on when the oil runs out, and genuine economic and political independence, that these states most need. Because industrial wealth may not come to them 'naturally', as it can with the Iran group, they feel that some sort of special arrangements may be called for. And although they are not yet certain what these arrangements might be, their preliminary thoughts on the subject are that the world should somehow 'co-operate' in making sure that in future a large part of its new industrial capacity will be installed in their own countries.

If the West does not like this proposed readjustment of the balance of world economic power, the producing states feel that it might as well stop paying lip-service to the whole idea of the Third World development. Anyway they are determined that the West should not be allowed to escape from this situation. In the absence of an 'accelerated or special development arrangement' the established manufacturing countries might hope to be able to do just this – because the surplus revenues paid to the producers would simply make a U-turn and come directly back on to the capital markets of New York, London, Tokyo and Paris to finance further Western industrial expansion, and neatly solve the consumers' balance of

---

*This is not meant to imply that Iran has been particularly unsuccessful in its development. In the late 1960s and early 1970s it had one of the fastest expanding economies in the world. The statistics were admittedly helped by enormous rises in oil prices and production, but there was also a very high rate of growth in industry, construction and services – especially in the private sector. The flaw in this glossy economic edifice, which the Iranian government tends to ignore, is that agriculture, which still employs the bulk of the population, has been badly neglected, and has put up a consistently miserable performance.

payments problems into the bargain.* Of course to a considerable extent such a U-turn will be unavoidable, but the producers do not want to see it emerge as any sort of unalterable and inevitable formula – the sum total of the oil money story. If, however, they do see the U-turn operating on too large and permanent a scale, and see themselves still making somewhat limited economic progress internally, the oil states claim that the only logical step for them will be to stop raising their output.

Whatever the producers were saying in 1973 and early 1974 it is by no means certain that in the long run they will translate the theory of their reasoning into action. But if the consumers decide that it is unwise to gamble on this chance they may have to offer some sort of package deal or other inducements to ensure that the oil keeps flowing in large enough quantities. Even without such arrangements though, the producers believe that the recent rise in crude oil prices might effect a movement of new industries in their direction more or less of its own accord. The basis of this movement would be that in a world of high oil prices (which were periodically increased to keep pace with inflation) a large amount of capital in the consumer countries will inevitably be directed into current expenditure. Consequently the industrial countries will not be able to continue their past rate of expansion without drawing on Arab capital; and if the Arabs show themselves more willing to provide capital for ventures in their own states than in the consumer countries, it will be in the Middle East that such industries will be built. The logic of this process is that the Arab states will gradually become industrially self-sufficient, while their manufactured goods will break into the Western domestic markets and into the West's traditional Third World export markets. This would constitute a major shift of industrial power away from the northern hemisphere.

On paper this train of thought sounds plausible enough, but, as the producers are well aware, there are a whole range of complications, and while their ambitions are still at the formative stage, one of the snags affecting both the surplus and non-surplus groups has

*In the last chapter and the conclusion of this book it is suggested that although the perpetuation of the U-turn phenomenon might appear at first sight to be the ideal solution to the consumers' problems, in the long run the industrial countries would do better to back the producers' ideas for special development assistance. The reason is partly that this would remove the danger of a disproportionate amount of Arab capital going to the richer consumers, and partly that a redistribution of industrial wealth among the Arab states, and other developing countries which may receive Arab investment, might stimulate world-wide a higher rate of real income growth.

already made itself felt. A rise in the government take on crude oil has the effect of increasing almost all prices in the consumer countries – in Britain, for instance, it is estimated that the price rises of October and December 1973 gave the economy an inflationary push of some five per cent. As the producer states are still enormously dependent on imports, of everything from food to heavy machinery, the policy of increasing their own export prices can rebound on themselves.

The classic example so far has been Iran, where by October 1973 a combination of internal and external pressures had forced inflation up to an annual rate of thirteen per cent for the population as a whole, and eighteen per cent for middle-class families. The external pressure, in the form of inflating imports, was not, of course, entirely oil-price driven. It included increases in the price of manufactured goods driven by such means as wage inflation in the West, and – more relevant to the Iranians' suggestions for a cure outlined in the following paragraphs – by price rises in raw materials imported directly and indirectly (via the industrialized states) by Iran.

In response to this situation the government ordered local manufacturers, wholesalers and retailers to put their prices back to the levels obtaining in the previous May – under threat of being closed down by the security forces. It also banned the export of twenty-five industrial products in short supply; and the Prime Minister declared that government office staff were to go without lump sugar in their tea, and write on both sides of a sheet of paper.

These measures were intended only as attacks on the symptoms of inflation (or as mere eyecatching gestures), not in any sense as a complete solution, and the government made clear its belief that part of the root of the problem lay in the oil price/imports costs vicious circle.

Recognizing this fact, in September 1973 the biggest English-language daily in Tehran, *Keyhan International*, published an article based on a senior ministerial briefing, under the headline: 'Everyone will lose out in oil price spiral.' This article argued that because of the vicious circle effect, price rises on the part of the producers of oil and other raw materials were not on their own the key to industrial progress. In fact for those underdeveloped countries not exporting the materials in question such increases only made industrialization more difficult. So the author claimed that what countries like Iran needed was an 'entirely new global strategy for trade', which would involve the present industrial powers going on a 'slimming diet', 'abdicating their selfish ambitions', and accepting a zero rate of growth. The consequent levelling-off of Western demand would remove or reverse the upwards pressure of raw materials prices and thus break the spiral.

But so that this should not put the oil and commodity producers back at square one – in other words without enough capital to industrialize anyway – it was suggested that there should be an international division of labour. The major powers should concentrate on exporting technology, sophisticated capital goods and plant, while the less complex forms of manufacturing should be left to the developing world – which would then use the proceeds of its industrial exports rather than its commodities revenues to finance its expansion.

5

OIL FOR INDUSTRY

The important point about the article in *Keyhan*, which, at the time it was published, attracted a good deal of attention and sympathy among both the Iranians and the foreign community in Tehran, was that it reflected thinking, not policy. And as David Housego, the Tehran correspondent of *The Financial Times*, commented when analysing the piece a few days later, the key question is: 'How does one translate such goals into negotiable terms?'

The answer is that the producers' ideas have been rather hazy, and when one looks at the problem as it bears on Saudi Arabia for instance, it is clear that to expect them to launch any massive political and economic programme to solve the money issue and change the economy of the world is out of the question. First, the whole problem is so new and it burst so suddenly. The Saudis perhaps had some inkling of what was coming, but the rest of the world only began to wake up properly to the situation in the autumn of 1972, when America became conscious of its 'energy crisis'.

Secondly, the Saudis in government are acutely aware that over the next ten years their particular generation is being asked to make a historic decision on the use of some two or three decades' wealth. Once their oil is gone there will, of course, be no second chance, and as the entire future of their country, and, to some extent, that of the rest of the world, depends on it, they know that their decision had better be the right one. The sense of responsibility felt by the government is overwhelming – and it was reflected in July 1973 by the remark of Hisham Nasser, the President of the Central Planning Organization, to two visiting American journalists: 'Frankly, I wish you could find some other sources of energy to take the pressure off us.'

64

Then, equally fundamental, Saudi Arabia is not a country with a system of government equipped to deal with this sort of issue. At the top during the past ten years there was only one policy maker – King Faisal, who held the positions of Prime Minister and Foreign Minister. Before he succeeded to the throne in 1964, by ousting his rather useless and extravagant brother, the late King Saud, Faisal was Minister of Finance from 1958 to 1960, and then, after a period during which his services were dispensed with and he retired to Taif, he became Prime Minister in 1962. As Minister of Finance it was Faisal who rescued his country from bankruptcy, and who brought in two of Saudi Arabia's most able administrators – Shaikh Ahmed Zaki Yamani, who first entered the Government as legal adviser to the Council of Ministers, and Anwar Ali, the Pakistani Governor of the central bank, the Saudi Arabian Monetary Agency. (Anwar Ali died in Washington on 5 November 1974.)

Beneath King Faisal there was a handful of men who had direct access to the monarch, and who were in a position to influence policy. The workings of the centre of the Saudi government are so shrouded in secrecy that it is difficult to be sure who were the most influential, but in 1974 the list might have run to nine. Most of them were members of the Supreme Petroleum Council: Prince Fahad bin Abdel-Aziz, one of the King's brothers, second Deputy Prime Minister and Minister of the Interior; Mohammed Abu Khil, the Minister of State for Financial and Economic Affairs; Hisham Nasser, the President of the Central Planning Organization; Omar Saqqaf, the Minister of State for Foreign Affairs (who died in New York only ten days after Anwar Ali); Shaikh Ahmed Zaki Yamani; Anwar Ali; and Prince Saud bin Faisal, the King's fourth son and Deputy Minister of Petroleum and Mineral Resources. To these names might be added two of the most influential figures of all: Prince Sultan bin Abdel-Aziz, the Minister of Defence; and Kamal Adham, the King's brother-in-law and chief adviser[1]. These men have little authority to make decisions on their own, except within the fairly close limits of policy laid down by the King – something which is hard to appreciate when ministers like Yamani are well known international figures seen travelling between the Western capitals and talking to the heads of foreign governments.

This system of one-man decision-making was more or less adequate during the 1960s, when Saudi Arabia played a mainly passive role in the world, but it is hardly suitable for the huge and complex responsibilities of the money problem. Even to begin to formulate a policy and take an initiative of the type suggested by the 'revo-

E

lutionary' nature of current Saudi thinking on this subject, would call for Western-style cabinet discussions – implying a more open exchange of ideas and some sort of collective responsibility. The existing Saudi cabinet, the Council of Ministers, is not this sort of body, and nor does it contain all the best men for this particular job.

Recognizing the cabinet's shortcomings, in 1972 the King formed a much more high-powered advisory working group, the Supreme Petroleum Council, but there are still doubts as to whether this relatively new body will be very effective. Although the men at the top in Saudi Arabia have a good general knowledge of most of the issues that confront them, they receive little backing from ministries, embassies and special committees (on which any Western government can draw), and there is virtually nobody on whom they can call for a detailed briefing on any specific aspect of a problem.

In different degrees all the other OPEC states suffer from the same difficulties – although only in Abu Dhabi and Qatar is the shortage of manpower quite as serious as it is in Saudi Arabia. As a result action by the producers on the money problem in 1972 and 1973 did not go much beyond periodic exercises in thinking aloud in public, while in 1974 their ideas were normally expressed in response to attacks on high oil prices made by the leaders of the consumer governments.

Collectively the speeches of the producer states' ministers added up to three separate diplomatic 'initiatives' – two aimed at the industrial consumer countries, and one aimed at promoting discussions among the Arab states themselves. These initiatives can be listed under the headings of: 'downstream operations', 'oil for industry', and 'inter-regional development' (discussed in Chapter 10). By early 1974 the second two initiatives were beginning to bear fruit (while the first had been temporarily or permanently abandoned) – but before these results are analysed it is necessary to start by examining the way in which each initiative was launched.

The Downstream Operations Initiative

The first of the three initiatives began on 6 October 1972 when Yamani was addressing the Conference of the Middle East Institute at Georgetown University in Washington D.C. The bulk of his speech was devoted to explaining the principles of Participation, then being negotiated with the companies in New York, but at the end he had this to say: 'In the light of the facts I have just mentioned, we in the Kingdom of Saudi Arabia extend our hand to the government of the United States of America and call for a commercial oil agreement between the two countries which would give Saudi Arabian oil a special place in this country. The agreement should exempt our oil from restrictions and duties, and encourage the increasing investment of Saudi capital in marketing the oil. In the last resort there will never be a substitute for Saudi Arabia in the field of oil, as indeed there will never be anything to parallel its friendly policies towards this country.' Later, during a period for questions, Yamani explained that the investments his government had in mind included refineries and probably petrol stations in the United States; and it was then also that he first mentioned the production figure of twenty million barrels a day.

What in effect Yamani was offering was a package deal. The idea was that Saudi Arabia would virtually guarantee the United States a supply of oil – because, as he pointed out, once the Saudis had launched themselves downstream they would hardly cut off the crude to their own refineries. At the same time the drain on the American balance of payments would be offset by the return of money on capital account to fund the Saudi investments, while for the Saudis themselves the arrangement would provide an outlet for some of their surplus revenues. The suggestion for tax exemption on supplies to Saudi refineries stemmed from a natural enough wish to maximize the return on their American operations, and avoid using their own oil to subsidize the U.S. Treasury, but this would not have been an essential precondition for a deal. In fact, Prince Saud, who first emerged into the limelight around this time, appeared to back-track on the issue a few weeks later when he explained to *Petroleum Intelligence Weekly* in Riyadh: 'This doesn't mean we're insisting on a specific treaty or a special preferential quota for Saudi oil.'

Inevitably these statements caused quite a sensation. Replying to the original speech, James E. Akins, then the Director of the Office of Fuel and Energy in the State Department, said that Yamani had made 'an extremely important proposal' which the American government should study carefully. But the State Department eventually decided that any formal agreement would set a dangerous precedent in dealings between producers and consumers, and Yamani's proposals were never taken up.

The 'Oil for Industry' Initiative

The next initiative, batted around by several OPEC ministers at odd intervals during 1973, was an altogether less specific affair, not addressed to any particular Western government. Again it was Yamani who launched the idea in February, when he suggested that instead of Saudi Arabia investing in America, it might be better if the industrial world were to invest in the development of Saudi Arabia. This would increase the West's exports of capital goods and construction machinery, reduce its future imports of oil, and save it from further pollution. In the end the process would involve the Arabian Peninsula becoming a sort of industrial base – an offshore Ruhr – for the affluent consumer societies.

Then at the Vienna meeting of OPEC on 16 March the Organization members examined this concept in more detail. The conference proposed that in future oil supplies should be made conditional on firm commitments by the industrial states: first to invest – through technical expertise more than cash – in the producer countries' industry, and secondly to open their markets to the products of these industries. It was, of course, the second half of this scheme that was recognized as presenting the main problems, and the Oil Minister of Venezuela, Hugo Perez la Salvia, whose paper provided the springboard for OPEC's discussions, went into some detail about what he had in mind: 'We would not be proposing unfair competition, we ask only for equal opportunities. We are not proposing that industrial states' industries reduce their share of the market to make way for our own. We ask that in the future expansion of markets, and in the corresponding future establishment of plant, we should be given a fair opportunity to take part in proportion to our needs . . . We would only be asking for fair conditions for our own industries to compete on equal terms with theirs.'

Three months later at the next OPEC conference, la Salvia's theme was taken up by Abdel-Rahman Atiqi, the Kuwaiti Minister of Finance and Oil[2]; Prince Saud, in an interview with *Middle East Economic Survey*, again stressed the importance of the West providing not only technology but markets as well. The *Survey* commented that OPEC seemed to have found a new banner – economic development. Or one might say that its attention was turning from the relatively straight-forward issue of prices – oil for dollars – on to the much more complex equation of oil for real industrial wealth.

But while saying that even if the West avoided announcing its hostility to these ideas, it would be obvious enough if it was not co-operating, on no occasion did the producers explain what exactly the industrialized countries were expected to do. It was not said whether OPEC would be content with the West playing a purely passive role by not devaluing its currencies or surrounding itself with tarriff barriers, or whether the producers were thinking of the

West doing something more active, like imposing quotas or taxes on its own exports.

The Inter-Regional Development Initiative

The third initiative emerged in Cairo at a meeting of the Arab League's Council for Arab Economic Unity (CAEU) in March 1973, when Abdel-Rahman Atiqi proposed that the producers' future policy should be to invest as much of their surplus as possible in the deficit Arab countries. As the Minister explained later, the thinking behind his suggestion was his desire to do away with 'these unsatisfactory relationships which make us a mere source of finance for economies stronger than our own'.

Atiqi's ideas were discussed in more detail at later CAEU meetings, and in early December 1973 Mahmoud Riad, the Arab League Secretary General, announced that it had been decided that two Arab-African development funds should be established, and that there should be a gradual transfer of funds invested in foreign banks to Arab investment institutions. Coming on top of the October oil price rise and the Arab production cut-backs, when this statement was reported in London it knocked nearly twelve points off *The Financial Times* Industrial Ordinary Share Index. But the market need not have worried, because in no way was the proposed long-term transfer meant as any version of a 'money weapon' designed to damage share values or undermine the parities of Western currencies.

Interspersed with the CAEU discussions there were a number of other meetings held by finance ministers, central bank governors and prominent Arab economists. These conferences all passed broadly similar resolutions, the most important of which were: (1) that Arab credit and investment guarantee organizations should be established to enable deficit Arab states to secure finance from surplus Arab countries; (2) that there should be an expansion in numbers and size of Arab development funds; (3) that Arab stock exchanges should be set up to facilitate direct private inter-Arab investment; (4) that deficit Arab countries should inform the surplus governments of domestic investment opportunities; and (5) that surplus central banks should hold Arab government bonds as part of their currency cover, and should encourage commercial banks to buy such bonds by accepting them as part of their legal reserves.

* * *

With the exception of this third initiative, all that the producers were doing with these expositions of their thinking was fishing – hoping to draw a response from some industrial power which would lead to negotiations. This in itself would amount to an acknowledgement by the consumers that there was something to talk about, and that at least part of the producers' ideas were worth taking seriously – and from the Arab point of view this would be half the battle. Once negotiations got under way they would feed off themselves, with the Arabs picking up some more specific and practical ideas and being able more easily to translate their thinking into policy.

Sometimes these tactics were obvious enough – as with the relatively straightforward proposals for downstream investments and tax concessions which Yamani made at Georgetown. But on other subjects Yamani's habit of expansive talking, often referred to as 'speaking in headlines', has given the misleading impression that what he was saying reflected definite Saudi intentions. When he first mentioned twenty million barrels a day his words were taken too much as an objective forecast, when in fact they were little more than part of the opening gambit in the hoped-for negotiations on downstream operations.

Similarly, there was no element of forecast in the statements he made during the cut-off crisis in November and December 1973, when Yamani's attempts to draw a response from the consumers on the 'oil for industry' initiative were mixed in with the more immediate aims of preventing a united consumer response to the embargoes and the October price rise, and providing the United States with an incentive to pressure Israel into withdrawing from the occupied territories, and agreeing to a satisfactory solution to the Palestinian problem. In London he announced that in the long term Saudi Arabia would only raise output in accordance with its needs, while two weeks later in the U.S.A. he assured the American public that once the Middle East problem was settled oil production would not only be restored to September levels, but doubled or even trebled. It would be naïve to assume that this contradiction indicated a sudden reversal of Saudi policy. Rather the Saudis were holding a carrot in one hand and a stick in the other, intending to show the West that they were still open-minded on the issue, and inviting the industrial powers to offer what inducements they could to influence the Saudi decision in their favour.

Nor, on the same principle, were Yamani's and la Salvia's rather sweeping suggestions for the world's future industrial development and the sharing of markets to be taken at face value. The two ministers were not stating a hard and fast negotiating position, and they never had any intention of defining exactly what the manufacturing countries were supposed to do in the way of giving the producers a 'fair share' of the market for industrial goods. Their ideas were thrown out partly in the hope that a Western power might want to do a deal on this basis in order to secure its oil supplies, and partly to show Western corporations that they would meet with a welcome response if they put up proposals to build plant in the producer states.

In effect, with both the Georgetown and industry initiatives, the producers were saying: 'We're letting you – the consumers – know what sort of terms we would like to get for raising our production. It's up to you to decide whether you want to take us up on our ideas, but if you do you can rely on receiving the oil you need in future.'

Seen in this context it is clear that the producers did not imagine that definite plans for their accelerated industrial development could be worked out in any vast multilateral conference – though in 1974 they repeatedly made it plain that they would welcome a big meeting of producer and consumer governments (along the lines of that envisaged by the French) to give general endorsement to their ideas, and to work out, in rather more detail, a solution to the surplus revenues' recycling problems discussed in Chapters 13 and 14. It was envisaged that the substance of any industrial development packages would have to be put together on a purely bilateral basis, where deals could be tailored to the varying requirements of the producers, and the different types of industry which individual consumer-states could offer.

* * *

Up to the end of 1973 the producers' initiative received very little response from any industrial nation except Japan, which in April that year agreed to the formation of a joint Saudi-Japanese committee to promote the development of Saudi industry. But soon after the October price rise and the beginning of the Arab cut-backs all the major European countries, bar the Netherlands and Germany, began queueing up to sign deals similar to barter arrangements. The deals were supposed to involve the sale of specific amounts of oil by the producer state, and an undertaking by the consumer to build industrial projects and supply capital and military goods worth roughly the same amount. The European countries hoped that these arrangements would enable them to ride out any further Arab cuts in 1974, and any subsequent limits on output which it was feared the producers were likely to impose for conservation reasons.

In late 1973 and early 1974 negotiations were held by France with Saudi Arabia, Kuwait, Iraq, Abu Dhabi, Libya and Algeria; by Italy with Saudi Arabia and Libya; and by Britain with Saudi Arabia. Although the Saudis eventually concluded straight crude sales contracts, unaccompanied by any industrial export package, with France and Italy, none of these proposed deals ever reached fruition – and some of the French negotiations never got beyond the most preliminary stages.

The only bilateral agreement ever formally concluded at this time was that signed by Mr Peter Walker, then British Secretary of State for Industry, and the Shah of Iran at St Moritz at the end of January 1974. This was worth only $290 million, and, unlike the deals discussed by the other consumers and producers, it contained no reference to the construction of new industrial plant. It involved the exchange of five million tons of oil for various commodities, such as textile fibres, plastics, chemicals, steel and paper, which the Iranians feared they might have difficulty in obtaining on the world markets later that year.

While these negotiations were under way they met with consistent opposition from the United States. Apart from wishing to unite the consumers in a hard-line stance which might discourage the Arabs from making further production cuts, the American government was anxious that the industrial countries should avoid doing anything which would give the impression that the high oil prices announced in December were in any way acceptable. In Washington's view barter-type deals not only endorsed the new price levels, but were liable to lead to a competitive bidding-up of prices.

By the end of February, however, the enthusiasm of all parties for any form of barter deals was waning. Some of the consumers, including Britain and Germany, had never liked the idea of bilateral agreements on the grounds that they did not have state-owned oil companies which could be ordered to purchase specific quantities of crude from specific sources, and/or were not accustomed to organizing the overseas operations of their major industrial contractors. As the Arabs began to relax their cuts these sentiments were reinforced by the fear of being committed to expensive crude supplies when the open market price of oil was falling.

From the producers' point of view there was an equally strong fear that barter-type deals would involve too hasty a commitment to projects and a limited choice of suppliers. It was these considerations, coupled with pressure from the United States, which prompted the Saudis to abandon their negotiations with Britain and France.

During the summer and autumn of 1974 there was a certain reawakening of the consumers' interest in bilateral deals – and the new generation of agreements represented a considerable improvement on the original barter formula, and appeared to tie in much more closely with the 'thinking' expressed in the producers' initiative of 1973.

One of the first of the new deals was that concluded by Saudi Arabia and the United States in June. This contained no reference to any specific quantity of oil, or to American oil supplies in general, but as Mr James Akins, the United States Ambassador in Jeddah, put it: 'The purpose is to show the Saudis that it is worth producing oil rather than keeping it in the ground.

The agreement took the form of a loose package, which included American offers of advice on the investment of the Saudi surplus, and arrangements for a special issue of US government securities. But the core of the deal was an apparently simple American commitment to the formation of various joint commissions – one to oversee the military assistance programme, and the others to draw up plans for the kingdom's industrial development – giving special attention to manpower training, technology, agriculture and the use of waste gas for fertilizer production. The Saudi government seemed to be looking to the Americans for impartial advice on choosing both between contending industrial projects, and between rival companies competing for the same contracts; while the United States government hoped that the commissions would ensure that American companies got their fair share of orders for new plant and equipment.

In this form the agreement did not represent any reversal of American policy in opposing barter deals, and in fact some such general agreement had been foreshadowed in a speech made by Dr Kissinger on 12 December 1973, when the Secretary of State proposed that 'a massive effort should be made to provide an incentive for the producers to increase their supplies'. (In this speech, at the Pilgrims' Dinner in London, Kissinger also suggested that the consumers should form an energy action group to develop alternative energy sources. The Secretary of State was, in effect, using much the same stick-and-carrot sparring technique as Yamani had used in his statements in London and New York.)

The establishment of the US-Saudi commissions was followed during the autumn and winter by announcements of the formation of a number of similar committees, involving the Japanese, Germans and British in Saudi Arabia, the Japanese in Iraq, the French in Abu Dhabi and the Americans in Iran. Although none of these committees were fully operational by the end of 1974, it seemed that they would probably be less active than the US-Saudi commissions (which are standing committees) and would be concerned with fewer, and probably smaller, projects.

During the second half of 1974 and January 1975 there were four further agreements (or series of agreements) of a rather different nature – containing a mention of individual industrial projects and a very tentative price tag – which can be thought of as being mid-way between the original barter-type ideas and the new American format.

By far the biggest transactions came in a series of Franco-Iranian deals valued at up to $10 billion, which involved nuclear power stations, an underground railway for Tehran, a special steels plant, a Renault motor car factory, the installation in Iran of the Secam colour television system, twelve liquefied natural-gas tankers, and the construction of 200,000 housing units with related school and hospital facilities. Two of the other deals were between Italy and Iran ($3.1 billion) involving a massive steel mill at Bandar Abbas and infra-structural projects in the coastal area stretching from Bandar Abbas to the Gulf of Oman; and Italy and Iraq ($3.0 billion) involving Italian help in training Iraqis for industrial jobs, irrigation and drainage work along the Tigris and Euphrates, and the construction of roads, bridges, low cost housing, a petrochemical complex, a power station, a steel cold rolling mill, a pipe plant, and several agro-industrial plants. The fourth deal, between Britain and Iran, was valued at $1.2 billion and involved the electrification of the Tabriz-Tehran railway, the sale of fifteen cargo vessels, the construction of silos, meat packing plants and warehouses, port development and the establishment of a training centre for agricultural engineers.

None of these deals contained any mention of oil supplies, and they confined the consumers' commitment to the various projects to the form of highly flexible agreements in principle, which allowed scope for the projects in the packages to be modified, enlarged, scaled down, replaced or supplemented by other projects, or dropped altogether.

*   *   *

The state-to-state bilateral agreements have been accompanied by massive joint venture projects concluded with Western industrial corporations. The most obvious interest has been in petrochemicals, where the rush of major companies to the Gulf has been big enough to lead to a significant scaling down of plans for petrochemical investment in other parts of the world, particularly Europe.

In other industries some of the best known deals have been in Iran, where, for example, it was announced after an Anglo-Iranian investment conference in November 1973 that a group of companies, including British Leyland, Hawker Siddeley, Massey Ferguson, Acrow (Engineers), and the British Steel Corporation, were to participate in projects valued at some $600 million. In Saudi Arabia meanwhile Nissan and General Motors have agreed to build truck and car assembly plants, and there have been proposals for the construction of steel mills from such companies as Broken Hill Proprietary of Australia, the Marcona Corporation of the USA, the Dutch-German group Estel, and the two largest Japanese steel companies, Nippon Steel and Nippon Kokan. In fact by December 1974 Petromin, the Saudi state oil and minerals agency, was thought to have signed nearly seventy letters of intent for major energy-orientated industries – including thirteen export refineries, a similar number of petrochemical plants, and various aluminium smelters, gas reduction steel mills and fertilizer plants.

In Bahrain there were plans for foreign participation in spin-off industries based on the Aluminium Bahrain (Alba) smelter. Alba itself is run off cheap local natural gas. It imports alumina from Australia, and exports almost all of its output – and it is a classic example of the type of plant envisaged by the producers in the original oil for industry initiative.

Some of the projects sponsored by Western corporations have been just as big as those included in the inter-government deals, and it might be assumed that the producers could continue to promote their industrial development by working with foreign companies on a normal commercial basis, leaving the consumer governments out of their plans altogether. The fact that the Arab and Iranian governments have virtually unlimited capital at their disposal, and are prepared to offer foreign investors tax concessions (or no tax at all), complete freedom in the repatriation of profits, and, in some cases, a large degree of management control, should, after all, be sufficient to encourage a large number of companies to build some of their export plant in the Middle East rather than in their home states. At the same time it should be possible for the producers further to encourage this type of investment through buying into the equity of big Western companies, and, as Iran did when it bought twenty-five per cent of the Krupp steel subsidiary, obtaining voting rights on their boards.

But in certain crucial respects ordinary commercial deals do not match up to the producers' requirements. Some of these short-comings were touched on by Yamani when he explained in May 1974 that negotiations with individual companies could not provide Saudi Arabia with all the technical assistance it needed, and would not necessarily lead to the establishment of the desired number and range of industries – because individual companies could not always guarantee export markets for all the products which Saudi Arabia would like to manufacture.

During 1974 the Saudis also found themselves bemused by the sheer numbers of companies with which they were dealing – even though some sixty foreign consultancy firms were being employed by different ministries. They complained that they did not have the manpower to deal with each company individually, and they stressed that they needed Western governments to help them through the jungle by shepherding together major corporations to undertake a group of projects and then seeing that these were carried out properly and on time. In this respect the Saudis were disappointed by the early performance of the American economic commissions, which ran foul of US industrialists when they tried to round them up for joint negotiations. It was hoped that the problem would be less likely to recur with commissions set up by European governments, which exercised a greater degree of state control over their eco-nomies.

*   *   *

Further co-operation from the consumer governments will be needed if the producers are to make satisfactory arrangements for dealing with the other part of their problem – the investment of their surplus revenues. Ideally the Arabs would like to be able to tie the invest-ment and industrial assistance aspects together in a few big inter-government packages.

This was arranged on a relatively unambitious scale as part of the US – Saudi deal in June 1974, but in the longer term the Arabs are hoping to negotiate rather more comprehensive agreements which would give their monetary reserves a measure of protection against devaluations and inflation. These agreements might involve the issue of indexed bonds, and possibly consumer government help in establishing new investment institutions, which would channel Arab money into inflation-proof real assets – like property, land and major holdings in industrial plant – requiring a larger amount of management expertise than most of the producers at present can muster.

This aspect of future packages will be almost as important to the producers as the industrial assistance element, because, whatever their long-term ambitions to become industrial powers, and however much they would prefer to spend their income, the U-turn pheno-menon is already beginning to operate on a colossal and unpreceden-ted scale. Over the next decade the U-turn is going to be the most visible feature of the Arab revenues explosion – and so the following chapters are devoted to examining the capital that is flowing to the West in more detail – and to discovering who owns it, who manages it and how it is used.

[1]After King Faisal's assassination on 25 March 1975 there were a number of changes in the Saudi government. The new King (who also held the positions of Prime Minister and Foreign Minister) was Prince Khaled bin Abdel-Aziz, one of Faisal's brothers and formerly Crown Prince and First Deputy Prime Minister. Prince Fahad became Crown Prince and First Deputy Prime Minister, while retaining his position as Minister of the Interior, and seemed certain to be the power behind the throne. Prince Saud became Minister of State for Foreign Affairs. Anwar Ali's successor at SAMA, named in late 1974, was Abdel-Aziz Quraishi.

[2]In the rearrangement of the Kuwaiti government after the elections of January 1975 the Ministry of Finance and Oil was split. Atiqi became Minister of Finance, and Mr. Abdel-Mutaleb Kazimi became Minister of Oil.

6

SPREADING THE WEALTH

One morning, Shaikh Shakbut bin Sultan al Nahayan, Ruler of Abu Dhabi, went down to the cellar of his palace to have a look at his oil revenues, and found, to his great dismay, that some £50,000 worth had been eaten by mice. He was so upset that he wrote to the British Political Agent in Dubai to ask if in future his revenues could be printed on poisonous and decay-proof paper.

Unfortunately for connoisseurs of Shaikhly anecdotes, this well known story is almost certainly untrue. Contrary to popular belief, Shaikh Shakbut did use banks. First he patronized the British Bank of the Middle East, and then when the manager offended him by transferring part of his deposit account to make up his current account overdraft, he switched to the Ottoman and Eastern banks. But the legend of the mice would probably never have arisen had it not seemed to sum up Shakbut – or rather Shakbut's popular image – so well.*

To be fair to Shakbut his reputation was not entirely justified. To write him off as an ordinary miser would be far too simple an interpretation of the man's character. At times it is true he was extraordinarily mean, lopping bits off his staff's salaries and refusing to pay their expenses; and certainly he spent very little money on himself, his most conspicuous luxury being a large chromium-plated espresso coffee machine given to him by Abu Dhabi Marine Areas,

*Shaikh Shakbut's full name – Shakbut bin Sultan al Nahayan – means roughly Shakbut, son of Sultan of the Nahayan family. The term 'Shaikh' in the Gulf states is applied only to members of the ruling families. In Saudi Arabia, where members of al Saud are Princes, the term denotes either a tribal leader, or, used more loosely, somebody who is held in respect – Shaikh Ahmed Zaki Yamani for instance.

and installed in a room on its own in his palace. He also had an appalling mental block over the uses of money. He was quite unable to
appreciate the necessity for commissioning a survey of the water
table in the Buraimi Oasis, because he said that he knew it contained
enough water to supply Abu Dhabi, and did not need to pay good
money to be told so by engineers. Similarly it seemed to him ridiculous that he should pay out $25,000 for a development plan – a mere
piece of paper. But beneath his eccentricities Shakbut did have some
sort of coherent philosophy on the subject of oil revenues. This was
that the money would not last for ever, and that the more he spent
the more he would need. The people of Abu Dhabi, whom he
referred to as 'al Raiia' – his flock – seemed perfectly happy as they
were, and he did not believe that they would enjoy life any more if
he started pumping millions of dollars into the state. Indeed, much to
his concessionnaire's embarrassment, Shakbut decided that the oil
companies needed the money more than he did, and for the first year
of production, in 1962, he would only accept payments on the basis
of the pre-1950 fixed royalty arrangements.

In financial terms Shakbut's definition of doing what was good for
his people extended as far as improving a few earth roads, installing
the water supply to Abu Dhabi town from Buraimi, and building a
power station, a couple of schools, and a small hospital which he
staffed with the cheapest doctors he could find. All these facilities
were provided free for his people, and, as Shakbut said, anyone who
fell really ill he would fly to London to be cured. Otherwise he
felt that his duty lay in ruling as best he could in the traditional
way.

It is personal contact between ruler and subjects which is the
cornerstone of the old-fashioned system of government in the Gulf.
Nowadays the increasing administrative burdens that wealth has
brought have made the rulers less approachable. In Kuwait the old
ways have disappeared – but in the lower Gulf states there are still one
or two days during most weeks when the people can come and talk
to the ruler in his Majlis (council chamber). They may simply
bring family news or problems for the ruler to give his opinion on,
or they may explain that they have fallen on hard times and would be
grateful for a little financial assistance, or that one of their children
is ill, and that they would like him sent to a specialist hospital abroad.
Foreign visitors may call to say how delighted they are to be enjoying
the hospitality of His Highness's country.

All this Shakbut excelled at. He knew every family in his state, he
was always available to receive his subjects, and he was a superb

listener. He guided his country skilfully through a small war with Dubai from 1945 to 1948, and through the Saudi incursion into the Buraimi Oasis in 1952. (It was on this latter occasion that his brother, Shaikh Zaid bin Sultan, who was then Governor of al Ain, turned down a Saudi bribe of $80 million.) For the whole of his thirty-eight-year rule Shakbut also maintained Abu Dhabi in a state of peace internally. In view of the bloodstained history of his family, which had involved most of the rulers since 1793 being either deposed or murdered, this was no small achievement in itself.

Nonetheless, for all his traditional wisdom, and his astonishing interest in matters scientific (including space travel), Shakbut's handling of money was an embarrassment to the protecting power. Although in the early 1960s Abu Dhabi's revenues were running at only a few tens of millions of dollars a year, they could hardly go on being put in the bank for ever, and so the British decided that Shaikh Zaid should take over. This Zaid was extremely reluctant to do, because long ago the brothers had sworn to their mother, the forceful and influential Shaikha Salaama, not to murder each other. But eventually Zaid agreed, and in 1966 Shakbut was removed. For some years Shakbut stayed abroad, but now he has been welcomed home by his brother, and he lives in retirement outside al Ain.

*   *   *

The purpose of this digression is not just to clear Shaikh Shakbut's name – though this is well worth doing because he is so often misrepresented. More important, Shakbut's story shows what an enormous break with the past the coming of oil revenues meant, and what a huge adjustment is called for on the part of the rulers. Simply to ignore the money, which was what in effect Shakbut tried to do, was not possible. The oil states had to set about adapting themselves from the life of small fishing/pearling/pastoral/trading communities to the habits of Western consumer culture in a matter of a few years. There were no precedents elsewhere in the world, nobody's mistakes to learn from, nobody to copy.

Faced with these same problems, the various states have found their own individual solutions – each has used and spread its wealth differently, and each has evolved into a different type of society. It is important to look at these differences and at the history of this process in each state because they provide some of the vital background to the money which is now being invested in the West. They explain how much is government money and how much is private, who owns the private money, how it has been earned, and how therefore it is likely to be invested.

KUWAIT

By far the most comprehensive philosophy of wealth and society in an oil state has been worked out in Kuwait. Perhaps this was inevitable because Kuwait ran into the problem earliest, and in its most sudden and acute form. Although production had begun just after the Second World War, by 1951 its oil income was still only $18 million. At this time Kuwait's revenues were paid one year in arrears (a system which continued until 1964), and so it was not until 1952 that the combined effects of the new fifty–fifty profit split and the surge in production caused by the Mossadeq crisis in Iran were first felt. In that year the state's revenues jumped to $56 million, and in the following year, when Kuwait became the biggest oil producer in the Middle East and fourth largest in the world, its income reached $168 million.

In the days before oil Kuwait (meaning 'little fort') was a small coastal settlement engaged in trade and pearl diving. The ruling al Sabah family, a branch of the Anazeh tribe, had migrated there from central Arabia in about 1750, along with the al Khalifa family who later moved down to Bahrain. The ruler himself was elected in rotation from the three branches of the family, al Salam, al Mubarak and al Ahmed, and his government was run on taxes levied on commerce, which by the late 1930s provided the exchequer with some $300,000 a year. In return for this levy the al Sabahs were expected to safeguard the security of the state, and their position was reinforced by the treaty of protection concluded by the British with the ruler personally in 1899. This treaty and those similar to it concluded with Bahrain, Qatar and the Trucial States, formed the basis of the British role in the Gulf. In essence the shaikhdoms bound themselves not 'to cede, mortgage, or otherwise dispose of parts of their territories to anyone except Her Majesty's Government, nor to enter into any relationship with a foreign power, other than Britain, without British consent'. In return, Britain undertook to conduct their defence and external relations.

Beneath the ruling family were the maritime and merchant communities. These men made up Kuwait's best educated citizens. Their elders were the ruler's advisers, and through their ability to withold loans from the al Sabahs they exercised a substantial in-

F

fluence on affairs of state. They also owned most of Kuwait's wealth, and their annual income was considerably above the $20 a head received by most of the population – which then numbered only 75,000.

The merchants' modest fortunes were based on the ownership of fishing and trading dhows, and their business received a severe setback in the 1930s when the pearl-diving industry collapsed under competition from the new cultured pearls of Japan. In fact the traditional maritime occupations of Kuwaitis did not revive until the late 1940s and early 1950s when there was a short boom in smuggling gold to India. Still, like the trading classes of Bahrain and Dubai, which has since taken over the gold 're-export' business, the Kuwaitis had considerable experience of the outside world – some of them maintaining representative offices in Bombay – and they were much better prepared for the influx of oil wealth than were the pastoral Bedouin peoples of Abu Dhabi and Saudi Arabia.

Fortunately the great surge in oil production in 1951 also coincided with the accession of a new and enlightened ruler, Shaikh Abdullah al Salem al Sabah, the man who made the early fundamental decision that Kuwait's wealth should be distributed among his people. However, despite the qualities of farsightedness, moderation and balance of judgement for which he had originally been elected, Shaikh Abdullah became depressed to the point of melancholia when confronted with family disputes, and he generally shrank from exerting his authority or overriding the decisions of department heads. So the development of Kuwait during the 1950s fell under the effective control of the ruler's half-brother, Shaikh Fahad al Salam, an aggressive hard-working man, much under the influence of his ambitious second wife, Shaikha Badriah.

Fahad dominated Supreme Council meetings (because he was virtually the only member to brief himself in advance), he eventually controlled five out of the twelve government departments, including the all-important Public Works Department, he became by far the biggest spender of public money and awarder of contracts, and he thus built up a large army of 'payrollers' and an impressive political machine. His strength was seen very clearly during the infamous land-grabbing scandal of the mid-1950s. To grab titleless land a claimant outlined an area with white barrels and painted his name on them – and Fahad's control of PWD trucks and empty oil barrels enabled him to facilitate to an enormous degree the fortunes of several family members and a considerable number of his other friends.

It was during the ascendency of Shaikh Fahad, when the Kuwaiti boom was at its most ostentatious, that the legends of huge shaikhly extravagance were born. And these were not entirely without basis. Fahad used to requisition millions from the Finance Department with no more than a hand-written chit, and little explanation of their purpose, and for his annual six- or seven-month excursions to Europe, during which Kuwait's development slowed down somewhat, he generally allowed himself $800,000, drawn from the National Bank in American Express travellers' cheques. But through all this the oil money was steadily spreading lower down Kuwaiti society, and the biggest agent of this process was (and still is) the land buying programme.

The programme stemmed more or less by accident from the very first meeting of the Development Board in January 1952, when General Bill Hastead, the ex-Indian Army Controller of Development, had his proposal to peg land prices rejected by the Kuwaiti members, on the grounds that when there was so much money to be made in gold, nobody would want to put their capital into patches of desert. Whether they said this from genuine naïvety, or whether they had spotted an opportunity to be in the know at the start of a very profitable enterprise, is open to question, but by 1953 land prices had started to climb.

When the government first began buying land for development in Shuwaikh, now an industrial area west of Kuwait city, it was paying under half a rupee* per square foot, but by the mid-1950s the price had risen to R500, and by the early 1960s in the present centre of the city it reached KD55, which meant that the space required to park a car cost $19,600. Anyone who found out in which direction the Development Board was going to expand, and could buy, or grab, the land in its path, stood to make a fortune – though there were also a lot of people who guessed wrong, or were deliberately told wrong, on whom the gamble turned sour.

Speculation however was not the main force behind the soaring price of land. The government itself over-priced land to cut its citizens in on the oil wealth to the maximum extent possible, and a very large part of what it bought was never earmarked for develop-

*Originally the currency in all the British protected shaikhdoms was the Gulf rupee, at par with the Indian rupee. At the time of the Indian devaluation in the early 1960s the Gulf states changed over to new currencies. Kuwait in 1961 adopted the Kuwait dinar, worth about R13, and until the devaluation of the pound in 1967 at par with sterling. In December 1973 one KD was worth about £1.40 or $3.30.

ment at all, but was intended from the start to be sold back to the public at a much lower price. The exact mechanics of this process have varied, but the net result is that from the early 1950s up to the 1972/3 financial year over KD800 million ($2,400 m) or nearly a quarter of total oil revenues have been distributed in this fashion. The system has been criticized as a crude means of spreading income, and since 1968 allocations have been considerably reduced and directed more specifically towards the lower income groups, but in the context of Kuwait in the early 1950s it is difficult to think of any practical alternative to land purchase, short of donations or handouts.

In a slightly less blatant manner the government has distributed a similar amount of money through the policy of overstaffing all its establishments and paying extraordinarily high salaries – for jobs which often require no more than symbolic effort or perfunctory attendance. In the 1972/3 fiscal year disbursements under this heading ran to over KD150 m ($450 m), or some twenty-eight per cent of the combined ordinary and development budgets. A primary school headmistress, for instance, would get KD4,000 p.a., and an office sweeper KD28 a week, which would easily be low enough to qualify him for an interest-free loan under the government's housing scheme. Nobody's income is subject to tax or social security contributions. All Kuwait's 160,000 odd primary and secondary school pupils receive free education, and the government will pay for anyone with sufficient qualifications to go to university abroad wherever he or she wishes. A special office is maintained in London to distribute grants to students studying in the UK. Health services are free, with a similar London office to pay for those sent abroad for specialist treatment. Local telephone calls are free, there is no purchase tax, cigarettes cost about eight pence or twenty cents a pack (only king size and larger available), petrol costs about the same, a small charge is made for water – all of which is desalinated from the sea – and alcohol is prohibited. The business community benefits from a ban on foreigners owning land or more than forty-nine per cent of any local enterprise. There is no corporation tax, and only nominal customs duties on a few items.

At the top of the tree the present ruler, Shaikh Sabah al Salem al Sabah, who succeeded Shaikh Abdullah in 1965, receives a civil list of KD8 m a year, out of which he pays a stipend to dependent members of the al Sabah family. In 1961, when Shaikh Abdullah formally separated his finances from those of the state, the sum was fixed at KD10 m, but this was cut in 1967 when Kuwait began paying subsidies to the front-line states involved in the war with Israel. In addition to the ruler's funds there are at least two other distinct fortunes within the family – that of Shaikh Jaber al Ahmed, the present Prime Minister, and his brothers,* who inherited the estate of Shaikh Ahmed al Jaber, the conservative ruler who died in 1951; and that of Shaikh Sa'ad al Abdullah, the Minister of Defence, who inherited the fortune of Shaikh Abdullah.

Since the early 1960s Kuwait has become a much more orderly state. The ruler finally curbed Shaikh Fahad's power in May 1959 when Shaikh Jaber was appointed to the Finance Department, and Fahad died a few weeks later on a pilgrimage to Mecca. In 1961 British protection was withdrawn, and in 1963 the first elected National Assembly was opened. For several years the government was still composed almost entirely of members of the al Sabah family, but the most recent administrations, formed in 1971 and January 1975, have established businessmen in the technical ministries, and have appointed members of the new educated class to the important ministries of Finance, Oil, Education and Cabinet Affairs.

The fifty members of the last two assemblies have included several merchants and backwoods shaikhs, a few committed leftists and a number of deputies who, for want of a better word, can be described as nationalists. Although there has never been a formal opposition bloc, at different times various combinations of deputies have been able to defeat the government on major issues. So far the assembly's most conspicuous concern has been the obstruction of government oil policy. In 1965 it refused to ratify the first OPEC agreement on royalty expensing; in 1971 it threw out a plan for a liquefied natural gas plant because it objected to the participation of British Petroleum and Gulf; in 1972 it pushed the government into putting the three million barrels a day ceiling on oil production; and in 1973 it rejected the Participation Agreement and demanded that the Kuwait Oil Company be nationalized. If he had used all the means at his disposal, Shaikh Jaber could probably have found ways to push Participation through the assembly, but, to his credit, he resisted the temptation.

Apart from echoing the radical currents of Arab politics, the rest of the assembly's attention has been focused on political liberalization – involving such issues as permission for political parties; votes for women; and better treatment for non-Kuwaitis, who make up over

*Shaikh Jaber's brothers include Shaikh Sabah al Ahmed, who is the present Foreign Minister and the majority owner of Gulf International, the Kuwaiti/Sudanese industrial group discussed in Chapter 12.

half the population, but are mostly excluded from citizenship, and are not eligible for some of the welfare benefits. At the highest level, the non-Kuwaitis, Palestinians especially, occupy senior advisory positions in the ministries. Palestinians and Egyptians provide most of the teachers, doctors and engineers; Indians and Pakistanis are clerks and mechanics; and Iraqis and Iranians, particularly Baluch, Bakhtiari and Qashqai tribesmen, form the manual labour force.

Considering the pressures it has been under as a small rich state in a turbulent Arab world, Kuwait has turned out to be a very pleasant and mature community – a place of sanity and gentility. It is the most democratic of all the Arab countries, bar Lebanon (where politics has a certain gangster tinge), it has a free press, and there is a good deal of open and objective thinking among its people. But the rule of 'Absolute Welfare' has not been without some bad side effects. Throughout society there has been a dimming of the relationship between effort and reward. Many young Kuwaitis become permanent students, and relatively few graduates have come home to work as engineers or doctors – preferring what they consider to be the more dignified life of business, where the profits are bigger. Outside the technical professions there is an appalling shortage of jobs for graduates in the government service, and as the men in the upper echelons of the ministries and state corporations are still in their thirties, the promotional bottleneck is likely to continue for many years to come.

The 'cutting-in' policy has also meant that the Kuwaiti public has more money to invest than the citizens of any other Arab state. Residents' bank deposits in December 1973 were $1,730 million – which can be compared with $1,100 million in Saudi Arabia, $150 million in Qatar, $195 million in Bahrain (in March 1973), $185 million in Dubai (in December 1972), and $120 million in Abu Dhabi (in December 1972).* Because of the oil price increases these figures, *and all figures listed for different types of private wealth in the rest of this book*, will expand enormously during the remainder of the 1970s. But given that it will take some time for the governments to re-gear their development plans and increase their spending, the new wealth may not begin to arrive in private hands on a really large scale until 1976. Meanwhile in 1974 it is probably still true to say that Kuwaiti residents' bank deposits and the Kuwaiti banks' foreign assets are as big as those of all the remaining Arabian

*Total deposits in December 1973 were: Kuwait $2,200 million, Saudi Arabia $1,190 m, Abu Dhabi $450 m (of which $233 m were government deposits), Dubai $300 m, Qatar $175m, and Bahrain (in March 1973) $230 m.

Peninsula states combined, while the direct private investments of the Kuwaitis in Europe and America are probably very much larger than those of the citizens of all the other states combined.

SAUDI ARABIA

In many respects the Saudi approach to wealth has been the exact opposite of Kuwait's. In part this is a measure of the country's bigger population and vast area, which until the recent explosion of revenues would have made the creation of a welfare state impossible. But equally important has been the austere character of King Faisal, and the Saudis' belief that too much money has made the Kuwaitis effete. After his accession in 1964 King Faisal bin Abdel-Aziz al Saud reacted strongly against the squanderings that marked the reign of his brother, cutting the stipends of the five thousand odd members of his family, and making it clear to the princes that ministries in his government were not sinecures, and had to be won by performance. The exact size of the al Saud income now is difficult to discover, though it is known that large parts of the princes' assets are tied up in local land, much of it at present unrealizable.

King Faisal himself was born in 1905, the third son of the founder of the kingdom, the great King Abdel-Aziz (ibn Saud) who died in 1953. He was a devout and ascetic man. Only recently, it is said, did he cut his working day from eighteen to fourteen hours. He ate rice and boiled mutton, taking his cook with him when he travelled, and he drove through Riyadh and Jeddah in the front seat of a rather old black Chrysler. By Arabian standards his domestic life was simple and modest. He had only four wives – one died and two were divorced, and he was with the surviving one, Iffat, for forty years.

The emphasis in King Faisal's rule was on gradual change, in which his people, as guardians of the Holy Places at Mecca and Medina, could retain their traditional Arab and Moslem values. It was not that the King despised Western culture. He wanted his country to become part of the community of Western powers, and he admired European and American society, but he did not want Saudi Arabia to adopt the more flashy and ephemeral ways of the consumer society, and he was anxious to avoid the mistake which other developing countries have made of abandoning their old culture in a rush to become as modern and 'Westernized' as possible. This philosophy was well summed up in the book *Farewell to Arabia*, where David Holden wrote that the King displayed 'the characteristic knack of the radical conservative for leading his people backwards into the future'.

Until recently this journey has involved keeping Saudi Arabia largely shut off from the world outside. Foreigners may only visit the country for pilgrimage or business, not tourism, and the resident Western community has been mainly confined to Jeddah, which contains the embassies and most of the foreign banks, and Dhahran, which is the headquarters of Aramco. The first year of television services was taken up entirely with readings from the Koran; alcohol, gambling and all forms of clubs are banned, foreign newspapers are censored, cinemas are out of bounds to Saudis, and women may not drive cars.

In the last two years things have begun to change, particularly in Jeddah, which receives a growing annual influx of pilgrims in the month of the Haj. The atmosphere has become more relaxed and friendly, and more Saudi women – from the wealthy families – are appearing outside their homes in Western dress. But the stern punishments of the Shariah law are still rigorously enforced in criminal matters, and a convicted thief may still have his hands cut off.

In economic matters the Saudi government holds an almost fanatical belief in free enterprise and the work ethic. The country has only some of the trappings of oil state economies, like free education and health services and no tax – except for the Jihad (Holy War) tax, levied between 1967 and 1970 to help finance the grants to Egypt and Jordan, and the two and a half per cent Zakat, a semi-optional religious tax which the rich pay to the Ministry of Labour to be spent on the poor. A few business enterprises have been given exclusive concessions to operate public utilities in the main provinces, though these were granted for the sake of convenience, rather than for the purpose of enriching Saudi citizens. In general, if a man was to get rich the King felt it should be through hard work, not handouts. Government salaries are slightly lower than those available in private companies, and land is bought at the going price as and when it is needed.

So Saudi Arabia has none of the gold rush, get-rich-quick atmosphere which once characterized Kuwait, and is still a feature of Abu Dhabi. Land prices are now rising fast, partly as a result of the Saudis bringing their money home during the currency crisis of 1971–73, and some people are leaving salaried positions to chance their arm at contracting for government tenders. But the private-sector boom is not very conspicuous because of the size of the country and the scattered population, and few of the big merchant houses are yet operating on a nationwide scale.

The banking habit is still new in Saudi Arabia. Deposits are little more than half of what they are in Kuwait, and despite the greater scope for domestic expansion and double the amount of imports, total advances ($675 million in December 1973) are only sixty per cent of the Kuwaiti figure. At the top level the biggest Saudi and Kuwaiti merchants are probably more or less equal in wealth. But lower down the scale, while all Kuwaiti middle-class families are 'rich', whether they have been successful in business or not, the Saudi middle class is only moderately prosperous.

QATAR

From the social point of view Qatar is less interesting than either Kuwait or Saudi Arabia. The emirate has always had a somewhat indistinct image, particularly when compared with its far more sophisticated neighbour, Bahrain, which has been enjoying a small oil income and free education since the 1930s. Qatar's revenues have never been very large, and, more important, until recently none of its rulers seems to have had the same definite ideas as King Faisal and Sheikh Abdullah on what sort of society they wanted to build.

There was one man who would have made an excellent ruler in the early days of oil – Shaikh Hamad bin Abdullah al Thani, who ran the government on behalf of his father through the difficult period after the collapse of the pearling industry. But Shaikh Hamad died prematurely in 1947, and for the next four years his father took direct control until old age forced him to retire. It had then been intended that Shaikh Khalifa, Hamad's son, should succeed, but Khalifa was only nineteen at the time, and he was passed over in favour of Shaikh Ali, a more distant relative. Shaikh Ali was not the shrewdest or most active member of the Al Thani family, his size suggested that he was unusually fond of his food, and over the years his rule became less and less effective. In 1960 the British sponsored his removal, and moored a gunboat off Doha, the capital, to ensure the coup's success.

The new ruler was Ali's son, Shaikh Ahmed. Quite a popular figure, but not hard working or gifted with an equable temperament, he did nothing to curb the extravagances of his family. He himself took about a quarter of the state's revenues each year, which in 1970 must have given him some $50 million. This he used, among other things, for the upkeep of his 3,000-ton yacht – formerly a Mediterranean cruise liner, and for chartering a VC 10 as his personal aircraft.

At the same time each of the five hundred-odd male members of the family received a stipend of $7,000 a year from birth, which meant that the al Thanis as a whole got through between a third and a half of Qatar's income each year. In practice the system was not quite as inequitable as it sounds, because with wives and daughters included, the ruling family accounts for a significant proportion of the true Qatari population (as opposed to the expatriates who make up over half of the total residents) – and a further large slice of the population is in the al Thanis' direct employ.

In February 1972 Shaikh Ahmed was overthrown while away on a falconing expedition in Iran, by Shaikh Khalifa bin Hamad, who by then had become deputy ruler and Prime Minister. The official pretext for the coup, given over Doha radio, was that Shaikh Khalifa had 'tried in vain to dissuade by advice and counsel those elements who had been indulging in profiteering and accumulation of fortune at the expense of the people', and that the resort to force was 'intended to correct conditions in the country and to remove the elements that had tried to hinder its progress and modernization'. But, as Richard Johns, the Middle East correspondent of *The Financial Times*, found out, what spurred Shaikh Khalifa into action were the activities of the deposed ruler's son, Shaikh Abdel-Aziz. This young man, who occupied the position of Minister of Health, held a well established reputation for violence. In the months before the coup Shaikh Abdel-Aziz had left no doubt about his pretentions to the succession and his claim to Shaikh Khalifa's title of Crown Prince, and the fact that at the time of the coup his palace was found to contain several lorry-loads of arms, an electric chair and a list of fifty prominent Qataris and expatriate Arabs working for the government, suggested that on this occasion he might have been planning to remove Shaikh Khalifa. Shaikh Ahmed and Shaikh Abdel-Aziz are now living in Dubai, as guests of the ruler, Shaikh Rashid bin Said al Makhtoum, whose daughter is Shaikh Ahmed's wife.

Shaikh Khalifa is the first ruler who has really set himself to do something for Qatar. Even before his accession, when he was Minister of Education in Shaikh Ali's time, it was he who built the schools and the first hospital, and later, when he was Prime Minister, it was he who exercised effective control over development. Now he models himself on his father, the much loved Shaikh Hamad. On coming to power he cut the salary he lived on as deputy ruler, and has since made do with $240,000 a year for himself and his immediate family.

In contrast to Shaikh Ahmed and Shaikh Abdel-Aziz, with their substantial investments in Switzerland, Khalifa owns no property outside Qatar – though he once had a modest house in London, near Paddington – and he seems to have few foreign investments of any other sort. The qualifying age for the al Thani male stipend was raised from birth to twelve years in 1970, but now it is thought that Khalifa may be reducing the amount of the payment as well.

Outside the ranks of the more prodigal al Thani members, Qatar's money is carefully spent. Up to October 1973 the state needed all the income it could get, and unlike the ruler of Abu Dhabi, Khalifa was firm in refusing the requests of other Arab states for hand-outs. At the time of the coup all mortgage obligations of Qataris who had bought subsidized houses on state loans were written off, and government salaries were raised by twenty per cent – though they are still well below the Kuwaiti level. Education and health services are free, there is no income tax for individuals, and only five per cent for companies' profits over 700,000 Qatar riyals – increasing to ten per cent at QR5 million.*

It is too early yet to judge what sort of a state Qatar will become under Shaikh Khalifa. All the larger emirates in the lower Gulf, with the exception of Bahrain, are still at the stage reached by Kuwait ten years ago. Although each has a personality of its own, as yet it is difficult to think of any of them as a nation (as Kuwait has now become) or as having evolved a distinctive social system.

ABU DHABI

Because of the newness and the size of its oil income, Abu Dhabi is changing faster than any other state in the Gulf. Since the end of 1971 it has been the leading member of the United Arab Emirates – Shaikh Zaid is the President – but it will probably take another five years before it can be seen whether the federation is going to hang together convincingly as a single nation. Its future really depends on how much the Union will become part of Abu Dhabi, rather than vice versa – and during 1973 and 1974 the momentum of events, encouraged by Shaikh Zaid, seemed to be in Abu Dhabi's favour. The state's wealth is a magnet to the population of the emirates in the north of the Musandam Peninsula. Even those who do not actually move to Abu Dhabi in search of jobs are leaving the

*Nine and a half Qatar riyals are worth about one pound sterling.

tribal life to settle near the schools, clinics and federal development projects which Abu Dhabi's money finances. As they do so the tribal authority of the local rulers falls into eclipse.

In Abu Dhabi itself Shaikh Zaid started spending the fairly modest amounts of money that his brother had accumulated in 1967, and for several years the emirate enjoyed dramatic expansion – ending with a severe recession in 1970, when the government's development budget was cut by a quarter, bank deposits dropped by thirty per cent, and building approvals almost halved. Since the recovery of 1971 and 1972 much of the government's money has been spread through giving citizens privileged opportunities to make money in property – though this is being done on a rather smaller scale than in Kuwait. There is a government-sponsored scheme for nationals to borrow money to put up accommodation, either for themselves, or (as is more often the case) for renting; and to cut down on contractors' profits the government is also building its own houses, and then selling them at cost price – either to owner occupiers or to landlords. Health services and education are free. Children at school are provided with free clothing, transport and mid-day meals, and their parents are paid a subsidy of between $15 and $30 a month (according to grade) for every child in class.

Shaikh Zaid used to receive about a quarter of the revenues himself, but since the Tehran Agreement this proportion has been steadily cut back, and in early 1973 it was thought to be running at about ten per cent. Of all the rulers in the oil states he probably has by far the largest expenses. His purse is much used in the cause of federal unity. Considerable sums have been given to Pakistan, for which state Zaid has a special affection, to the Palestinians, and in 1973 to Egypt – although in most of these cases government funds have been employed as well. The people of Abu Dhabi too have benefited from Zaid's generosity. In the month of Ramadan 1972, when Moslems fast by day and feast after sundown, Zaid imported enough livestock to halve the price of meat in the local markets – a popular gesture very much in the classic style of the traditional ruler.

*   *   *

In every state of the Arabian Peninsula there are a number of families who are almost as rich as their rulers – or, in the case of Bahrain, considerably richer. Most of their fortunes are based on import agencies, and on the enormous profits to be made from having the sales monopoly for companies like General Motors in countries with virtually no import duties, no company tax and thousands of affluent consumers. Even a relatively small operation, like that of Yusif Alyan, the food importer who sells Kuwaitis a hundred miles of Swiss roll each year, can achieve a turnover of two or three million dollars.

Complementing their agencies the bigger trading houses have a number of other interests, turning them into a sort of family conglomerate. In Saudi Arabia, Abdel-Aziz Sulaiman, one of the top five or six merchants and agent for Datsun and Scania Vabis (lorries), owns Jeddah's two biggest hotels, a contracting firm, Reem Construction, and a major interest in the Arabian Cement Company – his father Abdullah, the Finance Minister of King Abdel-Aziz, having been given the Hijaz cement franchise. Similarly, the richest Qatari merchant house, Kassem and Abdullah Sons of Darwish, who have extended their operations into Saudi Arabia, Abu Dhabi, Sharjah and Ras al Khaimah, now has travel agencies, cold stores, contracting companies, the Oasis Hotel in Doha and a catering concern at Qatar's international airport. Abdullah Darwish's fortune was originally built on supplying and contracting for the Qatar Petroleum Company, and the same principle has applied in Bahrain for Hussein Yateem, who provided a bargain rate labour force for BAPCO, and in Saudi Arabia for the Aramco merchants, Sulaiman Olayan, Qahtani and Tamini, whose operations are still largely confined to the Eastern Province.

As these examples show, the division between importers, contractors, industrialists and property owners is a hazy one. But rather separate from these enterprises is a group of merchants who are still operating in the old style, and who are best described as multi-billion dollar bazaar traders – men with a vast turnover, but no 'front' and very rudimentary finance and book-keeping techniques. In Saudi Arabia the obvious examples would be the three bulk food importers, Baeshen, Sharbatly and Bassamah, the last two of whom originally came to the Kingdom as houseboys from the Hadramaut. In much the same style are the two Rajhi brothers, Salah and Sulaiman, the exchange dealers. Sulaiman Rajhi, who became the manager of one of his brother's operations at the age of fifteen, is now thought to be perhaps the richest merchant in the Kingdom, and probably the biggest single investor in Saudi public companies.

Among both the traditional traders, like Rajhi, and the newer import agencies, a surprising number of the big names in the Gulf and Arabia today are not the descendants of pre-oil merchant families. In Saudi Arabia many of the most prominent businessmen

– the Juffalis (discussed in detail in Chapter 12), the Jumaihs, Sulaiman Olayan, the Bassams (who went to India), the Sulaimans, and the Rajhi brothers – came from inland during the early years of this century. Their original home was the area around Onaizah and Buraidah north of Riyadh – hundreds of miles from the traditional trading towns of the Hijaz, and al Khobar and Dammam in the Eastern Province.

Some of the principal families of Kuwait, al Ghanim, al Sagar, al Badr, al Roumi, al Shamlan, al Qatami – in fact, those who arrived with the al Sabahs in the mid-eighteenth century – used to be seamen rather than traders. One of the Qatamis even wrote a comprehensive manual of seamanship which is still available in the bazaar today. These families sailed the pearling dhows and carried goods, but they stayed out of marketing. They regarded shopkeeping as an inferior profession, and preferred to leave this business to the Indian and Persian communities, whose descendants include such modern merchants as the Ali Rezas of Saudi Arabia, Bahrain and Kuwait, the Zahids (the Ali Rezas' Saudi cousins), the Gharaballis of Kuwait and the Behbehanis, the Kuwaiti agents for Volkswagen. The fortunes of the principle Kuwaiti families, therefore, only began in the 1920s and 1930s, when the al Sagars started shipping dates from Basra, and Haji Ahmed al Ghanim,* the father of Yusif, the present head of the family (who got the General Motors agency) began importing kerosene from the Abadan refinery in Iran.

Although one still refers to the al Ghanims, al Sagars, Juffalis and others as 'trading families', this expression is becoming something of a misnomer, because some of these families are no longer associated primarily with their commercial interests. The classic example is that of the Ali Reza family, the oldest merchant house in Saudi Arabia.

The Ali Reza business was established well before oil by Abdullah, and it later made enormous profits out of the Ford and Westing-house agencies. General Motors it passed on to the Zahids. The Ali Rezas became probably the first Saudi millionaires outside the ranks of the royal family: but then in the 1960s their fortunes started to decline. The family confined its operations almost entirely to the Hijaz when other areas of the country were being opened up. At the same time Ford fell foul of the Arab boycott, and there was a general ebbing of commercial dynamism as its members, now

*Haji before a name denotes someone who has been on the pilgrimage, the Haj, to Mecca. In practice the title is only applied to a few people, normally those who made the journey in the days before modern transport.

second only to the al Sauds in status, branched out into other fields.

The Ali Reza enterprise is still one of the biggest Saudi trading houses, and it is undergoing something of a revival in a construction partnership with Wimpey and Laing, who have recently carried out defence projects and other major government building contracts – but only one of Abdullah's sons, Shaikh Ahmed Ali Reza, is directly involved in day-to-day management. The eldest son, Shaikh Mohammed, after a distinguished career in the government, is now the Saudi ambassador in Paris, and the second son, Shaikh Ali, a former cabinet minister, is now retired and is a friend and adviser of Prince Fawaz, the Governor of Mecca.

So the conventional merchant family arrangement, with the father, the founder, in a semi-retired position, and the sons running different branches of the business, is breaking up. This process has gone furthest in Kuwait, being the most advanced state, and members of the big families are now found in every part of the economy and in the government. Two of the best known figures in this respect are Abdullah al Ghanim, Yusif's eldest son, who is Minister of Electricity and Water, and Abdlatif al Hamad, the Chairman of the United Bank of Kuwait, Managing Director of the Kuwait Investment Company, and Director General of the Kuwait Fund for Arab Economic Development.

It is no longer true to think of the second echelon of Gulf and Arabian society as being a strictly merchant community. Although their money may originally have been made in trade, the people with the big private fortunes are now as likely to be in the government or government corporations, oil, banking, industry, investment or construction.

7

THE BANKING ESTABLISHMENT

As the oil revenues began to pour into Kuwait during 1952 a group of merchants decided that it might be profitable to open a bank. There was already one bank in the state, the British Bank of the Middle East, which had been granted a thirty-year concession in 1941, but this was only a branch office, and it did not provide any guide as to the proper procedure for setting up a nationally owned Kuwaiti bank. The merchants went to ask the permission of the ruler, Shaikh Abdullah, who immediately wrote them a charter, on a piece of paper torn from a school exercise book. Then they posted notices on the pillars in the bazaar, inviting other merchants to subscribe to the bank's capital, and, as an afterthought, they personally invited the ruling family to participate. In this way they collected the rather odd sum of 13,100,000 rupees. Finally they sent one of the al Ghanim family to Claude Loombe, who at the time was head of the Middle East department in the Bank of England, and who then became Chairman of the British Bank of the Middle East, until his retirement at the end of 1974. Loombe sent out one of his staff, Alan Medlycott, to be the first General Manager, and so the National Bank of Kuwait began business.

Since then the NBK has become the biggest bank in the Middle East. At the end of its first full year of operations its deposits came to 130 million rupees ($33 million) and its profits reflected a return on capital of more than twelve per cent; by 1966 it was big enough to consider baling out Intra, in the famous Lebanese bank crash that year; and at some point during 1972 its deposits passed the billion dollars mark.* As the leading bank in the richest, most sophisticated

*Although this figure is impressive in Middle Eastern terms, it puts NBK well below the two hundredth largest bank in the world. At the end of 1971 the world's

and most internationally minded of the oil producers, one might expect the National Bank of Kuwait to be a major and enterprising force in the development of the Gulf and in Middle Eastern regional finance – and yet between a half and two-thirds of its assets are conservatively deployed in London, chiefly on deposit with other banks.

The NBK is far from unique in this respect. The other British or American managed banks, the Commercial Bank of Kuwait, the Gulf Bank and the Bank of Kuwait and the Middle East,† also have between half and two-thirds of their assets abroad, and even the Alahli Bank, a much more dynamic and 'aggressive' institution, established under French management seconded from Credit Lyonnais in 1968, has been unable to lend much more than half of its resources locally. As a group in December 1973 the five Kuwaiti banks had $1,325 million or fifty-four per cent of assets totalling $2,443 million invested overseas. (These figures and all other figures for total assets quoted in this chapter exclude contra accounts.) At the same time in Saudi Arabia the banks had $386 million or twenty-seven per cent of their assets abroad, in Qatar $80 million (thirty-three per cent), in Abu Dhabi $292 million (sixty-two per cent), and in Bahrain (in March 1973) $98 million (thirty-seven per cent). In only one or two cases is this outflow a matter of voluntary bank policy – these being the Pakistani banks in the lower Gulf, which have been offering depositors rates well above the norm, apparently with the specific intention of funding their operations at home. Otherwise, for both the foreign and nationally owned banks, the huge foreign asset totals are a straightforward reflection of the chronic capital surplus in all the Arabian oil producers' economies.

The result of this situation is that every bank manager in the Gulf is haunted by the 'exchange risk'. Needless to say all the local

---

biggest bank, with deposits of $29 billion, was the Bank of America, followed by First National City, Chase Manhattan, Barclays, National Westminster, Banque Nationale de Paris, Dai-Ichi Kangyo, and the Deutsche Bank.

†When the British Bank of the Middle East's concession expired at the end of 1971, its assets were taken over by a new company, the BKME, owned fifty-one per cent by the government and forty-nine per cent by the Kuwaiti public. The BBME retains a management contract. There are Kuwaitis with sufficient expertise to become general managers, but the directors of all the banks prefer to employ Europeans or Americans. It is felt that customers will be more prepared to entrust their secrets to foreigners than to fellow Kuwaitis, who may have interests in competing merchant groups. As it is family connections between the directors of different banks and investment companies have a major influence on the pattern of Kuwaiti banking and on the policies of individual institutions.

G

currencies are extremely stable, with more than a hundred per cent backing, much of it in gold. Until July 1972 the currencies of Kuwait and the lower Gulf states were pegged to the pound (except in the devaluation of 1967), but since the sterling float began the Kuwait Central Bank, in order to maintain the dinar's purchasing power, has started quoting daily rates on the basis of an undisclosed weighted average formula involving all the major trading currencies. In effect the Bahrain dinar (worth just over one pound sterling) and the Qatar riyal and the UAE dirham (both worth exactly a tenth of a Bahrain dinar) move in the same way, while the Saudi riyal (about one-eighth of a pound) used to fluctuate with the dollar – though it did not devalue in December 1971 nor in February 1973, and in August 1973, when the dollar float dipped particularly badly, it was formally revalued by five per cent. In March 1975 the dollar link was dropped altogether, and replaced by a new parity based on the IMF's Special Drawing Right.

None of these currencies, however, can be considered as 'strong' in the sense that the deutsche mark and the yen have been strong in recent years. Their parities are not influenced by the market demand, and they do not respond to heavy inflows of capital nor to big balance of payments surpluses. The only factor likely to prompt a revaluation against all Western currencies, therefore, would be the authorities' desire to cushion the population against imported inflation – and these arguments in favour of revaluation are largely offset by the desire not to cause an exchange loss on government and private foreign assets, and to avoid weakening the competitive position of new local industries.

So the exchange risk derives from the 'stability' rather than the 'strength' of the Arabian Peninsula currencies – but this makes little practical difference to the problem confronting the bankers. If a bank has taken deposits in dinars, riyals or dirhams, while a large part of its assets are in the more unstable pound and dollar, it stands to make a considerable loss from any fall in the value of the two main investment currencies, which it will have to make up to depositors out of its profits or reserves. However the 'risk' is not as big as the figures for gross foreign assets (used above) would suggest; and to compute the banks' true exchange exposure a number of deductions should be made.

In most states the lack of comprehensive statistics makes this impossible, but, using the figures obtaining at the end of 1973, it can be done with a useful degree of accuracy in Kuwait. First there were foreign liabilities – borrowings from banks abroad and deposits of non-residents – to be taken into account. Some of these deposits might still have been in Gulf currencies, and therefore still have involved an exchange risk, but in the absence of a breakdown one can only deduct overall foreign liabilities – $453 million. Then there were deposits made by residents in foreign currencies, about $250/300 million, and lastly some $150 million of World Bank bonds denominated in dinars and perhaps roughly the same amount of KD international loans, both of which were included in the foreign assets. So when one subtracts these four figures (about $1,000/1,500 million in all) from the Kuwaiti banks' gross foreign assets of about $1,325 million, one comes up with only $325/275 million as the true exchange risk applying in December 1973.

Three hundred million dollars odd is still a fairly substantial figure, and, to make matters more difficult, whenever there is a currency crisis those Kuwaitis or Saudis who have invested abroad directly or have made foreign exchange deposits with local banks tend to switch back into their own currencies and put their money on deposit at home, which only increases the banks' exchange risk at the worst possible moment. As an example of this procedure, in the middle six months of 1970 when the exchange markets were relatively stable, dinar deposits in Kuwait dropped by nearly two per cent, while foreign currency deposits (yielding a higher rate of interest) rose by over seventeen per cent; but during the dollar crisis of 1971 KD deposits grew by almost eleven per cent, while foreign currency deposits fell by over nine per cent.

Not surprisingly, some banks have been hit badly, particularly in Saudi Arabia, where until the spring of 1973 the government did not allow the installation of telex, for security reasons. This put the bankers in an incredibly frustrating position. They received the exchange rates for the dollar and the European currencies on their Reuter teleprinters, or heard them on the BBC World Service promptly enough, but when it came to getting their buying and selling instructions out of the country fast, they were stuck. Consequently when the dollar went down in 1971 the Riyad Bank (one of the two nationally owned Saudi institutions) made no profits, and in the July 1972/July 1973 year, which saw the sterling float and heavy pressure on the dollar, National Commercial, the other Saudi Bank, suffered a similar fate. In the 1973 dollar devaluation two of the Kuwaiti banks lost $26 million.

To minimize this threat of being caught in the wrong currency at the wrong time the banks maintain an extraordinarily high degree of liquidity in their foreign assets – a practice which has the additional advantage of impressing their generally conservative shareholders and depositors.

In none of the Arabian Peninsula countries is the public financially sophisticated, and people tend to work very much on a cash basis. In Qatar, for example, the most popular denomination note after one riyal (about twenty-five cents) is a hundred riyals ($25), which suggests that citizens still keep a lot of money under their mattresses. Then in Kuwait the average size of a cash withdrawal from a bank is KD 250 (some $900) – and this is less a measure of the wealth of the population, than of the fact that shopkeepers do not like accepting cheques. By Western standards the number of cheques cleared per head of population each month is minute. So although over the past ten years there has been a considerable growth in customers' knowledge and confidence in banking – as shown in Kuwait by the drop in the proportion of deposits at call from fifty-three per cent in 1963 to twenty-one per cent in 1972 – the banks are still anxious not to do anything to discourage the banking habit, by levying bank charges, for instance.

Their caution is understandable, because there has also been a certain religious barrier to the development of banking, in that the payment of interest under Koranic law is regarded as usury, and prohibited. In practice there are now very few customers who will not accept interest, even among the devout populations of Qatar and Saudi Arabia – though there are still some people who are reluctant to pay, or who suggest devices which would enable them to salve their consciences without losing any money. The most common proposals are that they should neither take nor pay interest, in the hope that their credit and debit balances will more or less cancel each other out, or that instead of receiving interest they be given a preferential exchange rate on foreign currency purchases when they go abroad. The Saudi government however, has never admitted the legality of interest, referring to it euphemistically as 'commission'; and if a bank files a claim against a customer for repayment of a loan, the courts will deduct past interest charges. For this reason banks lend more on the basis of a client's reputation than on guarantees.

In Kuwait the commercial law puts a seven per cent ceiling on the lending rate, which normally means that the range of interest offered for deposits is between three and a half and five per cent. During 1971 to 1973 these restrictions were not too anomalous, because, despite the much higher interest rates obtaining in Europe, the instability of the currency markets encouraged Kuwaitis to keep their money at home. But in 1969, when high interest rates and currency stability abroad coincided with the new Alahli Bank's refusal to join the bankers' gentlemen's agreement on interest rates at home, the Kuwaiti banks were forced into a rate war. As much as six and a half per cent was being offered for one-year dinar deposits, and even then there were cases of Kuwaitis borrowing at seven per cent specifically to reinvest in Europe. The banks had to resort to charging an extra two per cent on loans as a fee of commitment – though this expedient was never tested in the courts, and it is doubtful whether it would have stood had it been.

Nonetheless the Central Bank was sympathetic, and the next year the government placed a bill before the National Assembly proposing that the seven per cent limit be abolished, and that the Central Bank be authorized to set the rate itself. Given that there is seldom any need for the regulation of credit in Kuwait, because the public's spending power is more easily controlled by the government's annual land-purchase allocations, it was envisaged that the determining factor in the Central Bank's policy would be the rates obtaining in Europe, rather than any of the domestic considerations that influence governments' decisions on interest rates in industrial countries. Anyway the bill did not get a very enthusiastic reception from the old Assembly in 1970, and under the new and more radical body elected in 1971 it lost some of its urgency during the following three years of currency crisis, and in 1973 it was eclipsed by the Participation debate. But the measure will probably be reintroduced in the fairly near future, and it is now expected to have a clear passage.

*   *   *

So the picture that emerges of banking in the Arabian Peninsula is a rather unique one. By Western standards the system remains unsophisticated, remarkably so considering the amount of money the banks are likely to be handling in future, and the philosophy of the bankers in the bigger and more important institutions is still very conservative. In part this is a matter of pure necessity – for example, the exchange risk forces the banks to maintain unusually high liquidity – but even at home their lending policy can hardly be described as enterprising.

In Kuwait during the latter half of 1973 and 1974 a number of factors combined to disguise this conservatism and give the impression of a much more aggressive banking system. The merchant community's expectations of higher government spending triggered off a boom, which was accompanied by a major build up of stocks, a big expansion of construction in the industrial, commercial and residential sectors, and the floating of a record number of new public companies – all of which caused a sudden increase in domestic lending. It happened that this boom coincided with a renewed outflow of private capital into dollars (reflecting the greater stability of exchange rates in Europe) and the beginnings of direct private dinar lending overseas – which together contributed to a very small growth in deposits. And when at the same time the Central Bank required the commercial banks to place with it large interest-free deposits (as a means of exerting a deflationary influence on the economy while ensuring that the banks maintained an adequate level of liquidity) the result was a tight credit situation and a big reduction in the proportion of the banks' assets held abroad.

These conditions were very untypical of Kuwaiti banking, and when the new oil revenues start to reach the private sector in late 1975 and 1976 it is expected that there will be a very big increase in deposits. It is most unlikely that this will be matched by a parallel expansion of local lending. The domestic business of banks through-out the Arabian Peninsula has traditionally been centred on financing trade; very few loans have been made to industry, and there is an extreme reluctance to accept any of the more ambitious commercial risks which a European or American bank might take in its stride.

The only exception to this general rule is the Alahli Bank of Kuwait. Right from the time it began operations in 1968 Alahli has been encouraged to invest more at home. This originally gave the other banks an opportunity to off-load some of their less reliable borrowers on to the new institution, and as Alahli's first general manager lent rather too generously, while the bank's aggressive tactics upset the older establishment, there were periodic rumours that Alahli was on the verge of collapse. But since then its performance has improved. In effect the bank has preferred to run a commercial risk at home to an exchange risk abroad, on the assumption that Kuwaiti debts are less often 'bad' than 'heavy' (in the sense that they linger on beyond the scheduled repayment date), and this approach has now been vindicated. At the end of 1973, when advances to local customers accounted for KD 66 million out of total assets of KD 135 million, Alahli's profits reached the healthy level of just over one million dinars.

Whether there is a big enough market for the traditional forms of lending in Kuwait and elsewhere to make it worthwhile for other banks to copy Alahli's approach is open to question. A single bank might be able to capture some of its competitors' customers, but taking each state as a whole the proportion of assets invested locally might not increase. But there may well be scope for the banks to develop Alahli's methods further – by expanding the actual size of the industrial lending market through giving businessmen ideas for new projects and encouraging them to come to the banks for finance. At present the banks are very weak in this area. None of them have project-appraisal or research departments worth speaking of, and although the foreign banks would argue that if they were asked to provide finance for a major industrial project they could summon the necessary staff from their head offices, the fact remains that so far they have shown little interest in this type of lending.

Instead of this at best 'passive' approach, the idea among the new technocrat class in the Gulf is that the banks should become a little more like modern European and American concerns, which are now involving themselves very closely with the complexities of their clients' businesses, and in some cases have set up different departments to monitor developments in individual industries. There are signs that a move in this direction would also be welcomed by governments. But both these parties are looking at banking from the point of view of the economic development of their area, and this is not necessarily how the bankers themselves see the situation. Their first responsibility is towards their profits and their shareholders, and if these are best served by continuing with a cautious and conservative approach, they are unlikely to change their ways just for the sake of appearing to be modern and dynamic.

So any progress towards more aggressive banking techniques will depend on the banks being given an 'incentive'. In Kuwait it would help if the interest rate restriction were removed, because the present seven per cent ceiling hardly encourages the more enterprising type of loan; and there may also be an argument for the Kuwaitis reviewing their effective ban on foreign banks, on the basis that some new arrivals might provide more competition for the existing establishment.

Developments like these would certainly increase the bankers' enthusiasm for industrial lending, but in all the states of the Arabian Peninsula their ability to pursue these opportunities would still be restricted by the familiar manpower problem, which shows up here in a chronic shortage of middle-management staff with experience in credit analysis and industrial finance. This is an area where change can only come gradually, and even then the banks would never be able to bring all their assets home. First, for the time being there are no inter-bank deposit markets, and no significant discount markets. In none of the Arabian Peninsula countries have treasury bills been issued, and although in Kuwait the Central Bank does in fact have a facility for discounting two signature trade bills of ninety days or less, none of the banks have ever used it. This means that almost all of the banks' liquidity – thirty per cent of total assets – will have to stay in London. Secondly, and more important in the long run, there will be limits to the money-absorbing capacities of the local economies, no matter how aggressive the banks become.

It is largely because they recognize this fact that the bankers' attention has been directed more towards a rather different innovation – accepting the inevitability of foreign assets, but reducing their exchange risk by lending abroad in their own currencies.

This type of lending was started in 1966 by Alan Medlycott, when he was still General Manager of the National Bank of Kuwait, but for some years the operation remained on a very small scale. Foreign customers were attracted by the low rates of interest, but they worried (unnecessarily) about how they would buy dinars when it came to paying back their loan, and with somewhat better reason they were concerned about the exchange risk – which here, of course, rests with the borrower. Then in September 1968 the World Bank made its first bond issue in Kuwait, and by the end of March 1975 there had been five further issues (the most recent in November 1973) worth a total of KD130 million, or about $440 million. All these issues were managed by the Kuwait Investment Company, but the commercial banks, and NBK in particular, have bought a great many of these bonds, and their arrival has done much to popularize and establish the principle of international dinar lending.

Led by Alahli and NBK, in the last four years Kuwaiti banks have made quite a large number of dinar loans, chiefly to foreign banks (including Triumph Investment which borrowed KD 2.50 million), and real estate companies (like Town and Commercial Properties which borrowed KD 2.75 million). In late 1973 and early 1974 there was a sudden surge in lending, both by the banks and by the larger merchants and public companies, and interest rates rose beyond the official seven per cent limit, to near euro-dollar levels.

With the exception of the World Bank borrowings and Kuwait government loans to other Arab states, the sums lent in dinars overseas are normally quite small – though there have been a few rather larger dinar bond issues in the KD 5/15 million ($17/50 million) range, for such clients as the Asian Development Bank, the National

Bank of Yugoslavia, and the Sudanese, Irish and Philippine governments. Large blocks of these bonds have been bought by the Kuwait government and placed in the state reserve. By mid-1974 it was thought that outstanding international dinar loans (excluding World Bank bonds) in the private sector might have been about KD 75 million ($250 million) due to the banks, and KD 25 million ($80 million) due to private and public companies (including investment companies) and to individual investors who had either bought dinar bonds or had managed their own direct loans to foreign borrowers.

None of the other Arab countries have made foreign loans in their own currencies which can compare with these figures. The Beirut banks are affected by the exchange risk almost as much as the Kuwaiti banks. The Lebanese pound, backed over fifty per cent in gold, is as strong as any Arabian Peninsula currency, and at the end of 1973 the banks had some $1,450 million, or fifty per cent of their assets, abroad. And yet the Beirut banks only began major international lending in Lebanese pounds in December 1972, when the State Bank of India borrowed LL 15 million ($6 million). A month later the World Bank floated a bond issue for LL 75 million ($30 million), and since then, in addition to various small borrowings, there have been major loans to Renlaut, the European Investment Bank and the External Bank of Algeria.

Elsewhere the Libyan Arab Foreign Bank has taken two privately placed World Bank dinar bond issues for LD 10 million and LD 30 million (about $135 million in all), and has managed a LD 15 million credit, underwritten by the state-controlled commercial banks, for the External Bank of Algeria. (The Libyan Arab Foreign Bank and the External Bank of Algeria are central bank subsidiaries, used to carry out overseas commercial banking operations on behalf of the Libyan and Algerian governments.)

In the lower Gulf there has been some small-scale lending in riyals and dirhams, mainly by Dubai banks; and in November 1973 the National Bank of Abu Dhabi and the Bank of Bahrain and Kuwait (owned half by Kuwaiti banks and investment companies and half by the Bahraini public) participated in a unique issue of $25 million worth of 'Arabian Peninsula currency related' bonds on behalf of the government of Oman. In effect, this was much the same as an ordinary dinar loan, except that repayment was to be based on whichever currency had appreciated most (or depreciated least) against the dollar during the six years for which the loan was due to run. The currencies included were the Oman, Qatar and Saudi riyals, the Kuwait and Bahrain dinars and the UAE dirham; but the list of underwriters, which was made up largely of Kuwaiti, European and Japanese institutions and Arab/European consortia, contained no banks from Qatar or Saudi Arabia.

Up to the middle of 1974 there had in fact been no international loans in Saudi riyals at all. Early in 1973 the British Bank of the Middle East and the First National City Bank in Jeddah were approached for a substantial ship finance loan, but the Saudi Arabian Monetary Agency (SAMA), which the banks had to consult before lending a sum of more than twenty-five per cent of their reserves to a single borrower, was not willing to guarantee the reconvertibility of the loan, and the idea was dropped.

SAMA policy on conversion is that it will buy riyals in exchange for dollars, but will not sell them – and this means that a foreign borrower, when he came to making his repayment, might have extreme difficulty in getting back into the Saudi currency. The SAMA policy may have had a certain logic in the 1960s, when the government did not want to increase its exchange exposure by holding more than a minimum of foreign currencies – but now that the state's reserves are climbing into figures of tens of billions of dollars, it has become irrelevant. It also constitutes a very serious barrier in the way of the development of Saudi banking.

The impossibility of buying riyals from SAMA means that Saudi banks can only repatriate their profits or their foreign assets by selling dollars and sterling to merchant clients who need foreign exchange to pay for imports. This is obviously an inefficient practice, and as the volume of deposits and the potential volumes of foreign assets and foreign profits in the Saudi banking system grow, it becomes more and more impracticable. In 1973 and 1974 Saudi citizens were repatriating large amounts of foreign investments (using the exchange dealers, who, like the banks, sell the foreign exchange to merchants), and the banks found themselves faced with a big inflow of new riyal deposits. Most of these deposits were at call, reflecting the Saudi public's continuing lack of financial sophistication. Domestic demand for advances did not match the build-up of deposits, and because there was no way in which the banks could be certain of being able to repatriate this money quickly in the event of there being a series of major withdrawals, it was impossible for them to invest their new deposits on the money markets abroad. So, over a period of many months, the ridiculous situation arose where the banks stopped offering any interest on new deposits, and, rather than lending abroad in either their own or foreign currencies, were forced to put enormous amounts of money (in the case of some banks over half of total assets) on interest-free deposit with SAMA.

*   *   *

The idea of making the type of local currency foreign loan discussed in the previous paragraphs leads up to one key question, much talked about in the Gulf these days, and that is: 'How does one turn the riyals, dinars and dirhams into "international currencies"?'

The expression is of course a vague one, but in simple terms a currency becomes international when it is used in trade – which means that most countries will be prepared to accumulate the currency in the knowledge that they will be able to use it to buy goods from the country of issue. There should also be a demand for investment in the currency, it should be easily obtainable on foreign exchange markets, and there should be a lot of it – all of which implies that the country of issue should have a large industrial economy and reasonable equilibrium in its balance of payments, so as not to cause a scarcity of the currency. It goes without saying that the issuing government must have adequate monetary reserves to guarantee the convertibility of the currency, but, on the other hand, the currency need not be as strong or stable as other convertible currencies that are not 'international'. By these criteria the main international currencies are obviously the dollar and sterling – and on a smaller scale, being less easily obtainable, the European currencies, the Canadian dollar and the Japanese yen.

None of the Arabian oil producers' currencies meet any of these conditions except convertibility, and even here the Saudi riyal does not qualify fully. The most fundamental problem is the lack of scope for using these currencies in trade, because the Gulf's only significant export is oil, and here prices are denominated in dollars and paid largely in dollars and sterling. The amounts of currency issued are small, the currencies are not readily available outside the Middle East, and local investment opportunities are limited. In most states, as part of the 'cutting-in' policies, purchases of shares or property are barred to foreigners, while treasury bills, which would be the normal investment for foreign governments holding Gulf currencies, do not exist. This problem is often overlooked by those who advocate internationalizing the Gulf currencies, but no state can be expected to accumulate a currency in its reserve, unless it is allowed to invest the money in something.

During 1973 a good deal of thinking was going into ways of getting round these barriers, and two rather tentative and ineffective schemes were put forward. One suggestion was that the producers should ask for their oil revenues to be paid in their own currencies. However, given that the Arabian states run a vast trade surplus, which would prevent any useful amount of their currencies leaving their own countries, there would be no way for the oil companies to buy the necessary exchange on the markets of Europe, and the end result would be the rather phoney system that obtains in Libya, where dinar payments are already part of the law. All that happens here is that the oil companies buy dinars for dollars from the Central Bank, and then hand the dinars over to the government – which amounts to the same as making revenue payments direct in the ordinary way. This snag was acknowledged in September 1973, when Abdel-Rahman Atiqi, the Kuwaiti Minister of Finance and Oil, went on record as saying that he could see no real advantage in the scheme – provided that the producers were compensated for any drop in the dollar's value, as had already been negotiated in Geneva.

A second train of thought was given rather more positive endorsement in April 1973 in a decision by the new Arab Fund for Social and Economic Development to make a priority study on issuing a single Arab dinar 'as an international unit of currency'. Then at the beginning of July the Council for Arab Economic Unity meeting in Cairo decided to join in the study, and three days later at a conference of Arab finance ministers, the Iraqis outlined a similar proposal for an Arab monetary fund which would issue an Arab dinar to be used side by side with existing Arab currencies, both internally and in foreign trade.

In practice these rather general ideas, which were still under study at the beginning of 1974, could involve any one of a number of different schemes. The easiest solution would be to restrict the issue of the new dinar to the Arabian Peninsula – though even here it is no foregone conclusion that the states would be prepared to give up their own currencies, especially as the outcome might be the domination of the area's money markets by Kuwait. In 1973 there was a move in the opposite direction, when the United Arab Emirates, which had previously used the Bahrain dinar and the now-defunct Qatar-Dubai riyal, started issuing a third lower Gulf currency of its own, the dirham. An even more fundamental difficulty is that any purely Arabian dinar would inherit all the limiting features of the existing currencies, and be of no more use internationally as a result.

The alternative, which would be to introduce the new dinar in all the Arab countries, would ensure a larger issue of the currency and more scope for international borrowing and investment, but it would still not get to the root of the availability problem, because even adding in the deficit countries, like Egypt, the Middle East as a whole is still in surplus with the rest of the world. There would be an inevitable tendency for the dinars to end up in the Arabian Peninsula, having been used by Egypt for instance to pay for European industrial goods, and then by Europe to pay for oil, and this would only be partially offset by the oil exporters investing in the other Arab countries.

Furthermore the broader scheme would give rise to a number of new objections. The issue of a common currency is only practical in countries which have arrived at an advanced stage of economic integration, with complete freedom of trade and capital transfers within the group – and this in turn can only be achieved if their economies are at roughly the same stage of development, with similar incomes per head of population, and similar combinations of state control and free enterprise. The Arab states are nowhere near meeting these conditions. Unless the dinar was intended solely for external use, which would present difficulties of its own, a whole series of 'internal' exchange and trade restrictions would have to remain, which would destroy much of the point of introducing the new currency in the first place. There would also be serious problems of valuation, because a few months after the date of issue some countries' economies might be demanding a revaluation of the dinar, and others a devaluation.

So all lines of approach on the international currency question lead into a circular argument, with the basic block being the Arabs' chronic trade surplus. For many of its exponents, who are predominantly Gulf Arabs, the purpose of making an Arab currency international is to create demand for that currency in order to transfer the exchange risk on to somebody else, and this is altogether the wrong starting point. There is no demand for Arab currencies because they are of no use in international trade and investment. If there were any demand for Arab currencies it would be because an entirely new industrial society had developed in the countries of issue, and in this case investors in the oil states would be able to keep their money at home. The whole issue of an exchange risk, foreign borrowers and international currencies might then never arise.

This is not to say that the volume of ordinary foreign lending in local currencies cannot continue to expand. It means only that demand for these currencies cannot be 'legislated into being', and that a better approach to increasing the attractions of dinar and riyal loans would be to encourage the development of more sophisticated and more useful money markets in the region.

According to current thinking in the Gulf and Saudi Arabia this might be done by such innovations as the issue of treasury bills and the establishment of proper stock exchanges; and by the removal of existing anomalies, like the Saudi Arabian Monetary Agency's policy on not selling riyals, the Kuwaiti interest rate restrictions, and the Kuwaiti ban on the banks dealing in foreign currencies among themselves. As the markets grow larger it is sometimes suggested that this last innovation would lead to the forward buying and selling of dinars, thus enabling foreign borrowers to hedge against the exchange risk.

These possibilities, which are bound up with the bankers' role in inter-regional finance (discussed in Chapter 11), lie some years in the future; and for the present the banks will continue to hold a large part of their assets in dollars or sterling on the markets abroad. It is the management of these foreign currency assets, and the over-seas holdings of private Arabian investors, that form the subject of the next two chapters.

8

THE ARAB INVESTOR

At least once during his time in Kuwait every bank manager has tried to work out how much capital is leaving the country to be invested abroad, and, more specifically, how much is not going out through his own bank. It is not that the answer would be of any vital importance to the running of the bank itself, but simply that the outflow is so obvious, and allegedly so big, that it would be interesting, on a purely personal level, to be able to put a figure on it. Leaving aside oil, foreign investment is after all the most prominent and most talked-about feature of the Kuwaiti economic scene, and the fact that it is a private and confidential process, surrounded by a mass of rumours, makes the search for the true figure all the more intriguing.

The logical starting point is to have a look at the balance of payments statistics, where the bankers should, in theory, find the answer they want under the heading 'private capital transfers (net)'. This item, however, is regarded as notoriously unreliable in any country, and as Kuwait has a free exchange market, where investors do not have to apply for permission to make a transfer, the margin of error here may be even bigger than usual. Furthermore, the bank managers know that much of the information that goes into the Central Bank's figures is provided by themselves, and they have no great faith in their own reports having been correct to start with. Their customers are under no obligation to state the purpose of a transfer, and the bankers believe that even if they are given an explanation this may sometimes be a slight 'embellishment' of the truth designed to keep a customer's investments totally secret. They may be told for instance that the money is to be used for 'a holiday', which would register in the balance of payments under 'travel', or that it is an allowance for the customer's children studying abroad, in which case it would be included in 'current transfers' – along with the private sector's invisible imports and the remittances of foreign workers. To make matters more difficult the substantial current and capital transfers made through the exchange dealers are both lumped in with the government's defence purchases under 'net errors and omissions'. This means that the real capital transfer figure may be mixed up with four different items (totalling a bit under $900 million in 1972/3) – and even then one is making the optimistic assumption that no capital has got into the imports figures, and that none has escaped being noticed at all.

So right at the beginning of their investigations the bankers realize that this theoretical line of enquiry is going to be a failure, and anyway, because the figures do not go back to the beginning of oil revenues, they are of no use whatever for finding out the answer to the equally interesting question of what might be the total worth of all private Kuwaiti foreign assets. At this point they are joined by their colleagues in Saudi Arabia, Qatar and Abu Dhabi, who occasionally use the much more rudimentary statistics provided by their own governments to go through the same exercise – though with less real interest in the result, because the outflow from these states is on a much smaller scale than it is from Kuwait. Instead the bankers embark on what might be called the 'empirical' approach.

First they look at the currency notes carried out (perfectly legitimately) in peoples' pockets – reflecting the strong cash emphasis in Arabian society, and the desire for complete secrecy. In Kuwait, with its relatively sophisticated population, this type of operation seems to be fairly small, and for the Saudis there is the disadvantage that the riyal is less easily exchangeable than other Arabian currencies. But in Qatar cash in the pocket may account for over half the total capital outflow. Some of the money goes to Beirut, but the bulk is taken to Dubai, and while the old Qatar-Dubai riyal was still in circulation this showed up very clearly in the issue and withdrawal statistics published by the Currency Board. In January 1973, for instance, the issue of new notes was QDR 13 million in Qatar and QDR 5 million in Dubai, while withdrawals from circulation were only QDR 1 million in Qatar, but QDR 14 million in Dubai.

The trade figures suggest that at the most ten per cent of this flow could be payment for Dubai's re-exports – and even this small figure is probably an exaggeration, because the majority of Qatari merchants would settle their accounts by cheque or by draft rather than in cash. Then a further small proportion may be taken out by Qataris going shopping for the wider range of consumer goods that

Dubai's stores offer – though because of the greater distance involved, these expeditions are probably much fewer than those made by Abu Dhabi citizens to Dubai. Together, these two current transactions can hardly account for more than fifteen per cent of the flow of riyal notes, which means that the bulk of the money must be capital attracted by the better interest rates offered by Dubai's banks – some seven and a half per cent in early 1973 against the four to six and a half per cent range available in Qatar. Part of the reason for these higher rates is that Dubai still needs to attract some outside funds, from Abu Dhabi as well as Qatar, to finance its entrepot trade. But the figures for foreign liabilities in the Dubai banking system show that the capital inflow is well in excess of the amount required to supplement domestic deposits – and so one can think of the bulk of the money from Qatar and Abu Dhabi as being channelled to London as part of the Dubai banks' foreign assets.

Next the bankers examine some of the different capital elements in the transfers made through their own banks and through the exchange dealers – those stemming from the operations of the American brokers in Kuwait, and the visiting brokers, fund salesmen and bankers. From their own experience and observations they then try to estimate how big these parts of the outflow might be, and whether they are large enough to give any guide to the total.

The first of these, the American stockbrokers' operations, were more important in the mid to late 1960s than they are now. Early in the decade three houses, Hayden Stone, Du Pont and Clark Dodge set up business in Kuwait, but they all left during the bear market of 1969/70 – which, together with the crash of Investors Overseas Services, Gramco and Consolidated Investors gave a very severe jolt to the Kuwaitis' confidence in equity investment. By 1971 the only remaining firm in Kuwait was Merrill Lynch, the biggest brokers in the U.S.A., who moved into the state as its competitors were moving out. In October 1972 Merrill Lynch also set up an office in Dubai.

Even at the height of the 1967/8 bull market there were never more than a few hundred Kuwaitis seriously interested in investment on Wall Street, and now, following the dollar devaluations, the numbers are even smaller. Merrill Lynch finds that its job is mainly educational, with the emphasis on fairly fundamental points like explaining the difference between buying for growth and buying for income. The office says that it would welcome the arrival of another broker to help in this work, but in 1973 the market was probably not big enough to accommodate a second firm – even if the applicant was prepared to put up the $750,000 bank guarantee now required

H

by the government under the Commercial Law of 1970. In both
Kuwait and Dubai Merrill Lynch's clients are made up largely of
institutional investors, American expatriates and a few of the merchant community – though much against the generally conservative
trend of Arab investment, these few Kuwaitis on Merrill Lynch's
books invest mainly in growth equities of the most speculative sort.

On an even smaller scale some of the British brokers, notably James
Capel, Fielding Newson Smith and Strauss Turnbull, do business in
the Gulf through sending one or two of their partners on periodic
visits to the area. Some of the accounts run by the British brokers
belong to members of the ruling families or the more wealthy merchants, but the main purpose of their visits is to arrange government
and institutional business. Fielding Newson Smith, for instance, now
does a certain amount of work for the Kuwait Investment Office
(discussed in Chapter 13) which is responsible for investing a large
block of the state reserve.

In contrast to the few active equity investors who form the core of
Merrill Lynch's business, it seems that the British brokers' private
clients are more representative of the conventional cautious Gulf
investors, and a lot of the securities they buy are various types of loan
stocks, bonds and debentures. Any reliable estimates of the value of
these purchases are difficult to come by, but most probably the
amount of private money that has been channelled to the London
stock exchange and Wall Street through the visiting British brokers or
the American brokers that have had offices in Kuwait would not
add up to more than a few tens of millions of dollars.

Before the market collapsed in 1969, the stockbrokers' operations
were complemented by the work of a group of mutual fund salesmen.
The last of these were a representative of the Real Estate Fund of
America, who made occasional tours through the area, and the
office of Gramco in Bahrain – which is believed to have done well
among the oil men in the BAPCO town at Awali. But compared
with the earlier impact of Investors Overseas Services in the Middle
East, Gramco and REFA were minor operations.

IOS, the organization that ran Bernie Cornfeld's various ill-fated
funds, had its regional headquarters in Beirut, and from there it
sent its salesmen down to the Arabian Peninsula.* As in South
America (which together with the Arab states was the main area of

*The information in these paragraphs has been drawn from *Do You Sincerely
Want to be Rich?*, the story of IOS written by Charles Raw, Bruce Page and Godfrey
Hodgson, and published by André Deutsch and Penguin.

sales before the company broke into the German and Italian markets in the late 1960s) the people to whom IOS was selling were not the small savers, who are the normal buyers of mutual fund shares, but the very rich merchant community with thousands to invest. On an expedition to Jeddah in late 1964 one of the salesmen sold enough shares in nine days to put himself second in the IOS annual sales contest, and is reputed to have made $173,000 in commissions.

These visits were never very popular with the Arab governments, nor with the small body of American and European financiers whom the central banks and finance ministries occasionally call upon for advice. But it was not until 1968 that the Arab League's Boycott Office formally expelled IOS from its member states, and then the reason was that the company had been running an (unsuccessful) operation in Israel. (Under the Boycott Office rules a company may trade with Israel, but it will be blacklisted if it invests in Israel, as IOS was planning to do.) By the time of its expulsion the Beirut region was no longer so important to IOS, but during the 'best' years from 1962 to 1966 a company official has estimated from memory that total Middle Eastern sales came to $80 million.

A third type of visitor are the foreign bankers commonly known as 'deposit filchers'. These men are severely frowned on by the resident bank managers. Not only do they take customers who are considered to belong properly to local institutions, but they also avoid the exchange risk by taking the bulk of their deposits in dollars or sterling. In Kuwait, which, being the richest market, is the most attractive to the visitors, the banks will avoid doing any future business with an institution which is caught filching their deposits, or if they already use that institution in their overseas business they may strike it off their list of correspondents.

Over the last ten years or so there have been only three instances of such steps being taken, two involving American banks and one a Swiss bank, but it is fairly obvious that a lot more money flows out of the region with visiting bankers than the number of these cases suggests. The trouble is that hundreds of bankers pass through the Gulf every year, and in most cases there is a perfectly above-board reason for them being there. Some banks have provided finance for industrial projects in the area, like Hambros with the Umm Said fertilizer plant in Qatar, and Guinness Mahon with Aluminium Bahrain. A few have interests in local banks – Hambros, again, owns part of the Dubai Bank and the Commerzbank has a share in the Commercial Bank of Dubai. Other visitors may be involved with Kuwaiti institutions in the management groups for bond issues, or may be calling on local banks with whom they have correspondent relationships to exchange ideas, pick up some more deposits from those banks, or discuss how their service can be improved. And finally a number of banks, like Chase Manhattan, First National City and Morgan Guaranty are involved in the management of the governments' reserves. Against this background of activity it is almost impossible to tell how much money may be going out 'on the side', with the initial approach coming from a Gulf resident rather than the visitor.

In the mid-1960s the money sent out of the Arabian Peninsula by the combination of all these channels – the brokers, fund salesmen and visiting bankers – may have amounted to some tens of millions of dollars a year. But since the stock markets fell in 1969/70 and the growing exchange risk discouraged visiting bankers from accepting deposits in local currencies, these operations have become relatively unimportant – too small to give any guide as to the total figures for private capital transfers. It seems, therefore, that the bulk of the outflow takes place on the individual customer's own initiative, without any connection with those channels that are 'visible' in the region; and this brings us back to the original problem of looking at the banks' and exchange dealers' total transfers, and trying to guess the size of the capital element within them.

At the lower end of the scale most of the exchange dealers are no more than one-man bazaar stores changing currency notes for travellers. It is only the two or three largest firms in each state, which have annual turnovers in excess of a hundred million dollars, that are concerned with foreign transfers. In Kuwait these are Abdel-Aziz and Ali al Yusif al Muzaini, a family business established in the 1930s, and the United Trading Group, set up in 1970 by Shaikha Badriah (the widow of Shaikh Fahad) and managed by two former Muzaini employees who had found that working for a family group offered no prospects for promotion. In Saudi Arabia the biggest dealers are the two Rajhi companies, followed by Abdel-Aziz al Khaaki, Mohammed and Abdullah al Subaie and Abdel-Aziz Sulaiman Mukairn; in Dubai there are the Hemchard brothers and Middle East Exchange and Trade; and in Qatar the al Fardan Banking and Finance Corporation. These larger companies like to think of themselves as merchant banks, and Muzaini has given itself this title on a brass plate outside its office, but in practice they are barred from most of the normal commercial banking activities. They may not open letters of credit nor accept deposits, and their profits are made by buying and selling foreign currencies at more competitive rates than those offered by the banks. The bulk of their transfers are done with drafts drawn on their correspondents in Europe and America.

Like the bankers the exchange dealers have no way of knowing for certain how much of the money they transfer is capital and how much current account – though because they are more attuned to local gossip they are better able to guess. In 1972 Muzaini transferred $153 million, which included $17 million to Switzerland (where its correspondent is the Swiss Bank Corporation) $71 million to New York (mainly through the Irving Trust Company), $43 million to London (through National Westminster and Kleinwort Benson), $12 million to Beirut, and $20 million to Bahrain, Qatar, Dubai and Saudi Arabia. All of the transfers made within the Arabian Peninsula, except perhaps some of those to Dubai, could be accounted for by trade and travel, and there would also have been a large element of these current transactions in the Beirut and London transfers. So Muzaini believes that much of the capital must have been in the New York and Switzerland figures, and from experience it suggests that its total capital transactions in 1972 may have been about $45 million, or some thirty per cent of all transfers. The United Trading Group's figures would be roughly the same. In Saudi Arabia from mid-1972 to mid-1973 the two Rajhi operations both transferred about $170 million, considerably more than any of the other exchange dealers, but the breakdown was estimated at fifty per cent trade, thirty per cent remittances of salaries by foreign workers, and twenty per cent travel. In that year capital transfers were insignificant.

It is generally thought in Saudi Arabia that the transfers of the exchange dealers each year are only slightly smaller than the combined transfers made by the twelve commercial banks.* So if the largest exchange dealers believe that in 1972/3 the capital outflow through their own offices was negligible, then it is fair to assume that the same would apply with the banks and the other dealers.

In Kuwait the normal rule of thumb is that Muzaini and the United Trading Group each handle about as many transfers as any one of the five commercial banks. So if the Muzaini figure is simply multiplied by seven – making $300 million odd – and $100 million

---

*In very rough order of size the banks in Saudi Arabia are: National Commercial, Riyad, First National City, Algemene Bank Nederland, Arab Bank (Jordanian), British Bank of the Middle East, Banque de l'Indochine, National Bank of Pakistan, United Bank of Pakistan, Bank Melli (Iranian), Banque du Liban et d'Outre-Mer, and Banque du Caire.

is deducted for repatriations, it would appear that total capital transfers in 1972 might have been $200 million, or KD 60 million. This is an extremely crude calculation; but $200 million is at least a plausible sum for 1972 (in 1973 the total was probably rather smaller), and there is no way of getting anything more accurate.

In Qatar it is impossible to give even this sort of guesstimate figure. The bankers are fairly sure that most of the transfers they make are for trade or travel; but they believe that for the sake of secrecy most citizens prefer to make their capital transactions either through the exchange dealers, or through taking the money out in the form of riyal notes in their own pockets.

Although it is possible to work out very approximate figures for the annual value of capital transfers from the Arabian Peninsula countries, one cannot do more than guess at the total worth of privately held foreign assets. The rough outflow calculations already made cannot be repeated for every year over the past two decades (even if it were possible to get any evidence going back that far) because the accumulation of foreign assets is affected by a number of external gains and losses. On the credit side it is thought that many Kuwaiti and Saudi agents for foreign contracting firms may have their commission paid direct into foreign bank accounts, and there is certainly a large amount of interest that is reinvested abroad as it is earned. On the debit side there would probably be some imports paid for by merchants drawing on foreign bank accounts, and on top of this there must have been substantial capital losses – particularly from the collapse of Intra Bank in 1966, and the failure of some of the mutual funds in 1970.

So in Kuwait at the end of 1973 the standard figure given for individually held foreign assets (excluding the investments of the ruling family) was a very well rounded $2,000 million; and to this can be added the net foreign assets of the five commercial banks – $870 million – and the foreign assets of the Kuwait Investment Company (KIC) and the Kuwait Foreign Trading Contracting and Investment Company (KFTCIC) – $190 million – to give a combined total for private Kuwaiti foreign assets of $3,060 million. (In order to give a figure which reflects only the private sector participation in KIC and KFTCIC, the government shareholding in each company has been deducted from foreign assets.)

In Saudi Arabia direct private foreign investment (excluding the unknown fortune of the al Saud family) may be as little as a quarter of the Kuwaiti figure, or about $500 million, which with the banks' net foreign assets of $300 million odd at the end of 1973 would add up to total private foreign holdings of only $800 million.

In Qatar the sum would be smaller still, but rather than trying to pin-point a figure for foreign assets, the bankers are mainly concerned to find out what has become of private Qatari wealth as a whole. Residents' bank deposits ($150 million at the end of 1973)* are remarkably small for a state that has had an oil income, albeit a modest one, for over twenty years. One reason might be that the ruling al Thani family, which until the accession of Shaikh Khalifa in February 1972 used to receive between a half and two-thirds of Qatar's oil revenues, keeps most of its money abroad. But by itself this explanation would not be sufficient. A large part of the missing money must have been taken out of the country in the form of riyal notes and put on deposit in Dubai; and a further sum – about $20 million or some $200 per head of population – may be hoarded under mattresses. With this sort of mentality still common it seems unlikely that very much money can be traced to ordinary Qatari citizens having built up investments in the West. It is thought that there are only two Qatari families with substantial assets in Europe and America – the Darwishs, the richest of the merchant community, and the al Thanis.

Similarly in Abu Dhabi the only really large holders of foreign assets must be the al Nahayans – though here the small amount of private foreign investment is mainly a measure of the newness of the state's wealth, and of the considerable scope that still exists for investing locally in building and other enterprises.

*   *   *

If the four main Arabian oil states are taken together the combined foreign holdings of their citizens and the foreign assets of their banks and investment companies at the end of 1973 might have been $4,200 million, though this estimate must be subject to a margin of error of at least $500 million either way. If a further $2,000 million is added as a guess at the overseas investments of the members of the ruling families, there would be a grand total of $6,200 million.

This figure is a good deal smaller than some of those that have been put forward outside the Middle East. But when it is remembered that up to December 1973 the revenues paid to these states

*At this time there were ten commercial banks in Qatar: the Qatar National Bank, British Bank of the Middle East, Chartered, National and Grindlays, Arab Bank, First National City, United Bank of Pakistan, Bank Saderat (Iranian), Bank of Oman (Dubian), and al Mashreq (Lebanese).

since the beginning of oil production had amounted to roughly $40,000 million, and that some $8,000 million of this was in the governments' reserves, $6,200 million as an estimate of total private savings abroad seems about right.

In terms of the investments held by the Western public six billion dollars is a very small sum – being considerably less than the deposits in any of the bigger American or European banks, and not much more than one per cent of the value of shares quoted on the London stock exchange in March 1973 – but it is still large enough to have a major impact on the money and exchange markets if it were managed in a disruptive and unstable fashion.

In trying to find out where this money is invested it is easiest to start with the foreign assets of the commercial banks, which at the end of 1973 stood at a combined total of $2,100 million gross.* Most of this money, $1,300 million, is controlled by the five banks in Kuwait. The four British- or American-managed Kuwaiti banks would normally place about three-quarters of their money in London, while Alahli would have about half in London, thirty per cent in Paris, and ten per cent in Brussels. Because of the eight-hour time difference between Kuwait and New York very little money is placed direct in the U.S.A. A small percentage of the foreign assets is invested in euro-bonds – with Alahli holding proportionately more of these than the other banks – United Kingdom treasury bills, and an insignificant amount of equity shares. But the bulk of the money – about eighty per cent – is either in certificates of deposit or on the inter-bank deposit market. In late 1972 and early 1973 much of this money went to the newly established American banks in London (because they were offering attractive rates at that time), but generally it is difficult to single out any particular group of institutions as having more of the Kuwaiti banks' funds than others.

In order to play a more direct role in placing their funds on the London market, and at the same time maximize their profits from this operation, four of the banks, National, Commercial, Gulf and Alahli, and two of the Kuwaiti investment companies have opened a London subsidiary called the United Bank of Kuwait (UBK). This bank was set up in 1966 on the initiative of Alan Medlycott, who,

---

*Figures given earlier in this chapter for the commercial banks' foreign assets were *net* totals – denoting only that part of the banks' foreign holdings which might be considered as belonging to Arabian citizens. The figures quoted in the following paragraphs are *gross* assets – applying to money which, whatever its origin, is managed on overseas markets by Kuwaiti, Saudi, Abu Dhabi or Qatari banks, or by banks that have branches in these states.

since his retirement from Kuwait, has become the National Bank's investment adviser in London, and Abdlatif al Hamad, who was then acting in his capacity as Managing Director of the Kuwait Investment Company, and has since assumed the additional post of UBK's Chairman.

The Kuwait Foreign Trading Contracting and Investment Company and the other banks (with the exception of Alahli, which joined when it was founded in 1968, and the British Bank of the Middle East, which at that time still had a branch in Kuwait) were invited to put up equal shares of UBK's capital. But they showed no great interest when they accepted the offer – and since then the feeling has grown that UBK tends to work mainly to the advantage of the National Bank, and, to a lesser extent, the Commercial Bank. This may be because it is the National Bank which has given UBK the most support – but the outcome is that the Gulf Bank has set up a London representative office of its own, while Alahli channels more of its business to the UBAF Limited consortium bank,* which is partly owned by Crédit Lyonnais, the bank which has seconded Alahli's management.

At the end of 1973 some $350 million of UBK's total deposits of $530 million was due to the bank's shareholders (much of the rest being due to the Kuwait Investment Office and the Kuwait Fund for Arab Economic Development) and it is probably fair to assume that most of this $350 million was deposited by the National and Commercial banks. In all over a quarter of the Kuwaiti banks' gross foreign assets were deposited with UBK, and about ninety per cent of UBK's assets were on the London money market.

In Saudi Arabia, where there are only two nationally owned banks whose foreign assets can be analysed in this manner, the picture is rather simpler. The National Commercial Bank in February 1973 had about $146 million, or thirty-five per cent, of its assets abroad, and the Riyad Bank in July 1973 had about $90 million, or thirty-four per cent, of its assets abroad. Most of this money was placed in London, and in each case over ninety per cent was on deposit. Although one cannot give a precise comparison, because the Riyad and National Commercial balance sheets are published on different dates (neither of which corresponds exactly to any of the dates on which the Saudi Arabian Monetary Agency publishes a

*UBAF Limited is the London associate of the Paris-based consortium Union des Banques Arabes et Françaises. It is owned fifty per cent by UBAF in Paris, twenty-five per cent by the Libyan Arab Foreign Bank and twenty-five per cent by Midland.

consolidated report), the two Saudi banks, which between them have well over half of residents' deposits, would probably account for about eighty per cent of the foreign assets of all the banks in the Kingdom. This would leave the ten foreign branch banks in mid-1973 with foreign assets of about $50 million.

The surplus money from these banks, and from the foreign branches which dominate the banking system in the Lower Gulf, would automatically be merged into the pool of funds controlled by each bank's main office overseas, where it would be indistinguishable from the money derived from any other source in that bank's network. Compared with the foreign assets of the big Kuwaiti and Saudi banks, the amounts of private Arab money held abroad by most of the nine American and European banks with operations in the Arabian Peninsula would be insignificant. This would apply particularly to the Algemene Bank Nederland in Saudi Arabia and Dubai, Banque de l'Indochine in Saudi Arabia, Chase Manhattan in Bahrain, Banque de Paris et des Pays Bas in Abu Dhabi, the First National Bank of Chicago in Dubai, and National and Grindlays, which entered the Middle East through taking over the Ottoman Bank in 1969, and now has branches in Qatar, Abu Dhabi, Dubai, Sharjah, Ras al Khaimah and Oman.

Two other banks, Chartered, formerly known in Arab countries as the Eastern Bank, and First National City, have rather larger networks – but their surplus funds would not be as big as the number of their branches might indicate. Chartered's best established business is in Bahrain and Qatar, both of which have relatively small banking systems; while First National City has its biggest operation in Saudi Arabia (where it is the only non-Arab bank to be allowed a branch in Riyadh) and here it has managed to lend an unusually high proportion of its resources locally. Of the foreign concerns it is only the British Bank of the Middle East (BBME), a member of the Hongkong and Shanghai Banking Corporation with branches in thirteen Arab states (including the northern emirates of the UAE), that holds really large quantities of Arab money outside the region. There is, of course, no breakdown in the bank's balance sheet of which assets are in London and which in the Middle East, and any estimate is complicated by the unknown amount of foreign assets belonging to the Bank of Kuwait and the Middle East that would be on deposit at the BBME head office, but out of total assets of $1,310 million in December 1973, those funds in London that were derived from its own branches in Saudi Arabia, Qatar and Abu Dhabi might have been rather over $100 million.

So in the four biggest Arabian oil states the bulk of the banks' foreign assets – $1,500 million plus out of $2,100 million in 1973 – is controlled by eight institutions: the British Bank of the Middle East, the National Commercial and Riyad banks in Saudi Arabia and the five Kuwaiti banks. And because all of these banks are prepared to say, in general terms, where they have invested their assets abroad, the money is not too difficult to trace. But when it comes to tracking down the direct private investment, the money involved in the banks' and exchange dealers' capital transfers, it is largely a matter of sifting through bits of circumstantial evidence, and then guessing. This means looking at some of the 'general principles' of private Arab investment, and at the financial mentality and background of the investors themselves.

The society in which the Arabian investors have made their money is, of course, very much less financially sophisticated than that of the industrial West. In Europe and America anyone who has built up a fortune will inevitably have gained some experience of the technicalities of Western finance and business in the process, and he will be accustomed to Western investment regulations and Western tax. His wealth will be matched by a certain amount of investment expertise. This the Arabian investor in Europe lacks. In most cases his money will have been made originally in trade (or in Kuwait by selling land to the government) and not in industry or finance. Furthermore he will have been working in a rather free-wheeling and unusually profitable environment, where there are a few government controls, virtually no tax, and no formal capital market. This background is hardly an appropriate training for foreign investment, and consequently the Arabs' approach is marked with some caution and apprehension – especially regarding the matter of tax, and how to avoid it.

There has been an emphasis on tangible assets, such as property, and on investments that guarantee the safety of capital and a predictable income, such as bank deposits. Where possible, the Arabs also prefer something which yields a quick return – though this trait, which reflects the merchant background, is less pronounced in their Western investments than it is in their dealings in the Gulf and Beirut. With a very few exceptions they have avoided making direct investments in Western industry or commercial enterprises, which might involve them in taking management responsibility. If a Gulf Arab is induced to invest in such a project, he will often require the person who has put forward the idea to prove his good faith by contributing an equal share of the capital.

In the first few months of 1975 there was evidence that Arab investors were becoming somewhat bolder in their overseas investment. There were announcements of individuals or groups of investors purchasing or negotiating to purchase blocks of shares in Occidental Petroleum; the British construction company Costain, in which the total Arab interest, made up of several holdings was twenty-one per cent; the British mining and finance company Lonrho, in which the issue of new shares to Gulf International in December 1974 (see Chapter 12) was followed by news of an unnamed group of Kuwaitis negotiating for a separate and larger holding; and the Detroit-based Bank of the Commonwealth, the sixth biggest bank in Michigan, in which Mr Gaith Pharaon (a Saudi of Lebanese origin) was bidding for a stake of thirty-five per cent. At the same time a group of investors from Saudi Arabia, Kuwait, Bahrain and Hong Kong bought out the tea and rubber properties in Sri Lanka of the British company Pelmadulla Holdings.

These deals, however, were still somewhat exceptional. Most private investors in the Arabian Peninsula retain a deep-seated cautious and conservative attitude, and this is reinforced by the lessons of recent experience. During the late 1950s and early 1960s many Kuwaitis and Saudis were taken for a ride by rather unscrupulous Europeans and Americans peddling their own 'patent' schemes for guaranteed big profits. But even since the Arabs have grown wary of these people (who are by no means entirely unheard-of in the Gulf today) their fingers have been burned in various investment fashions of a more conventional sort. First the idea that Beirut was the perfect haven for their money received a severe setback when Intra, the biggest bank in the Lebanon, crashed in 1966. Then there was the mutual fund fashion. As explained earlier in this chapter Investors Overseas Services had its best years in the Middle East at a rather earlier date, from 1962 to 1966, and so most of the Arab buying in the later 1960s was concentrated on other funds. But it was still IOS that had sold most shares in the area, and when it collapsed along with Gramco and the Real Estate Fund of America in 1970 the Arabs probably lost more money than they did in the Intra affair. The disaster was felt to reflect on the mutual fund business in general, and the Arabs have since steered clear of this type of investment.

Inevitably the decline on the London and Wall Street stock exchanges which triggered off the crash of IOS also undermined the confidence of those relatively few Arabs who had put their faith in a more direct form of stock-market investment, dealing either through the conventional brokers' offices in Kuwait, London or New York, or through the ill-fated omnibus account run by Consolidated Investors. This 'omnibus' or 'consolidated' account differed from a mutual fund in that investors could put in random amounts of capital and exercise discretion over which shares were bought with their money. The client's instructions, however, always went through Consolidated Investors (as the company running the account), and as with a mutual fund, the firms of stockbrokers in New York who did the actual buying and selling did not know the identity of the individual clients whose money they were handling.

Consolidated Investors was established in Kuwait by a member of the al Sabah family and two Palestinians in 1964, and in the following year it opened an office in Beirut. For several years it did rather well – building up quite a reputation for picking the best of the speculative conglomerate stocks – and at one point the market value of its accounts in New York reached $11 million. But in 1969 conglomerate prices collapsed. Most of the accounts of Consolidated Investors' clients still held a heavy concentration of these shares – particularly AMK, Susquahana and Ling-Temco-Vought – and because their purchase had been financed in part with money borrowed from New York banks (which had of course to be paid back in full) the dramatic fall in their value meant that Consolidated Investors went bankrupt.

After this fiasco the Kuwait government, which tries to protect its citizens from rash speculations overseas, introduced regulations in the 1970 Commercial Law designed to discourage the use of the leverage principle in foreign investment transactions.* Dealings in consolidated accounts were forbidden, and commodity accounts were made illegal, except for those citizens who were actually importing or selling the particular commodity which was the subject of their contract. In other words, if a Kuwaiti is now to buy cocoa futures, he should be importing chocolate – or possibly running a sweet shop.

After 1970 there was a big movement of Arab funds into European deposit accounts (which had always been a popular form of investment) and, on a rather lesser scale, into euro-dollar bonds. The classic Arab technique was to swap money from one currency to another to chase the highest interest rates, and investors would frequently do this

*The principle of leverage, as used by Consolidated Investors, involves the investor buying stock with his own capital – say $1,000 – and with a bank loan of up to twice this amount – $2,000. If his shares rise in value by only thirty-three per cent he will therefore double his money. If his shares go down by thirty-three per cent he will be wiped out.

for the sake of a quarter per cent or less. But there was very little switching between European currencies and dollars in order to speculate on parity changes. In fact, during the dollar and sterling crises of 1971/3 most Arab investors in those currencies either stayed put and took their losses, or brought their money home for a time. These movements showed up in soaring domestic land and share prices, and big rises in bank deposits – though in the balance of payments statistics covering a period of one year, they would appear as a decline in the normal outflow, not as a net inflow.

During 1972 and 1973 a part of this inflow could be attributed to more positive motives. There was a feeling throughout the Arabian Peninsula that the region was heading for a period of major industrial expansion, which investors were anxious to cash in on; and in the lower Gulf there was an additional element of relief that the British withdrawal in 1971, which caused a larger than usual capital outflow that year, did not lead to the political and economic disruption that some investors had feared. Compared with defensive motives though, these positive factors in the return of capital were fairly small – and, predictably, as the dollar began to recover in the autumn of 1973, there were signs that some of the funds that had returned were going out again.

For the banks the result of these periodic inflows of private capital was in an increased exchange risk – and, unlike the private investors, the banks do make great efforts during monetary crises to get their foreign assets into the stronger European currencies. In the weeks leading up to the dollar devaluation of 1973 it is estimated that the Kuwaiti banks, and those few private Kuwaiti investors who were prepared to shift their money within Europe, moved some $250 million in this way – though, as explained in the last chapter, the banks still made a substantial loss on the devaluation.

Compared with the sums moved by the European financial community at this time, $250 million is not a very large figure; and even when one adds the private money moved out of dollars into dinars one still does not get a picture which would tie in with the rumours of massive Arab speculation which occasionally sweep through the City of London. Although the distinction is a blurred one, the Arabs are better classed as the victims than the villains of currency upheavals – and this applies even more with the governments' reserves, which are hardly ever moved, than with private-sector capital.

One effect of this catalogue of misfortunes, from the crash of Intra to the devaluations of the dollar, has been educational. It is now better realized in Kuwait and elsewhere that foreign investment is not inevitably 'a good thing' with success guaranteed; that it is more important to choose and supervise an investment carefully than to opt for what may appear to be the safest possible investment and then forget about it; and that the return on almost any investment will be marginal, which implies that unless the investment is carefully managed the marginal profit will vanish, and a marginal loss will appear instead. At the same time, more investors have discovered that there is no point in blindly copying the investments of other members of their families or friends, as many Kuwaitis have done, on the assumption that these people must 'know something' that they themselves do not.

So in the long run the experience gained in the last few years may help promote a more discriminating and more 'active' style of Arab investment overseas, but for the time being the emphasis with most of those funds that are abroad is still on extreme caution. It is thought that the bulk of the Arabs' money remains in deposit accounts, chiefly in London. Probably the largest proportion of these deposits would end up with the big four U.K. clearing banks, National Westminster, Barclays, Midland and Lloyds; rather less would be with the branches of American banks in London; and a little would be with those merchant banks that have a well established Middle East connection – like Hambros, Morgan Grenfell (which in 1974 went into a joint venture with the Arab Bank), and Kleinwort Benson. Generally the Arabs are slightly afraid of merchant banks, because they have the impression that many – without being sure quite how many – are Jewish-controlled, and would therefore be liable to lend Arab funds to Israel.

The United States would rank a poor second to Britain in the amount of private Arab investment it has received – though the Saudis, who have had a traditionally close relationship with America, may have placed a larger proportion of their investments in the U.S. than the Kuwaitis, Abu Dhabians and Qataris. It also seems possible that the al Saud and al Sabah ruling families would have made big deposits with the head offices of those American banks that have had a long connection with their governments' official reserves. (A large amount of the al Sauds' private fortune is also thought to be with the Algemene Bank Nederland – another of the banks holding part of the Saudi reserve. The Algemene Bank was the first to be established in the Kingdom – its original purpose being to provide a service for pilgrims from the Dutch East Indies.)

Much of the remaining Arab money in America would be in property (discussed in the next chapter) or on Wall Street. In view of the Arabs' distrust of equity investment the amount of money involved here would not be large in absolute terms – but taking into account the portfolios managed by the Swiss banks, the smaller sums handled by the Merrill Lynch offices in Kuwait and Dubai, and the money placed direct by Arab clients with brokers' offices in New York, it would be safe to assume that there is considerably more Arab money on Wall Street than on the London stock exchange.

Part of the reason why Britain and the United States have attracted the largest amounts of investment is that most educated Arabs in the Gulf and Saudi Arabia speak English. The United States is a bit remote from the Middle East, but this language advantage makes Britain the first choice (after Lebanon) for their long summer holidays, and therefore the obvious country in which to buy a second home and hold investments. But the Arabs are not so familiar with the European countries and Japan – and, apart from this cultural disincentive to investment, in the last few years they have been deterred by a number of practical difficulties as well. Up to 1972 there was a certain amount of money being moved around Europe and Japan to take advantage of interest rate differences, but during the currency crises of 1972/3, when most of these countries imposed restrictions on foreigners making deposits in their currencies, that part of the flow of Arab deposits which had been in the European currencies and the yen (as opposed to euro-dollars) dried up. The restrictions, which were designed to prevent speculative inflows of foreign money, generally involved depositors receiving no interest, or having to place half their money interest-free with the central banks.

For two years this confined the Arabs to investing in euro-dollar bonds and deposits or in euro-sterling deposits, and in property – chiefly in Spain, Italy and France – and in the European and Japanese stock markets, though in some countries there were also restrictions on foreign purchases of domestic securities. Added to the fact that the stock exchanges of Europe and Japan are considerably smaller and less well known than those of London and New York, these restrictions meant that in practice the amount of private Arab money going into European and Japanese shares of any type must have been negligible. (On 30 March 1973 the market capitalization, or the current market value of all shares quoted on the world's four big stock exchanges was: New York $985 billion, London $435 billion, Tokyo $181 billion, and Paris $63 billion.)

Early in 1974, however, the restrictions on both deposits and securities transactions were being lifted, because the dollar had

Faisal bin Abdel-Aziz al Saud, King of Saudi Arabia, 1964–1975, and President Amin of Uganda visiting the Ripon Falls near the source of the Nile in 1972

King Khaled bin Abdel-Aziz al Saud receiving the oath of fealty from Saudi dignitaries at the royal palace in Riyadh, 26 March 1975. On the King's right is Prince Fahad bin Abdel-Aziz, the new Crown Prince, and on the left is Prince Sultan bin Abdel-Aziz, the Minister of Defence

Shaikh Abdullah al Salem al Sabah, Ruler of Kuwait 1951–1965

Shaikh Sabah al Salem al Sabah, the present Ruler of Kuwait

Shaikh Jaber al Ahmed al Jaber al Sabah, Crown Prince and Prime Minister of Kuwait

Shaikh Shakbut bin Sultan al Nahayan, Ruler of Abu Dhabi 1928–1966, in his palace talking to his European adviser Mr. Bill Clark

Shaikh Zaid bin Sultan al Nahayan, the present Ruler of Abu Dhabi, with the Saudi Arabian Ambassador's horse, Whistling Glory, at Newmarket in 1969

Shaikh Khalifa bin Hamid al Thani, Ruler of Qatar

Shaikh Rashid bin Said al Makhtoum, Ruler of Dubai

Shaikh Isa bin Sulman al Khalifa, Ruler of Bahrain

Above Left: Prince Saud bin Faisal, the fourth son of King Faisal. Appointed Saudi Arabian Minister of State for Foreign Affairs in March 1975, formerly Deputy Minister of Petroleum and Mineral Resources. Above Right: Mr. Hisham Nasser, President of Saudi Arabian Central Planning Organization

Shaikh Ahmed Zaki Yamani, Saudi Arabian Minister of Petroleum and Mineral Resources, whispering to Belaid Abdessalem, Algerian Minister of Industry and Energy, during a Japanese Press Club luncheon in Tokyo in January 1974

Mr. Abdel-Rahman Atiqi, appointed Kuwaiti Minister of Finance in January 1975. Formerly Minister of Finance and Oil

Mr. Abdlatif al Hamad, Director General of the Kuwait Fund for Arab Economic Development, at home

Mr. Khaled Abu Saud, Director of Investment at the Kuwaiti Ministry of Finance

Two members of the Abu Dhabi Investment Board, Mr. Mohammed Habroush, Minister of Finance, and Mr. John Butter, Director of Finance

Mr. Mohammed Mehdi Tajir, Ambassador of the United Arab Emirates, with the Honorable Major General Sir Michael Fitzalan-Howard, Marshal of the Diplomatic Corps, on his way to present his credentials at Buckingham Palace, June 1972

Mr. Saeb Jaroudi, President of the Arab Fund for Economic and Social Development, addressing an Arab League Boycott Office conference in December 1970, when he was Lebanese Minister of National Economy. On Jaroudi's left is the Egyptian Commissioner General of the Boycott Office, General Mohammed Mahgoub

Shaikh Sabah al Ahmed al Sabah, the Kuwaiti Foreign Minister and founder of Gulf Fisheries (left), talking to the Lebanese President, Mr. Sulaiman Franjieh at the United Nations in December 1974

Shaikh Sabah al Ahmed's son, Shaikh Nasser al Sabah, of Gulf International and Gulf Fisheries, and Dr. Khalil Osman Mahmoud of Gulf International, at a Lonrho shareholders meeting in London, December 1974

become stronger, and most countries were anxious to attract foreign capital to offset the current account payments deficit caused by the rise in oil prices.

The same sort of restrictions that were temporarily in force in some EEC countries and in Japan during 1972 and 1973 were also applied in Switzerland. From June 1972 to January 1974 the Swiss barred foreigners from all purchases of domestic property (which had previously been very popular with Arab investors) or Swiss franc securities. In July 1972 they also supplemented an earlier ban on the payment of interest on new short-term Swiss franc bank deposits made by foreigners, by levying a two per cent per quarter negative interest or 'commission' charge on any increase of more than SF100,000 in these accounts.

So almost all recent private Arab investment dealings with Switzerland have been in money which does not stay in the country, but only passes through it. About half of this investment has been in dollar or sterling fiduciary deposits – where the recipient bank passes the money on to London or some other centre in its own name. Unlike the interest received on ordinary foreign currency deposits made by foreigners in Switzerland, the income from fiduciary deposits is not subject to a thirty per cent withholding tax. Much of the rest of the Arab money invested through Switzerland has been placed under the banks' management in portfolios of non-Swiss franc securities. In most cases it seems that the Arab customers leave the choice of shares to the banks' discretion – though in the general guide lines that customers lay down there is a predictable emphasis on fixed-interest stocks and bonds.

Some investors also include gold in their portfolios, but the amounts are small. Since 1971 the Arabs have been a declining influence in the gold market, and the main force behind the soaring price is thought to have come from European speculators, investors and hoarders who have lost their faith in depreciating paper money. Because the Arabs prefer earning interest on a fixed capital sum to speculating in the hope of capital gains, the metal is not popular in the Middle East as an investment. In fact it is thought that the small quantities included in the Swiss-managed portfolios would constitute a large proportion of all the gold bought in Switzerland by Arabs for investment (as opposed to hoarding) purposes. Nor does gold have very much appeal to the merchants of the Gulf as a store of constant value or as a hedge against inflation – and even in Saudi Arabia, which is traditionally supposed to contain vast hoards of gold, the Monetary Agency's balance of payments statistics over the last

I

decade show private-sector imports averaging only $14 million a year.

By far the largest Arab buyers therefore, have been the Dubian merchants engaged in 're-exporting' gold to India. The merchants' purchases reached a record 259 tons in 1970 but have since slumped to under 100 tons in 1973. The reason for this decline has been partly that in unstable price conditions the merchants risk having a significant part of their profit margin knocked off the value of their cargo while it is still on its one-week voyage by dhow across the Indian Ocean. But it has also been found that each recent surge in the price has caused an immediate drop in demand on the subcontinent, which has been followed by only a partial recovery.

It seems that the decline in Arab demand has taken place more at the expense of the London Gold Market (composed of Samuel Montagu, Johnson Matthey, Sharps Pixley, Mocatta and Goldsmid, and N. M. Rothschild) than of the Zurich Gold Pool. The three big banks which make up the pool, Union Bank of Switzerland, the Swiss Bank Corporation and the Swiss Credit Bank, all have substantial connections with the Arab world – and within Switzerland the Arabs take infinitely more of their business to these three than to the 500-odd smaller Swiss banks.

It is also noticeable that the Arabs have a marked preference for Geneva over Zurich, which is by far the larger centre. It is estimated that about eighty-five to ninety per cent of Arab deposits are placed initially in Geneva – and it is no coincidence that Geneva has been chosen for the branches of the British Bank of the Middle East, National and Grindlays and most of the other Arab or Arab-orientated banks that have set up offices in Switzerland. The reasons for this may be that the Arabs like the relaxed and cosmopolitan atmosphere of Geneva, or that some of them have bought lakeside property, or simply that while many of them can speak French, few can handle German. But perhaps in the final analysis they are attracted by a characteristic discovered by Alexandre Dumas, who wrote: 'The Genevese are the leading financiers of the continent, and they have what for this profession is the most important of all virtues, the ability to spend less in a day than they earn.'

9

THE APPEAL OF PROPERTY

In 1968 Shaikh Jaber al Abdullah al Jaber al Sabah, the Governor of the Kuwait Oil Company town at Ahmedi, bought himself a large mansion at Esher in Surrey. In 1969 he had it painted, in 1970 he furnished it, and finally in 1971 he went to live in it for ten days or so. The story goes that his visit was very slightly marred one evening when he took a walk in his long white dish-dasha down a nearby lane and terrified a courting couple who thought he was a ghost – but more serious was his discovery on his way to see his brother in the London Clinic that the traffic fumes made his dish-dasha dirty. This he mentioned to a friend in the Kuwait Embassy, and, on his friend's suggestion, he then bought a penthouse flat in Portman Square, as a pied-à-terre in which, on future visits to the metropolis, he would be able to change.

Since 1971 Shaikh Jaber has in fact lived in his Esher residence quite frequently – coming over to England for Ascot, and cultivating a rose garden – but the stories of the original purchase of the mansion and the Portman Square flat provide fairly typical examples of the Kuwaitis' style of buying and the type of property they favour. The Kuwaitis and the Arabs of the lower Gulf – Bahrainis, Qataris, Abu Dhabians and Dubians – now own a very large amount of property in Mayfair – particularly in South Street, Mount Street, South Audley Street and Green Street; and in recent years Brighton, rural Sussex and the Thames valley have become popular with the older generation as out of London retreats. Shaikh Zaid of Abu Dhabi has bought Buxted Park, a former Sussex health hydro; and further away from London, in Somerset, a group of Kuwaiti investors has bought Cricket St Thomas, a Georgian house surrounded by nearly a thousand acres of farmland and a wild-life park containing a variety of species including elephants, leopards, pumas, llamas and camels.

On much the same scale there have been substantial purchases on the Costa del Sol in Spain; in Italy; in Switzerland – where the deposed Shaikh Ahmed of Qatar owns a particularly conspicuous palace at Versoix on Lake Geneva; and in France – notably in Paris, the Riviera and Evian – which is not far across the border from Geneva, and became popular when the Swiss imposed their restrictions of foreigners buying property in 1972. Some of the bigger property buyers have a whole chain of foreign residences; Mehdi Tajir, for instance, the United Arab Emirates' Ambassador to Britain and former chief adviser to Shaikh Rashid of Dubai, has bought houses in Mayfair and in Avenue Foch in Paris, Windelsham Manor, where the Queen and Prince Philip lived immediately after their marriage, Mereworth Castle near Tunbridge Wells in Kent, and such commercial properties as the Tajir building in Rue Clemenceau, Beirut.

It is cases such as these, where the main emphasis is on buying a home, that account for the vast majority of all Arab purchases of property outside the Middle East; but apart from giving a long list of individuals' houses, which might be a rather pointless invasion of privacy, there is little more that can be said about this aspect of property buying. There is, after all, no great difference between a Kuwaiti buying a house outside his own country, and, say, a Brazilian buying one; and given the income bracket of Kuwaitis, and such other factors as their ability to speak English, the type and location of the houses they buy is fairly predictable.

There is, however, an additional investment element in buying any type of property, including the primarily residential properties described above, and this lends itself to a more detailed examination. The Arabs' belief is that one cannot go wrong in buying property, and that even if one only lives in the house for a few weeks each year, the building still makes a good, solid worry-free investment. The Arabs feel that they 'know' property – because, unlike bonds and share certificates, it is something they have seen in their own states and have been aware of from birth. Property satisfies traditional instincts, particularly among members of the older generation. (For example, it is said of Ebrahim Juffali, the eldest brother of the merchant family discussed in Chapter 12, that however much money he has, his life is still centred on his farm near Mecca.) Above all, property is reassuring and tangible – and the Arabs would generally much pefer to be able to look at a building and say to themselves 'that's all mine', than to contemplate the significance of their owning a minute proportion of some big public corporation. They have therefore been especially disillusioned when they have made losses on property, because although they acknowledge that there is a risk with stocks and shares, they feel that a building 'should not let them down'.

The flaws inherent in this approach when it is applied to buying property purely for investment (as opposed to investment-cum-residential) purposes have been shown up very well by the experience of Arabian investors, mostly Kuwaitis, on the Beirut property market. During the early and middle 1960s a large number of office and apartment blocks were bought on Hamra (the Regent Street or Fifth Avenue of Beirut) and in the south-western area of the city around Rauche and Pigeon Rock. Many of the buildings were not very well constructed, and in order to obtain a quick return their owners had them rather skimpily decorated inside. In most cases the running of these blocks was left to the banks – which in Beirut will arrange letting, recruit a concierge, and provide other necessary management. This service though is not particularly efficient, and, given the more fundamental drawback in the generally poor quality of the buildings themselves, there have been many occasions when investors have either received only a very small return or have actually made a loss. Where the big profits hoped for have material-ized – as in the centre of Jeddah, Manama (the capital of Bahrain) and Kuwait, as well as Beirut – these have often been due to a largely fortuitous soaring of land values, accelerated in recent years by investors repatriating their money at a time of currency crisis.

It is now better appreciated that if an owner is going to regard his property solely as an investment he must adopt a wholly professional approach, because although the building may look reassuring and may well retain or increase its capital value, it will not guarantee an income. In Beirut it is a waste of time to aim for a spectacular rate of return, because even a well managed and properly built block is unlikely to yield more than five to five and a half per cent per annum. So in the last few years, since 1970 perhaps, there has been more emphasis on buying land only with a definite and well appraised scheme in mind.

Because foreigners may now own no more than 10,000 square metres of land in Lebanon, the recent trend has been towards Lebanese/Arabian joint ventures centred on large-scale develop-ments. The most spectacular of these operations to date has been the St Charles Centre complex, mostly owned by Shaikh Saad, the Kuwaiti Defence Minister, and containing the tallest building in the

Middle East – which is to be run by Holiday Inns as a hotel. Another big project being planned during 1973 involved a Lebanese/ Saudi group, with a development scheme near the Coral Beach to the south of the city, incorporating a hotel, a swimming pool and a shopping centre.

The mistakes made in Beirut have had their parallel on the European and American property markets – though here much investment buying has been conducted through foreign sales groups rather than off the individual investor's own bat. Two of the biggest companies selling in the Middle East have been Mackle Brothers, owned by the Deltona Corporation of Florida, USA, and the General Development Corporation, both of which set up offices in Beirut during the mid-1960s. Their operations, which were backed by some highly professional and glossy advertising in Lebanese newspapers and television, were confined to selling plots of undeveloped land in Florida. Mackle sold in Deltona itself, and in five other places given the enticing names of Sunny Hill, Citrus Springs, Pine Ridge, Marco Island and Marion Ox. On his plot the buyer could build whatever he liked – a house, or some small commercial property, like a shop, which he could either live in himself or let – and the idea was that in time completely new semi-urban communities would grow up. Needless to say this concept appealed most to retired American couples, and, equally predictably, the most advanced of the new townships, Deltona, has developed a highly organized community life.

It is very doubtful whether the Arabs were much attracted by this sort of life, and yet Mackle alone sold around a thousand plots to Middle Eastern customers, with roughly half going to Kuwaitis and a third to Saudis. The secret of their success was that in Beirut both Mackle and the General Development Corporation presented their land as an investment opportunity. In a sense this was fair enough, because when each community had become fully developed, and the investor found himself owning land in the middle of a town, he would indeed be able to make a substantial profit if he sold. But the snag was that the investor had to wait many years for his land to appreciate to this extent (by which time he might be dead); while if he decided to sell earlier he had to compete against the sophisticated machines of Mackle and the General Development Corporation selling almost identical plots on attractive terms in the same area. So the popularity of the two companies in Beirut waned rapidly. The General Development Corporation has long since moved out, and what remains of the Mackle operation is geared to selling apartment leases in an area described as 'the exclusive Benyamina district of Torremolinos, Spain'. Buyers may either live in their apartments or sub-let them at a guaranteed twelve and a half per cent return.

At about the same time that Mackle and the General Development Corporation began business in the Middle East, another rather different American property organization, Keyes Realty Incorporated, moved into Beirut. Keyes (pronounced to rhyme with 'eyes') was not involved in development property of any sort, and dealt only with large commercial buildings, like office or apartment blocks, shopping centres and warehouses. Once a customer had bought one of these properties, legal and management services were provided by other companies in the Keyes organization – which included mortgage, insurance and accountancy firms, a domestic sales group, an overseas sales group and two property management concerns. All of these were owned by the Keyes Companies of Miami, the largest corporation of its type in the southern United States.

Keyes first became interested in the Middle East during the 1950s and early 1960s, when it received some welcome but entirely unsolicited business from Arab and Iranian private investors; and during the course of flying in and out of Beirut, Tehran and Kuwait, the company's executives decided that the area looked promising. So in 1965 Keyes established a permanent representative in Beirut. Business went well. The Arabs had previously tended to think of buying property with 'cash on the barrel', and they were impressed to discover that in the USA at that time they needed to put up only twenty per cent of the capital required, and were able to borrow the balance in some cases at a rate of as little as four and a half or five per cent, with repayment spread over twenty-five years. They were also impressed by the fact that many properties which Keyes was selling had an established 'track record' – and, in the case of some of the shopping centres, had rents tied to the value of turnover, which meant that the owners' income kept pace with inflation.

In particular, there was the advantage that after 1965 Keyes conducted all its transactions with non-US residents through Curaçao, the largest island of the Netherlands Antilles, where business of this sort benefited from a unique treaty signed between the Netherlands and the USA in 1964, under which companies resident in either of the signatories' territories were exempted from withholding tax on profits earned on investments held in the other. Investors working through Curaçao were still not immune from US income or corporation tax, but because they were able to deduct mortgage interest and depreciation from their profits, in the early years of their investment it worked out that their actual tax liability was virtually nil. When these deductions fell much below the level of their income, investors would generally sell, repatriate their capital gains without paying the thirty per cent US withholding tax, and then carry out the operation again on some other building.

The largest part of Keyes Middle Eastern business came from Iranians, whom the company found to be by far its most sophisticated clients – knowing many of the technicalities of gearing and tax before they approached Keyes. Most of the other clients were Kuwaitis and Lebanese. Between 1965 and 1969 Keyes did six one-million-dollar-plus deals with individual Arab investors. Four were shopping centre interests sold to Kuwaitis in Florida, Alabama, New Orleans and Kansas, and two were apartment blocks – one in Ohio sold to a Kuwaiti and another in Texas to a Saudi. In a more modest transaction with an institutional investor Keyes sold a share in a further apartment block in Houston, Texas, to the Kuwait Investment Company; and in another deal in 1969 one of the al Ghunaim family of Kuwait (not to be confused with the al Ghanims) bought interests in shopping centres in Texas and Florida, and an apartment-block complex in Texas. In all these cases Keyes looked after the management of the properties.

In 1969/70, however, Keyes Middle Eastern business began to slow down. In part this was because the less professional investors were moving their money out of property and into euro-dollar deposits, which were at that time offering particularly attractive rates of interest; but at the same time sound investment property in the United States had been made scarce by the activities of REFA and Gramco. For its more sophisticated buyers, Keyes simply ran out of properties which it could recommend, and so in 1971 its Middle East office was closed.

Other property sales organizations in the Middle East have worked on an altogether smaller scale than Keyes. In the late 1960s there was a Canadian concern, with a Beirut office selling apartment houses in Montreal, and slightly later a Canadian real estate fund called Investpool made a brief appearance. But neither of these companies did well in the Middle East, because mortgage rates were then two per cent higher in Canada than in the USA and, in the absence of any Curaçao-style arrangement, investors were hit by a fifteen per cent withholding tax. Elsewhere various Italian and Spanish companies have done some Arab business by sending representatives on periodic visits through the Gulf; but there have apparently been no British companies selling in the area. The reasons presumably are that foreign investors in the United Kingdom would get a rather smaller mortgage on commercial property with higher interest rates, and that the tax-bite on non-residents' profits in the UK is bigger than in America.*

What remaining commercial properties private Arab investors own outside the Middle East have been bought on the initiative of the individuals themselves, and there are few examples of such deals. Mubarak al Hasawi, a member of the Kuwait National Assembly, and for many years a big landowner in his own state, has invested in several houses in Hertford Street and Berkeley Square in Mayfair; another big Kuwaiti property magnate, Khaled Marzoukh, in partnership with the Lebanese banking family Audi, has bought a huge area of development land in Montreal; the Saudi businessman Adnan Khashoggi, whose companies are discussed in Chapter 12, owns a number of different commercial properties spread all over the world; and Sulaiman Olayan, one of the 'Aramco merchants', is believed to have done substantial land deals in Florida. On a rather more exotic plane, the late Badr Mullah, a brilliant young Kuwaiti with a playboy reputation, used to own a share in the London discotheque Annabel's. (Another of Badr Mullah's claims to fame was a copy of a James Bond car, known in Kuwait as the 'al Mullah car', which offended the French police by releasing pink and green smoke on the Champs Elysées.) More recently, in late 1974, a group of investors from Abu Dhabi and Dubai bought the Park Tower Hotel in the Knightsbridge area of London.

This is obviously not a complete list, but it is very difficult in the Middle East to distinguish between fact and the mass of very plausible rumours which many Kuwaitis and Saudis tend to present as fact. It is, for instance, widely, but wrongly, believed that Mehdi Tajir and Shaikh Rashid own the Carlton Towers Hotel, and that Shaikh Zaid has bought Balnagowan Castle in Scotland. Similar myths attach themselves to newly established investment companies, like the Kuwait Real Estate Company (promoted by Khaled Marzoukh), which within months of its foundation in July 1972 on a fully paid-up capital of only $10 million, was being credited with having bought

*In early 1975 two British partnerships of chartered surveyors, Debenham Tewson and Chinnocks and Jones Lang Wooton were setting up offices in the Middle East, but their purpose was not to sell property in Britain. Debenham Tewson and Chinnocks (in Bahrain) was planning to act *for Arab buyers* of overseas property, while Jones Lang Wooton (in Beirut) aimed to provide professional services in carrying out valuations, arranging the letting and selling of local properties, and project management.

apartment blocks in Montreal, enormous areas of land around the Hudson Bay and in Alaska, and a 'skyscraper' in London. In fact at the time of these rumours – in mid-1973 – the company owned one large apartment building, called Louloua Marzoukh, and was planning a marina complex, a parking lot and a shopping centre – all in Kuwait. An even more remarkable story appeared in October 1974, when *The Sun*, a popular London daily, reported that the Shah of Iran was investing £200 million in the reconstruction and expansion of Southend pier into the biggest leisure centre in Europe.

A few of the rumours may be caused by the habit of laying false scents, which some investors, particularly members of the ruling families, use to disguise the true whereabouts of their assets; but a more common explanation is that they stem from ideas for future deals which individual investors have confided to their friends, or from transactions which were once being negotiated, but which were never successfully completed. In this category there was an example in 1969, when a Saudi very nearly bought a large area of Pimlico, and in 1972 it appears that a Kuwaiti put in a bid for the Dorchester Hotel. Another perennial rumour, which has been circulating for ten years or so, came from a Kuwaiti ambassador's suggestion that some enterprising person should build a Kuwait centre in London to contain the Embassy, the Health Office, the Military Office, the Cultural Office (which finances Kuwaiti students in Britain), a number of flats and a nightclub or discotheque.

*   *   *

Among institutional Middle Eastern investors (other than governments, which are discussed in Chapter 13) the most spectacular properties are owned by the Intra Investment Company, which was formed in December 1970 to take over the assets of Intra Bank. The Intra Investment Company is, of course, a Lebanese institution, but its shareholders include the Kuwait government (which was the biggest single depositor at the time of the crash in October 1966) with eighteen per cent, the Qatar government with three per cent, and a number of Kuwaiti, Saudi and Qatari private citizens. Up until 1966 Intra was a major force in Middle Eastern finance, and even since that date the memory of the crash has had a significant and conservative influence on the development of the area's banking system. So the story of Intra and its investments is worth running through in some detail.

Intra Bank was founded in 1951 by Yusif Beidas, a Palestinian refugee from the 1948 war, who was to be the bank's Chairman, Managing Director and sole decision-maker for fifteen years. The bank grew out of an exchange dealing operation, the International Traders Company, but within two years of beginning business it had entered less conventional banking fields by contributing part of the capital of a local chocolate factory, Chocolaterie President SA. In the early 1960s, after ten years of steadily expanding its branch network in Lebanon and other Arab countries, Intra moved into Europe and America.

In 1962 it bought a skyscraper on Fifth Avenue, changing the building's name from Canada House to the House of Lebanon. It was intended that the skyscraper should house Intra's New York branch, and the representative offices of Middle East Airlines (MEA) of which Intra owned sixty-five per cent, Casion du Liban and various other Lebanese companies. In 1963 Intra bought a large area of land, over 4,000 square metres, on the Avenue des Champs Elysées next to *Le Figaro* newspaper offices and the corner of Rue de Pothieu. Here the plan was to demolish the existing buildings and put up a new commercial centre to be known as 'Maison du Liban', which would have much the same purpose as the House of Lebanon in New York. In the following year the bank bought some eighty per cent of the shares of Chantiers Navals de la Ciotat, the second biggest shipyard in France. Other overseas assets acquired during this period included banking interests in Nigeria, Switzerland and Brazil, further properties in France, Britain and Switzerland, and small industrial companies in France, Britain and Panama. In its own country Intra took major shareholdings in Radio Orient (the Lebanese telecommunications company), Casino du Liban, the Phoenicia Hotel, Baalbeck Studios, Lebanese television, freight handling at Beirut port, and a number of smaller industrial, real estate and banking assets. One of Intra's associates, the Alahli Bank, bought the Londonderry Hotel in Park Lane. (The Alahli Bank closed at roughly the same time as Intra, and the Londonderry Hotel was subsequently sold.)

By 1965 Intra was by far the largest bank in Lebanon, with deposits of some LL750 million ($300 million), or about one-fifth of all deposits in Beirut if inter-bank money is excluded – but it was already becoming clear that Intra was having difficulty in sustaining its phenomenal rate of growth. The bank was unable to marshal the sophisticated management skills needed to run its overseas investments, and this began to show up in a loss of profitability. Instead of trying to remedy the causes of this situation, Intra's directors concentrated on covering the appearance of such bad results.

Then in the summer of 1966 the strengthening of the pound and the dollar and a big rise in interest rates in Europe triggered a major movement of funds out of Lebanon, losing Intra some sixty per cent of its bankers' deposits in the nine months between 1 January and 30 September. From July onwards Beidas was in contact with the authorities at the Bank of Lebanon (the central bank) with the object of raising a loan which would be secured on such assets as MEA and Casino du Liban – but whatever view one takes of the crisis it cannot be said that the government went out of its way to be helpful. Indeed, because of Intra's reputation for aggressive and unrelenting competition, certain members of the Lebanese establishment and most of the older and more conservative bankers regarded it with a fair degree of hostility.

Gradually it became known that Intra was in serious trouble. During early October there was a sharp increase in the rate of deposit withdrawals, culminating in a run on the bank and rumours of massive amounts of money being taken out by the Moscow Narodny Bank and by rich Kuwaitis and Saudis. The Bank of Lebanon came forward with only LL 15 million ($6 million) – and this at a rather late stage; while an eleventh-hour bid by the American shipping tycoon Daniel Ludwig, the President of National Bulk Carriers, to buy Intra lock, stock and barrel for the sake of acquiring MEA and its unused traffic rights in America, was turned down on the night before the crash. On 14 October Intra was forced to suspend payments, leaving some 16,000 depositors with their money still trapped inside.

After the crash the authorities' first moves were directed to re-opening Intra as a commercial bank. At different times there were discussions with Ludwig, Stavros Niarchos, who also wanted to take over MEA, the commercial banks and the government of Kuwait, and a syndicate of European banks put together by the New York investment bank, Kidder Peabody. There was even a rumour a few days after the closure that the Russians, who had tried to buy Air Liban in 1964 before it merged with MEA, were hoping to gain control of Intra by putting in a bid through Moscow Narodny.

But by early 1967 it had become obvious that none of these schemes was going to work. Intra was declared bankrupt, and legal proceedings were instituted against various board members, including Beidas. At the time of the crash Beidas had been in New York, but later he had disappeared. In January 1967 he turned up in Brazil, where he was admitted to a São Paulo hospital after a heart attack

In April the Lebanese authorities formally charged him with embezzlement and fraud, and in November that year he was arrested in Lucerne. He died in Geneva in 1969.

The bank was placed under an interim 'Management Committee' charged with preserving Intra's assets while the London accountants, Cooper Brothers, worked to establish Intra's deficit, and the government decided what was to be done. Intra's true condition proved extremely difficult to unravel, and for nine months after the crash very few decisions were taken. Instead there developed the first manifestations of the 'wait and see' attitude, which since that time has remained the largest stumbling block in the way of Intra's progress. In August 1967, however, a new committee was formed under Elias Sarkis, the Governor of the Bank of Lebanon, with the specific mission of finding a solution to the crisis within two months. Negotiations between Kidder Peabody (which had maintained contact with the authorities throughout the summer of 1967) and the Sarkis Committee moved forward swiftly, and in early October a protocol was signed under which Intra was recapitalized as an investment company. Shares in the new institution were distributed to creditors in proportion to their claims, which gave the Kuwait government a thirty per cent stake, the Qatar government five per cent, the Lebanese government (which had provided LL50 million to pay off small depositors in the previous December) eleven per cent, and the Commodity Credit Corporation of the United States government (which in 1966 had loaned Intra $22 million to finance wheat shipments) fifteen per cent.

It was originally expected that the new company would be established within a year or six months, but owing to continuing valuation difficulties and the time taken in sorting out more than two thousand law suits and claims, the Intra Investment Company did not come into being until December 1970. Since that date, while trying to get its shares quoted on some major stock exchange (so that those creditors needing cash can realize their claims) the company's policy has been to sell off some assets in order to gain liquidity, but to keep most of its investments together and attempt to attain sufficient growth to make its shares rise by enough to indemnify the original depositors. This is not an unrealistic target, because whatever may be said about Beidas as a commercial banker, his major investments – and MEA in particular – have proved extremely profitable. Those important assets liquidated have been the House of Lebanon in New York, Radio Orient, Intra Geneva, bought by Kleinwort Benson in May 1971, and the land on the Champs Elysées, which was sold to the governments of Kuwait, Qatar and Lebanon in 1973 in a deal involving a reduction in these states' shareholdings in Intra. Meanwhile the commercial banking side of Intra's operations was reopened in September 1971, with the formation of the al Mashreq (Levant) Bank, in which Morgan Guaranty has since acquired a controlling interest.

In aiming for growth the Intra Investment Company was faced with a choice between two separate paths. It could become a conventional investment company, holding only marketable portfolio investments in bonds or shares – in which case it might by now have emerged as a major force in the development of the inter-regional financial system discussed in the next chapter. Alternatively, it could establish itself as a conglomerate – which is what it has most resembled since 1966. Despite pressure from Kidder Peabody, who have been retained as the company's advisers, no definite decision has been taken on this issue, but in practice it appears that Intra is travelling along the second path. The investments that have been sold, most of which might be classed as 'miscellaneous' assets, have left the company with two distinct groups of holdings – a series of inter-related domestic investments in tourism and transport, such as MEA, Beirut port, the Phoenicia Hotel and Casino du Liban; and Chantiers Navals de la Ciotat, where Intra has retained control, in the face of strong pressure from French interests in 1971 and 1972, by doubling the shipyard's capital with the help of a loan from MEA. The expansion potential of the first group of assets need hardly be stated, while La Ciotat, which is already highly experienced in the construction of liquefied natural-gas tankers, is in a good position to exploit the growth of Arab tanker fleets which is bound to follow on the development of the area's natural gas reserves.

* * *

No other Arab company has owned real assets overseas on the same scale as Intra. In fact the only institution that can even be compared with Intra is the Kuwait Investment Company (KIC), which was established in 1962 with its capital subscribed half by the government and half by private citizens. KIC's early investment policy was extremely conservative, and until 1966 well over half its assets were kept in deposit accounts. The company's only well-known overseas investment during this period was its participation in the World Banking Corporation, a Bahamas-registered investment bank set up in 1964 by the Bank of America, and Robert Anderson, the United States Treasury Secretary under President Eisenhower.

In the mid-1960s however, Abdlatif al Hamad was brought in as KIC's Managing Director, and the company's investments became more ambitious. In 1968 it entered the property business in the USA when it bought a major share in the Novor Corporation, one of Keyes Realty's companies in Curaçao, which owned a controlling interest in 'The Hermitage', a twelve-storey apartment block in Houston, Texas. Oddly enough, KIC at first insisted that its share-holding should be confined to the nine per cent fixed interest notes which made up two-thirds of Novor's capital. This excessively cautious decision meant that KIC was excluding itself from the profits that would accrue to Novor when the building was sold, and was therefore wasting much of the benefit of operating through the Netherlands Antilles and being exempted from U.S. withholding tax. In December 1969, however, KIC took the equity shares as well – raising its holding to a hundred per cent – and when Novor was sold in 1971 KIC described its profits as 'very satisfactory'.

The company's other major real estate operation in the late 1960s was somewhat less successful. In 1968 KIC went into a joint venture with a Californian salvage concern called Murphy Pacific, and, with the help of a Uruguayan of Syrian extraction, the two companies bought a building site in the fashionable South American beach resort of Punte del Este. Here they built a fifteen-storey block, containing forty-five luxury apartments, to which they gave the rather grandiose name of 'Opus Alpha'. The idea was to sell long leases to the American millionaire market, but although the sales programme continued throughout 1969 and 1970, KIC and Murphy failed to let a single apartment. Officially, KIC blamed the political troubles caused in Uruguay by the Tupamaros, but it also seems that the company had chosen the wrong part of Punte del Este – or an area which the tourist boom had not yet reached. In 1972 Opus Alpha was put up for sale, and in its annual report that year KIC announced that it was doubtful whether it would recover its total investment, and that the building had therefore been written off.

Since the Opus Alpha project began KIC has been in three further foreign real estate ventures. In 1970 the company announced that it had concluded an agreement with American Airlines, the Chase Manhattan International Investment Corporation and Williams Holdings (New Zealand) for the construction of a 250-room luxury hotel in Wellington. It was thought at the time that this might lead to the establishment of a chain of three hotels in New Zealand and a resort hotel in the Fiji Islands, but since 1970 the project seems to have faded out. Then in 1971 the company entered into a programme with one of America's largest real estate syndicates, and more recently, in 1973, KIC and Trammel Crow launched an $84 million joint venture in Georgia, involving the construction of a Hilton Hotel with over a thousand rooms, a twenty-nine storey office block, and a shopping centre.

Although projects like these are impressive, overseas property does not in fact make up a very large proportion of KIC's investments. The bulk of its money is in equity portfolios, convertibles, bonds, venture capital companies, and loans to companies and governments – but the work for which KIC is best known is the management, placement and underwriting of bond issues (discussed in Chapter 11). In 1973 it placed some $56 million of bonds (many of them with the government), and underwrote $27 million worth – spread over more than sixty per cent of all euro-currency issues placed during that year.

On a lesser scale this has also become one of the major activities of the Kuwait Foreign Trading Contracting and Investment Company. The KFTCIC, which is eighty per cent state owned, is a rather smaller and much less ambitious concern, with assets totalling $124 million at the end of 1973. Most of its funds are deployed in small loans and in blocks of bonds, equity shares and debentures. At various times it has participated in financing a machinery leasing company in the U.S.A., a refrigerated gas storage plant in Spain, a steel company in Mexico, two cement plants in Canada, a copper project in Mauritania, a public utilities company in the Philippines, Destiny Tankers – the owners of an oil product carrier called *Sea Griffin* – and property companies in Spain and Germany. In its early days KFTCIC also participated in Molder-Vogem, a Dutch company investing in warehouses; but this concern proved unable to meet its mortgage commitments, and KFTCIC had to write off both the loan it had advanced and its shares in the company.

In almost every case KFTCIC's loans and investments have been worth under $3 million – but then the purpose which its promoters had in mind when the company was established in 1965, was not the management of major investment operations in the style of KIC, but the direction of resources towards inter-regional and African finance. For some years KFTCIC did not make a very big impact in this area, but in the past few years the idea of inter-regional finance has undergone something of a resurgence in the Arab world, and it is around this theme, which is the subject of the next two chapters, that the main development of Arab capital markets is now taking place.

10

ARAB MONEY FOR ARAB DEVELOPMENT

During its first few months of full independence in 1961 Kuwait was applying to join the United Nations. Membership of this body is one of the major aspirations of any newly independent country – but in Kuwait's case the government was particularly anxious for a prompt and trouble-free admission, because no sooner had the British left in June that year than the Iraqi regime of General Kassem had revived an old territorial claim to the state. To raise support for its application the government despatched diplomatic missions across the world in an attempt to dispel the then popular image of the Kuwaitis as Bedouin nouveaux riches, and on their return these missions recommended the establishment of an international aid fund, which would show Kuwait to be a responsible and outward-looking member of the world community.

So in December 1961 the government set up the Kuwait Fund for Arab Economic Development (KFAED) on a capital of KD 50 million, or about $165 million. This figure was raised to KD 100 million in 1963 and to KD 200 million in 1966 – though the increases were not paid up immediately. In 1974 a further addition raised the authorized capital to KD 1,000 million, of which KD 400 million was due to be paid by the end of March 1975. Given that the Fund is permitted to issue bonds of up to twice its paid-up capital plus reserves (which are intended to be twenty per cent of capital), if and when the new authorization is fully paid up this will give the KFAED total potential resources of KD 3,600 million – or nearly twelve billion dollars.

The Fund's first Director General was Abdel-Aziz al Bahar, a member of one of the big Kuwaiti merchant families, but at the end of 1962 he was succeeded by his new assistant, Abdlatif al Hamad – a young Kuwaiti who had previously been attached to the diplomatic mission in New York.

Abdlatif al Hamad had graduated from a small college near Los Angeles and had taken a degree in international relations at Harvard. In 1962 he had been offered a career in the Kuwaiti Foreign Ministry, but he felt that the diplomatic life was not sufficiently creative, and although he then knew relatively little about economics he joined the Fund instead. At first he had only one assistant and no secretary, and was forced to do everything from arranging loans to moving the office furniture; but this modest beginning also allowed him to build up the Fund in accordance with his own philosophy of development, and to impose on the Fund the imprint of his own personality and methods. In the process of this work al Hamad has become the shrewdest, and perhaps the most respected and influential member of the Kuwaiti financial community.*

When al Hamad became Director General of the Fund, three loans (one to the Sudan – for the expansion of the railway network, and two to Jordan – for a project on the Yarmouk river, and the development of the al Hasa phosphate mines) had already been given without any serious economic appraisal, and there was a distinct danger that the Fund would become a government agency used to hand out money in response to political pressures. However, assistance was obtained from the World Bank, which sent out one of its staff on a two-year secondment to advise on loan procedures, and al Hamad set to work developing the Fund along lines which resembled the World Bank, but which incorporated a more human and nationalist style geared to the particular needs of the Arab world.

This first involved demonstrating the Fund's political independence – something which became very necessary only a year after operations had begun. In 1963 a mission from the newly independent Algerian government (then the heroes of the Arab world) came to Kuwait in search of finance to help in rebuilding their war-torn economy. The Foreign Ministry summoned al Hamad home from an international conference and told him that the Fund must sign a loan agreement before the Algerians left. This he refused to do, but eventually a compromise was worked out. The Fund made an agreement in principle to provide loans worth KD10 million, while the specific projects on which the money was to be spent were left to the normal procedure of negotiation and appraisal. In the event

*Much of the information on the Kuwait Fund in this chapter has been drawn from *The Arabs' New Frontier*, a study of the Fund and Arab economic development written by Robert Stevens, and published by Maurice Temple Smith.

three-quarters of the money was allocated in 1964 to the first stage of an oil pipeline, and the remainder financed the completion of the same project in 1967.

By the end of March 1973 the KFAED had approved loans totalling KD 120 million ($400 million) spread between twelve countries, or all those Arab states, bar Oman, which do not run a major payments surplus. In most cases the Fund has provided only the foreign exchange cost of the projects, which it pays, in effect, by picking up the bills of the foreign contractors or suppliers as the work proceeds. Interest rates and the average duration of loans vary from four per cent and fourteen years for industrial and most infrastructural developments, to three per cent and twenty-three years for agricultural projects – though in the two Yemens, which are the poorest Arab countries, the rate has been reduced to as little as half per cent, covering only the Fund's service charge; and the repayment of one loan, for an agricultural survey of Southern Yemen, has been spread over forty-nine years.

A government wishing to apply for a loan must submit a feasibility study explaining not only the finances of the project itself, but also its place in the overall development of its economy. If the Fund decides that the scheme looks promising – which is not always the case, because governments have frequently provided rather weak reports or have submitted a whole range of projects in the hope that just one or two will prove acceptable – a Fund mission is sent to carry out an on-the-spot appraisal. The team will make a careful technical and financial study of the project, and will judge its priority according to its contribution to the expansion of the country's productive capacity, its impact on the balance of payments, the recipient government's ability to bare the local currency cost without undue strain, and its effect on employment. During their visit the Fund staff will also decide on the amount of the loan and its terms. The project will then be discussed both formally and informally at the Fund headquarters, and the appraisal team will submit a proposed agreement to the board. Finally the borrower is asked to visit Kuwait for the signing ceremony. Throughout the appraisal process, from application to signature, the Fund has established a reputation for working considerably faster than the World Bank and the various national aid programmes of the American and European governments.

The speed of its operations though, is not the only advantage that the Fund enjoys in Arab countries. Its staff, who are mostly former engineers, civil servants, and economists, have been recruited on a personal and informal basis from a variety of Arab states, including Egypt, Palestine, Iraq, Lebanon, Sudan, Syria, Kuwait and Yemen. They speak most Arab dialects; they have an intimate first-hand knowledge of many of the recipient countries, and know personally some of the people with whom they are dealing; they understand Arab ways of doing business; and, unlike most of the staff of aid organizations based in the industrial world, they share the aspirations and attitudes of developing nations.

The Fund is bound by few of the formal restrictions that apply to the World Bank. When in 1963 the Bank had to withdraw from a power station project at La Goulette because the Tunisian government was still involved in a compensation dispute over nationalized French utilities, the Fund was able to step in. Similarly, the Fund's informal approach has allowed it on more than one occasion to put forward its own ideas for projects without having received any formal loan application. In the Sudan, for example, the Fund has prompted the government to undertake studies for a co-ordinated national transport system, and in Southern Yemen it has promoted a fish-meal project. This second initiative stemmed from a report on Southern Yemen's fish potential which the Food and Agriculture Organization had sent, as a matter of routine, to one of the Fund's economists. The government in Aden had seen the report but had not followed it up. The Fund, however, made an analysis of the project, and then wrote to the Southern Yemen government saying that although further studies were needed on marketing aspects, it liked the idea, and was prepared in principle to offer finance. The outcome was that in February 1972 a KD 50,000 grant was made for a detailed appraisal – on the assumption that the Fund would later be making a loan to finance the construction of a fish-meal and fish-oil plant.

Arab governments have been strongly impressed by the technical performance of the Fund staff, which in many cases has been infinitely superior to anything which their own personnel could provide. The delegations which have come to Kuwait to sign loan agreements have also been struck by the emphasis on professionalism and team work (which makes the Director General, in effect, only *primus inter pares*), by the very modest building which until recently has served as the Fund's headquarters, and by the mid-morning gatherings over coffee and biscuits – when the entire staff meets for a general exchange of ideas. In the field the advice of the Fund's appraisal missions has often been sought on problems of overall economic planning, and on projects other than those which are being studied for a loan. The opinions given on these occasions have been purely informal, and the Fund has never exerted any kind of pressure on governments to adopt particular economic policies, as other aid organizations have sometimes been accused of doing. But the Fund still maintains close touch with its projects while work is being carried out, and has occasionally been able to help maintain the impetus of progress when it has been threatened with delay by bureaucratic inertia or other obstacles. In some cases it has even advised and obtained changes of management, as it is entitled to suggest under the terms of its loan agreements.

The Fund has made a number of criticisms of Arab economic administration. Speaking in 1972 at a United Nations Economic and Social Office conference in Beirut, Abdlatif al Hamad stressed that he would like to see improvements in: the standard of feasibility studies submitted in support of loan applications; the response to the Fund's needs for information concerning both candidate projects and the overall economic situation and prospects of the borrower country; a greater recognition of the importance of the time factor both in administrative and legislative procedures, and in the execution of the project; and an improved understanding that management, both before and after the completion of a project, is the main determinant of success or failure. The fact that the Fund has been able to make comments such as these is a measure of the goodwill it has built up in the Arab world over the last twelve years or so. Its influence has been felt not only in the direct benefits of individual projects, but in a growing Arab acceptance of the rules of the game of international aid, and in the help it has given in introducing Arab states to other lending institutions.

For Kuwait itself the Fund has proved equally beneficial. Along with the gradual introduction of democratic institutions in the state, and the government's mediation in inter-Arab disputes, the Fund has done much to earn Kuwait the respect of other Arab countries and to establish the state as one of the leaders of the Arab world. In this indirect and intangible manner the Fund has turned out to be of much greater political advantage than it would have been had it grown along the lines which appeared most likely in 1961 and 1962. In those days, when Arab countries were considerably more divided and their politics considerably more extremist than they are now, Kuwait was on the defensive, and the obvious prediction would have been that the Fund's disbursements would amount to straightforward protection money. The attitude of the radicals to Kuwait's wealth was summed up at the First Arab Petroleum Congress in 1959, when the Egyptian delegate announced: 'We are not asking for a gift, but for a natural right – and if the oil-producing countries refuse to share with us the gift which God has bestowed upon them, then the time will come when we will get our share through force.'

The Kuwait Fund was not the only regional aid or investment operation to be established in this atmosphere of political distrust. There were two other aid programmes, a regional bank and two investment companies (one successful and one unsuccessful) promoted at this time, and these can be listed as follows:

Government Loans

In 1960 the Kuwait government began making special loans from its reserves for reasons which in many cases were blatantly political. Normally the official purpose of the loans was to finance balance of payments deficits or fill gaps in budgets, though two of the loans given to Egypt were allocated to specific projects – the restoration of the Abu Simbel temples, and the construction of residential quarters for the armed forces. None of these loans carried interest rates of more than four per cent, and in a few instances, as with the $100 million advanced to Iraq at the time of Baghdad's recognition of Kuwaiti sovereignty in 1963, they carried no interest at all. Unlike the Kuwait Fund's aid, however, these disbursements had to be ratified by the National Assembly, and in 1965, by which time the government had committed a total of $400 million, the Assembly voted to stop further loans.

Gulf Permanent Assistance Committee

Several years before these loans began Kuwait had instituted a rather less political system of outright grants to Yemen and the Trucial States – which were then without oil. The programme started in 1952 when the Kuwaitis opened the first modern school in Sharjah, and in 1962 it was institutionalized with the creation of the Gulf Permanent Assistance Committee. GUPAC followed two grants policies – one with a relatively short-term emphasis on the problems of health and illiteracy, and the other designed to yield long-term benefits through surveys of soils and water resources. In 1965 Kuwait was running thirty-two schools (with mostly Egyptian and Bahraini teachers), two hospitals and seven clinics in the Trucial States. But by then oil was flowing in significant quantities from Abu Dhabi, and in the following year GUPAC was replaced by the General Authority for Southern Arabia and the Gulf States, which is involved more in running the existing Kuwaiti services than in providing new ones.

Arab African Bank

In 1964 the Kuwait government started a mainly commercial regional investment scheme, when it concluded an agreement with the Egyptian government setting up the Arab African Bank, the capital of which is owned by the two founders, the governments of Qatar, Iraq, Algeria and Jordan, and Arab private citizens. The purpose of the Bank, which is based in Cairo and is exempted from certain Egyptian taxes and exchange controls, is to 'support the economic development of Arab and African countries', but at the end of 1973 the bulk of its resources, $260 million, was committed to trade credits. At the same time the Bank's investments in Arab and African development projects amounted to only $21 million – of which about $16 million was divided between Egypt and Algeria. At the end of 1974 it was decided that the Arab African Bank should be managed by the Arab Fund for Economic and Social Development discussed later in this chapter.

Kuwait Foreign Trading Contracting and Investment Company (KFTCIC)

A few months after the Arab African Bank began business, the Kuwait government sponsored the establishment of the Kuwait Foreign Trading Contracting and Investment Company. Like the Fund the KFTCIC had its origins in Kuwait's application to join the United Nations, when the government suggested that in return for African votes it might promote an African-orientated investment company. Strictly speaking, KFTCIC was intended to be a purely commercial institution, but because the government originally owned some ninety per cent of its equity (now reduced to eighty per cent) the Foreign Ministry has occasionally been able to influence the company's investment decisions.

The government's participation however, has not prevented KFTCIC from having a rather limited impact both in Africa and elsewhere. Part of the reason for this has been the difficulties that the company has experienced over its capital. When KFTCIC was floated in 1965 it was given an authorized capital of KD 20 million (KD 16 million government and KD 4 million private), but at that time Kuwait was going through a mild economic recession, and less than a tenth of the shares offered to the public were taken up. In 1969 the company's capital was reduced to KD 10 million, and it was not restored to KD 20 million until 1972, when the company made a rights issue in which the government reduced its holding by not taking up its full entitlement. Since then, as discussed later in this chapter, KFTCIC has been much more active.

Kuwait Northern Nigeria Investment Company

At about the same time that KFTCIC was set up, one other scheme for African investment was being promoted. The idea seems to have stemmed from some Lebanese who wanted to sell various assets in northern Nigeria, including a bank, a match factory and a transport company, to the Nigerian government. As a means of facilitating their transaction, it occurred to them that if they were able to persuade the Kuwaitis to set up a Nigerian investment company, and this company were to give a loan to the Nigerian government (which was not then receiving large amounts of oil revenues) the authorities in Lagos and Kano might look favourably on their proposition. The Kuwaitis apparently responded to the idea. The Prime Minister of the Northern Region, Sir Ahmedu Bello, was invited to see Shaikh Jaber al Ahmed (who was then Minister of Finance), and the two men agreed to establish the Kuwait Northern Nigeria Investment Company, with a capital of $14 million. However, on 15 January 1966, within days of his return to Nigeria, Sir Ahmedu Bello was assassinated, and although his successors wanted to go ahead with the deal, the Kuwaitis let the idea drop.

*   *   *

Throughout the second half of the 1960s the four successful organizations described here – the Kuwait Fund, the General Authority for Southern Arabia and the Gulf States, the Arab African Bank, and the Kuwait Foreign Trading Contracting and Investment Company – remained the only officially sponsored inter-regional aid or investment institutions. When the special reserve loans are also taken into account, the aid (as distinct from investment) element in the funds disbursed by Kuwait during its first decade of independence absorbed the equivalent of between fifteen and twenty per cent of the government's budgets and seven to ten per cent of national income. This made Kuwait the world's seventh biggest giver of aid in absolute terms (after the U.S.A., the U.S.S.R., Britain, Germany, Japan and France) and by far the largest in proportional per capita terms. It was the only country in the world whose aid consistently attained and exceeded the famous target of one per cent of national income suggested by the United Nations Conference on Trade and Development in 1964.*

*The aid given by the World Bank (which operates on a larger scale than any government bar the United States) cannot be compared with the Kuwaiti programme because the Bank is a multi-national institution. From 1968, when the

The reasons for Kuwait's generosity compared with Saudi Arabia, Qatar and Abu Dhabi during this period was not just political. Before the Tehran Agreement of February 1971 Kuwait was the only Arabian oil producer with a big enough surplus to be able to mount large-scale foreign aid and investment programmes. But since the 'revenue explosion' began, a large number of new institutions have appeared, and this 'second generation' of aid funds and regional development companies has a much more idealistic and less political background. Their foundation reflects the Arabs' current economic-cum-political 'thinking' on the energy crisis and the surplus oil revenues issue, and the spirit of the resolutions passed at the meetings discussed under the heading of 'The Inter-Regional Development Initiative' in Chapter 5.

The idea for the first of the new funds, the Arab Fund for Economic and Social Development (AFESD), was originally put forward by Kuwait in August 1967 at a conference of Arab finance ministers in Baghdad, but progress in getting the scheme off the ground was slow. In May 1968 the Arab League's Council for Arab Economic Unity, which had thought of a similar plan back in the 1950s, gave the Fund its official approval, and a month or so later Kuwait pledged KD 30 million towards the Fund's KD 100 million authorized capital. For the next two and a half years the project lay dormant – until December 1970, when Kuwaiti officials lobbied the other Arab governments and raised total pledged subscriptions to KD 81.5 million or about $270 million, which is where the figure stood at the beginning of 1974. Apart from Kuwait the biggest contributors were Libya – KD 12 million, Egypt – KD 10.5 million, Iraq – KD 7.5 million, Abu Dhabi – KD 5 million, and Algeria – KD 4 million. Smaller amounts were subscribed by all the other Arab states bar Saudi Arabia. Initially the Saudis claimed that the subsidies they were paying to Egypt and Jordan under the Khartoum Agreement (see Chapter 13) prevented them from undertaking further financial commitments, and later it seemed that their attention was focused on their own scheme for the Islamic Development Bank, and on giving loans or grants on a direct bilateral basis. Saudi Arabia finally joined the AFESD at the end of 1974.

Bank made its first dinar bond issue, to 1973, Kuwait was the fifth largest source of World Bank funds. In 1974, when there was a major expansion of borrowing, most of the Bank's funds were raised through direct OPEC government loans – rather than through the conventional bond issues. The most generous contributors were Venezuela and Iran.

The Arab Fund eventually set up its headquarters in Kuwait early in 1973, with Saeb Jaroudi, a former KFAED official and Lebanese Minister of National Economy, as its President, and Abdlatif al Hamad as one of its directors. The AFESD's aims and methods are very much like those of the Kuwait Fund, except that it will be laying additional emphasis on three areas where the Fund has not been particularly active.

First it will give priority to inter-Arab projects – such as roads, shipping and big river developments – and to complementary ventures where, for instance, one state might open up an iron ore deposit, while its neighbour would build a steel mill. Secondly, AFESD hopes that it will act as an agent for channelling private Arab capital into Arab development, partly by putting together groups of banks and individuals to provide additional finance for projects which it is backing itself, and partly through selling bonds, which, like the Kuwait Fund, it is authorized to issue to an amount worth twice its capital and reserves. And thirdly, as its name implies, part of AFESD's investment will go towards social projects, like schools and hospitals.

This is a relatively new fashion in development circles. During the 1950s and 1960s the traditional wisdom was that money would best be spent on building up a country's agricultural and industrial productive capacity, since it was on this that a higher level of welfare services would ultimately depend. But in recent years there has been growing support at the World Bank and the Kuwait Fund, as well as at AFESD, for the theory that social expenditure will help create a more flexible and less traditional attitude of mind in the people of the recipient country, and that this in turn will make the population more receptive to technical and modern agricultural training, encourage self-help, and bring the point of economic take-off closer.

By February 1974 AFESD had made three loans: KD 3.2 million for part of the fish-meal plant sponsored by the Kuwait Fund in Southern Yemen, KD 2 million towards the cost of fifty-two oil product storage tanks in Syria, and KD 2 million for a power station in Tunisia. However, much of the attention that AFESD has received has stemmed not from the size of its disbursements but from the special studies that have been assigned to it and from the numerous recommendations that various bodies have made to the Fund. These have ranged from the proposal that AFESD should consider the establishment of an institute for technical, economic and management research, which would help draw back into the Arab world some of those highly qualified Arab citizens who are now working overseas; to the suggestion that the Fund should set up a special department for long-term low-interest loans, rather like the International Development Association in the World Bank group.

It may be that this stream of advice, which, given the number of Arab countries participating in the Fund, has probably been unavoidable, will divert a considerable amount of AFESD's resources of time and manpower from the purpose for which the Fund was originally established. To some extent the Fund may be able to compensate for this by co-operating closely with the KFAED – in carrying out joint feasibility studies, in providing loans for projects on the basis of each other's studies, and in exchanging information on individual projects and on the state of recipient countries' economies. This collaboration is likely to extend to a further new institution, the Abu Dhabi Fund for Arab Economic Development (ADFAED).

The decision to establish the Abu Dhabi Fund was taken in July 1971, a few months before Britain's withdrawal from the Gulf – and underlying the government's reasoning at the time must have been the thought that if an Arab development fund had served Kuwait's interests, the same might help promote the security of Abu Dhabi. The new Fund's capital was authorized at 50 million Bahrain dinars (which since the currency change has been increased to 2,000 million dirhams – BD 200 million or $500 million), and, like the two other funds, ADFAED is permitted to issue bonds to an amount not exceeding twice its capital plus reserves. By February 1974 the Fund had made seven loans worth just over $24 million, the biggest of which were $11 million for part of the Banias electricity project in Syria, and $5.4 million for the King Talal dam on the Zarka river in Jordan.

The success of ADFAED under its Egyptian Director General, Dr Hassan Abbas Zaki, will depend partly on how much Shaikh Zaid will be able to resist demands for direct hand-outs from his own government's purse, and partly on whether the Fund will be able to establish the same reputation for detailed project appraisal and political neutrality which the Kuwait Fund enjoys. If its resources of experienced manpower are stretched, it can always provide additional finance for projects which have already been given loans by the Kuwait Fund, the Arab Fund or the World Bank – as, for instance, the Banias electricity project had already received the backing of the World Bank when ADFAED made its loan, and an Egyptian fertilizer plant, which ADFAED agreed in principle to finance in February 1974, had the support of the World Bank and the Arab Fund. It was in fact the Abu Dhabi Fund, in June 1973, which made the first formal proposal that the three Arab-backed funds should co-ordinate their operations.

By the end of 1974 the Arab Fund and the Abu Dhabi Fund were the only two of the 'second generation' of regional development organizations to have begun business, but during the previous twelve months there had been announcements of the formation of many more new institutions. These included the Saudi-sponsored multi-national Islamic Bank, which is to be established in Jeddah; the Iraq External Development Fund; a Saudi fund which will lend mainly to non-Arab developing countries at interest rates ranging from two and a half per cent to zero; and at least four African-orientated aid funds or semi-commercial investment banks.

The arrival of the new development banks has been accompanied by a recharging of two existing institutions. First there has been the expansion of the activities of the Kuwait Foreign Trading Contracting and Investment Company (KFTCIC), following the restoration of the company's capital to KD 20 million. During the last three years KFTCIC has spawned three new subsidiaries: the Sudan Kuwait Investment Company, owned fifty-fifty by KTFCIC and the Sudan government; the Banque Senegalo-Koweitienne; and the Afro-Arab Company for Investment and International Trade (AFARCO). At the same time KFTCIC has been acting as an agent for placing certain Kuwait government loans and investments, such as the $33 million advanced to the Sudan in 1972 for the purchase of metal pipes and fertilizers from Kuwait, and the government's $60 million participation in the Suez-Mediterranean (Sumed) pipeline in Egypt. In 1973 KFTCIC also arranged the sale of KD 7 million ($24 million) of bonds issued by the Sudanese government to finance the construction of a pipeline from Port Sudan to Khartoum.

The second, and at first sight more significant, change has been the increase in the Kuwait Fund's authorized capital to KD 1,000 million – dwarfing all other regional funds and development banks. This was accompanied by permission for the Fund to lend to developing states outside the Arab world, and by a spate of new loans, including the biggest single loan yet – $33 million for the reconstruction of the Suez Canal.

During the period since the oil price rises at the end of 1973 the Arab producers have pledged well over $5 billion to the capital of new or existing regional and Third World development banks. This total seems impressive, but it is quite possible that some of the funds proposed in 1974 will never get off the ground; and there are also considerable doubts as to whether a multiplication of the traditional type of development bank, granting loans related to specific projects, will be the best method of distributing Arab aid. (These doubts apply to bodies like the KFAED and the Islamic Bank, rather than to the more commercial institutions like the KFTCIC, the Arab African Bank and some of the new African-orientated investment companies.)

The most fundamental problem (discussed in Chapter 14) is that the developing countries are now less interested in project aid than in receiving long-term credits to finance higher current expenditure caused by the increases in the price of oil and other basic commodities. But there are also a number of difficulties within the field of project aid itself. Apart from the arrival of so many new funds involving a duplication of effort by countries experiencing a serious shortage of trained manpower, it seems likely that the strict appraisal criteria applied by the World Bank will result in many candidate projects submitted by the poorest and least developed countries being turned down. If at the same time the more efficient and credit-worthy countries continue, for reasons of self-respect, to prefer drawing on the euro-dollar market or on investment companies such as the KTFCIC for finance, the Arab development banks will probably be unable to lend more than a small proportion of their total resources.

Abdlatif al Hamad, for one, is aware of these problems, and has said on several occasions that he doubts whether the traditional World Bank philosophy is still appropriate for development lending in the 1970s. This may mean that the KFAED and the other Arab funds are considering changes in their approach – but, if as a result of a small relaxation of standards, there is a dramatic increase in the number of projects found suitable for loans, the development banks are likely to experience a shortage of manpower.

*   *   *

During the expansion of inter-regional development activities in the last few years there has been in the background a rather different but equally important scheme for an investment guarantee company. The original proposal for this company was put forward by Abdlatif al Hamad when he was addressing the First Arab Industrial Development Conference in 1966. Although the conference was rather sceptical at first, it was eventually won over to the idea, and instructed the Kuwait Fund to produce more concrete plans. In November 1967 the Fund convened a meeting of Arab financial 'experts'* who discussed three related topics: investment insurance, the settlement of disputes between foreign Arab investors and the governments of recipient countries, and the need for an inter-Arab investment code. In subsequent discussions it was decided that the investment code idea should be shelved for the time being, while it was felt that rules for the settlement of disputes might be incorporated in individual insurance policies – but the investment guarantee scheme itself was followed up by a second meeting of experts in March 1970.

After this meeting the Kuwait Fund prepared a convention setting up the Inter-Arab Investment Guarantee Corporation, which by the beginning of 1973 had received the support of fourteen Arab states. The exceptions were Saudi Arabia, which felt that if guarantees were needed they should be given by the recipient countries, and three other governments, whose decisions on joining the Corporation had for various reasons been delayed.

The Corporation's authorized capital was fixed at KD 10 million, a considerably smaller sum than its promoters had originally hoped to raise, and in early 1973 only some KD 7 million of this total had actually been promised by member governments. On the basis of the full authorized capital the Corporation will be able to issue policies to the value of KD 50 million or about $170 million.

It is envisaged that most of the Corporation's business will come from investors taking out policies against nationalization and related threats, but the Corporation will also underwrite two other categories of non-commercial risks: damage caused by war, civil disturbances and coups d'état; and losses incurred through restrictions on the repatriation of profits – provided that such restrictions are imposed after the investor has committed his capital. The parties insured may be private citizens, public companies, state-controlled corporations or governments – though it is thought that 'strong' parties, like governments, will not need to use the Corporation because they will be able to retaliate against nationalization and moratoriums on debts by cutting off the flow of new loans or grants. If it wishes, the Corporation may refuse to insure investments in particularly high-risk states (which are fewer in the Arab world than they were five years ago) – but it may not charge an investor a higher premium purely on the basis of the political system of the recipient country.

It was hoped that the Corporation, which had been taking shape

*The expression 'expert' is a favourite Arab word. It is used almost as if it had the same fairly precise meaning in English as the words 'banker', 'economist' and 'engineer'.

under the auspices of the Kuwait Fund, would move into its own offices in Kuwait in the summer of 1973, but it did not begin business until the end of 1974. Part of the reason for the delay was the lack of Saudi interest – which was rather more serious for the Corporation than it was for the Arab Fund. For AFESD Saudi Arabia's absence meant only a large reduction in capital – but for the Corporation, whose charter prevents it not only from underwriting assets placed in non-signatory states, but also from underwriting external investments belonging to citizens of these states, the non-participation of Saudi Arabia removed one of the two largest sources of clients.

The failure of the Inter-Arab Investment Guarantee Corporation (IAIGC) to begin operations was reflected at the beginning of March 1974 in one of the resolutions of a meeting of economic 'experts' sponsored by the Council for Arab Economic Unity, which called for, 'the establishment as soon as possible of a financial institution to guarantee Arab investments'. It may have been that the economists at the CAEU hoped that their recommendations would give a new impetus to the IAIGC, or that they expected some totally new scheme to emerge – but either way the meeting was right to give its time and attention to the channelling of capital from the surplus to the deficit Arab states within the private sector.

11

INTER-REGIONAL FINANCE

There would be a good case for arguing that a big inter-Arab investment guarantee company – with a capital nearer KD 100 million
than KD 10 million – would be a more useful innovation in inter-
regional development than any of the new funds or banks. There is
enormous potential in the Arab world for encouraging the surplus
countries to invest their wealth in their deficit neighbours, not just
through development aid at concessionary rates of interest, but
through strictly commercial dealings in bonds, shares, loans and
direct investments.

As described in Chapter 8, at the end of 1973 the citizens of Kuwait,
Saudi Arabia, Qatar and Abu Dhabi were thought to own investments in Europe and American worth about $2,700 million, while
the four ruling families might have held a further $2,000 million
between them, and the commercial banks were known to have gross
foreign assets of $2,100 million. In addition to these holdings there
were substantial sums deposited in bank accounts in Lebanon. The
Beirut banks had gross foreign assets of $1,450 million, and the
direct overseas investments of Lebanese citizens might have been
roughly $400 million. Altogether there must have been some $8–9
billion of Arabian and Lebanese private money which was invested in
Europe and America, but which could, in theory, be channelled into
the poorer states of the Middle East.

Compared with the tens of billions of dollars in the oil-producing
governments' reserves (which can be put into the capital of state-
backed development banks), $8–9 billion is not a very large sum –
but if this money were invested within the region, it could have a
much bigger impact than government aid.

This is mainly because smaller amounts of money directed into medium-sized businesses in the deficit Arab states may have more long-term potential for bringing these countries to the point of economic take-off than vast government-backed infra-structural and industrial projects. But almost equally important is the familiar manpower problem. At the top level not all of the new development funds are likely to get the same inspired management that the Kuwait Fund has, and, lower down, however much money is available, there will still be a limit to the amount of appraisal work that the staff of the funds will be able to carry out. At the receiving end there are also limits to the number of projects that government officials are able to conceive, plan and submit as worthwhile candidates for loans. It is partly because of this bottleneck that in its first twelve years of operations the Kuwait Fund made, on average, only four loans a year.

In private finance the manpower problem still exists, but it is much less acute. In the case of relatively small transactions, companies and individuals may do their own appraisals and handle their own investments, and for major loans and bond issues the resources of all the commercial investment companies and the more aggressive banks are available. In effect, the job of investing surplus oil money can be spread among thousands of individuals rather than hundreds.

Until the beginning of the 1970s the investors of the Arabian Peninsula oil states were so distrustful of the political systems in the more radical Arab countries, with major development potential and big populations, that what money they were prepared to invest within the Arab world was confined almost exclusively to bank deposits and property in Lebanon. But during the last four years, which have seen more liberal economic regimes introduced in Egypt, Sudan and, to a lesser extent, Syria, there has been a major surge of interest in inter-regional finance. Naturally enough it has occurred to bankers throughout the Arab world that the surplus money of the oil states and the development potential of the deficit states should be put together in a regional capital market, which would handle not only private funds, but, hopefully, a large amount of the producer governments' reserves as well.

If a Middle East capital (or euro-dollar) market is going to develop on the scale envisaged by some of its supporters, it is going to need a recognized centre. The existence of a centre would not exclude all other banking communities from conducting a parallel inter-regional business – but there would be obvious benefits in having a single Arab capital where borrowers would make their first enquiries, and where those banks drawing on the funds of other banking cities

L

would establish their regional base. Such a centre will not be created in a hurry (as the capital market supporters sometimes appear to assume), and the speed of its development will depend not on the volume of funds available for lending by the surplus states, but on the economic growth of the borrowing countries, and particularly the private sectors within these countries. As the demand of the borrowers expands, so will the facilities of the lending centre.

The centre might be located in Dubai, Kuwait or Beirut. All of these well established banking cities have their supporters, but each also has certain serious drawbacks.

The most unlikely contender of the three is the small Gulf emirate of Dubai, ruled by its wily merchant prince, Shaikh Rashid bin Said al Makhtoum. The foundation of Dubai's prosperity since the early 1960s has been its entrepot trade, carried by dhows based in the creek which runs through the centre of the city. Much of this trade, including that with Abu Dhabi, the northern emirates and Oman, is perfectly legitimate, but a large proportion still goes under the counter. In 1973 the most profitable lines in smuggled goods were rice and cigarettes to Iran, medicines and textiles to India and Pakistan, and, above all, gold bullion and gold Swiss watches to India. (In recent years Dubai has been importing the equivalent of fifty gold watches for every man, woman and child in the emirate.)

The emirate's development has been stimulated by Shaikh Rashid's maxim that what is good for his merchants is good for Dubai – and this has shown up in liberal commercial and financial regulations, and an almost total absence of civil servants, paperwork, and restrictions on foreign ownership of local industrial and commercial enterprises. Until recently, what government there was in Dubai, including the offices of the ruler and his advisers, was located in the customs building overlooking the creek – and from there Shaikh Rashid ran his emirate more as if he were the owner of a large holding company than a head of state. His own and the government's finances were merged, and before oil came on stream in 1969, public expenditure was financed by a small levy on imports. The management of many public utilities, which in most countries would fall under government control, has been placed in the hands of private enterprise – with International Aeradio running the massive airport and the internal telephone system, and Gray MacKenzie, a member of the Inchcape group, running the sixteen-berth port near the mouth of the creek. When Dubai's dry-dock, which like the port will be the largest in the Middle East, is completed in 1977, it too will be privately operated.

The ease with which foreign companies can do business in Dubai (plus the fact that by Gulf standards Dubai is an attractive state, has excellent international telecommunications – like all its neighbours bar Saudi Arabia – and does not prohibit alcohol) has encouraged a number of groups to establish their regional headquarters in the emirate. Shell and Caltex have moved in from Doha and Manama, and J. Ray McDermott, the American oil-rig and production-platform engineers, have arrived from Beirut, and set up a fabrication yard beside the creek. At the same time Dubai has attracted a Merrill Lynch office and over twenty banks – more than any other state in the Arabian Peninsula. Competition between these banks has been unusually fierce for the Gulf, and from 1963 (the year in which the British Bank of the Middle East's monopoly was ended) until late 1970 there was a particularly savage rate war, with the interest paid on deposits being pushed up as high as ten per cent, and several banks operating with dangerously little liquidity.

One of Dubai's problems in becoming a regional financial centre is that, despite the size and vitality of its banking system, it does not have very much surplus money which it can pump into foreign lending. The state's modest oil revenues are committed to paying for such projects as the port, the dry-dock, the airport, the tunnel under the creek, the hospital and a cement works; and although many of the Dubian merchants are very rich, most of their money is tied up in the entrepot trade. (It is significant that bank advances to residents at the end of 1973 were bigger than in Abu Dhabi and Qatar combined.) In future the amount of surplus money in the Dubian banking system may be increased by the growing wealth of Abu Dhabi and Qatar, whose citizens deposit large sums of money in Dubai to take advantage of the higher interest rates, but as yet the Dubian banks (with the exception of the new Oryx investment bank) are showing few signs of any major desire to lend inter-regionally.

More serious problems for Dubai's future financial development derive from the impression that the emirate is something of a freak – a temporary point of convenience, or a 'pirates' cave' as some Kuwaitis refer to it – and that when Shiakh Rashid dies it may lose much of its dynamism. It is also uncertain how far Dubai will be sucked into the orbit of Abu Dhabi, which has the headquarters of the new currency board, and to what extent the growth of federal authority within the United Arab Emirates will destroy Dubai's individuality. Until the answers to these questions are known Dubai's chances of becoming the centre of a Middle East dollar market are small, but in any event it seems likely that the Dubian merchants will maintain their trading business (which the Kuwaitis mostly failed to do after the advent of oil) and that Dubai will remain as the banking centre of the lower Gulf.

Two of the major qualifications for the position of regional financial centre which Dubai lacks, Kuwait has in large measure. It contains an enormous amount of private and government surplus money, and it already has substantial experience of inter-regional lending. All its banks have underwritten Arab bond issues at various times, the Kuwait Investment Company and the Kuwait Foreign Trading Contracting and Investment Company are building up some expertise in the management of bond issues and big inter-national loans, and in 1973 and 1974 three new companies set up business with the stated intention of carrying out roughly similar operations. These were two investment banking consortia, Inter-national Financial Advisers and the Arab Financial Consultants Company, and the Kuwait International Investment Company – an entirely privately owned Kuwaiti concern.

There are, however, a number of barriers in the way of further progress in Kuwait, and these are incorporated in a body of unsubtle commercial law designed more to protect innocent Kuwaiti investors than to regulate a sophisticated financial machine. The most obvious of the restrictions is the seven per cent limit on interest charges, which discourages aggressive lending, and works against the banks gaining experience in industrial finance. Then there is the ban on foreigners investing in local property or setting up any new commercial enterprises unless they have majority Kuwaiti participation. Recently there has been some relaxation in this area by allowing citizens of Saudi Arabia, Oman and the lower Gulf states to buy shares in Kuwaiti companies, but as a whole the ownership restrictions stop Kuwait from handling any significant volume of funds from the other Arabian Peninsula countries.

The same restrictions also prevent the establishment of branches of foreign banks. In theory an American or European bank could move into Kuwait by registering itself as an associate of the parent group and selling over half of its equity to Kuwaitis – but even then there is a strong possibility that unless the company intended to carry out purely investment banking operations (like International Financial Advisers), the authorities would not grant it a licence. It seems that the reason for this is the Kuwait government's belief that if it were to pursue an open-doors policy, there would be a massive influx of banks, and that this would lead to an unstable and unsound banking system. At the same time the Kuwaitis, who have a residual fear left over from the 1950s and early 1960s of being exploited by foreigners, wish to keep the substantial profits from handling their own money to themselves.

Until recently this view had much to recommend it, but now, if Kuwait is to be the Middle East's financial centre, it seems obvious that those banks wishing to enter the inter-regional lending business should be allowed to set up branches. The arrival of foreign banks might also be beneficial in providing more competition for the existing institutions, and in spreading the burden of the Kuwaiti banks' very heavy exchange exposure.

Changes in the interest rate law and in official policy on foreign investment and the admission of foreign banks, might be regarded as removing 'artificial' barriers in the way of Kuwait's financial development. But there are two further innovations suggested by some of the Kuwaiti business community which would themselves be somewhat 'artificial', and which would most likely prove ineffective.

One of these suggestions is that the Kuwaiti banks be allowed to deal among themselves in foreign exchange – on the assumption that this would produce the beginnings of a forward market, enabling the banks to hedge against the exchange risk to some extent. In practice, such reasoning would be shown to be too simple. The ultimate logic of a forward market is that on any given day one should be able to find buyers and sellers of the same currency with complementary needs, and at present the Kuwaiti banking and trading system is not big enough for this always to be possible.

The second suggestion is that the Central Bank should issue and discount treasury bills, as a means of creating a Kuwaiti discount market. The supporters of this idea argue that in any city with a claim to be a financial centre, the banks should be able to invest in liquid assets locally and not have to resort to the London market, which is what the Kuwaiti banks are forced to do at present. Up to now the only way in which a bank has been able to gain liquidity within Kuwait has been by making use of the Central Bank's facility for discounting two signature trade bills with a maturity of ninety days or less – and as these bills are not very common the scope for raising money on them is limited. The banks have requested that the authorities should accept World Bank dinar bonds, but this too would provide only a small volume of liquidity.

So if the Central Bank wishes to encourage the growth of a really large discount market in Kuwait, it will have to issue and accept its own securities – and because the government does not need to borrow money from its citizens, any move in this direction would amount to little more than an extension of the 'cutting-in' policy. In effect, the government would be borrowing and paying interest in dinars, while running an unnecessary exchange risk by having to invest the money it received in its dollar or sterling reserves.

Apart from these 'technical' shortcomings, one of the fundamental problems in the way of Kuwait becoming the base of a regional dollar market is that it handles very little of its neighbours' money. The restrictions placed on foreigners buying domestic assets are only a small part of the reason for this. The Saudis and the Arabs of the lower Gulf are often suspicious of the Kuwaitis, who are felt to be somewhat overbearing;* and while their own states are building up adequate banking systems (which in many cases pay slightly better rates of interest than are available in Kuwait) they have little reason to make use of Kuwait's facilities. The only development which might change this would be the introduction of an Arabian Peninsula dinar – because then the mere fact that borrowers would probably make their first enquiries in Kuwait, would tend to establish the Kuwaiti banks as the main organizers of dinar loans and bond issues.

In the near future the chances of Kuwait becoming the banking centre of the Middle East, or even of the Arabian Peninsula, are small. In the view of Abdlatif al Hamad, who reflects the thinking of the Central Bank and the Finance Ministry in this respect, Kuwait should aspire more to being an important centre in its own right. Rather than embarking on some sort of financial development plan, the authorities feel that the emphasis should be placed on evolving a system where the requirements of borrowers can be met fast and efficiently (which the Kuwaitis rightly maintain does not always happen in Beirut and other Arab banking centres), and where the local banks and investment companies can develop a close working relationship with leading financial institutions the world over.

By a process of elimination, therefore, it seems that the city with the best chance of becoming the regional centre is Beirut. The Lebanese capital would have a number of major advantages in this role. It is strategically situated half way between the Gulf and Europe; it has excellent air communications – with its own airline, MEA, having cornered a large proportion of the total traffic in and out of the Middle East; it has a big port, which handles much of the trade of Syria, Jordan, Iraq and the Arabian Peninsula; and with a vigorous free press, it has established itself as the news and informa-

---

*This is not necessarily a just criticism of the Kuwaitis. The Kuwaitis themselves often do not have a very high opinion of their neighbours, whom they feel to be generally backward and unsophisticated; and nor, for that matter, do most of their neighbours care much for each other.

tion centre of the entire Arab world. Beirut can also claim to be a very much more attractive place for a foreign banker than any of the Gulf states. It has excellent hotels, restaurants, theatres and cinemas, a beautiful mountainous hinterland, facilities for swimming and skiing, several important universities (including the American University of Beirut, which is one of the best in the Middle East), and a variety of big stores and supermarkets.

As a banking centre Beirut has the advantage of size, with deposits at the end of 1973 totalling some $3,280 million (about $1,100 million more than in Kuwait), and foreign assets (which could be diverted into inter-regional lending) of $1,450 million. In all there are now seventy-three banks in Beirut, twenty less than there were before the collapse of Intra in 1966. Of this total about forty are foreign branches or mixed Lebanese/foreign banks, which together hold well over seventy per cent of all deposits. Because the government decided after the 1966 crisis that the number of banks should be limited, any foreign bank that wishes to establish itself in Beirut must now do so through buying a share in an existing Lebanese or mixed bank.

Lebanese banking is now a much more orderly affair than it was before 1966, when the official feeling was that as Beirut had grown up and thrived on complete banking freedom, any government interference could only be harmful. Soon after the Intra crash some of the weaker institutions were closed down, and ten of the smaller banks were merged into the Banque de Crédit Agricole Industriel et Foncier. Since then the Banking Control Commission, which was set up in 1967, has made monthly checks on each bank's liquidity, and on any other features of a bank's position which it may consider need detailed examination.

Generally the Commission's work is unobtrusive, and the financial community in Lebanon still enjoys much greater freedom than it does in most other Arab countries. There are, for instance, no restrictions on the banks dealing between themselves in foreign currencies – though as yet the banking system is not big enough for there to be more than the beginnings of an exchange market in the city. The best established foreign firm of dealers in Beirut, Guy Butler International (which arrived in 1973), has been more active in the money market than in exchange.

The limited size of the exchange market is only a minor flaw in the system, and it will presumably become less serious with time. Meanwhile Beirut has a number of more important faults as a banking centre. One of these is the disincentive to foreign depositors provided by the various taxes and insurance fees, levied on all deposits other than savings accounts, which in early 1974 would have cut by more than a quarter the interest paid on a three-month deposit of LL 100,000.

But much more serious is the way in which finance in Lebanon is inextricably mixed up with local politics and private business interests. On big international loans too many people want to be involved for reasons of personal prestige, and the result is that deals are arranged more slowly and less efficiently than they are in Kuwait. The younger generation of bankers, who are the main supporters of the dollar market concept, are generally more professional in their approach – but these men are too few and mostly too inexperienced so far to have made much impact.

The habit of playing banking and politics simultaneously was a major factor in the Intra fiasco; and despite the reforms of the Banking Control Commission and the attraction of the banking secrecy laws, the memory of 1966 has helped scare away the Kuwaiti and Saudi money which was responsible for much of Beirut's growth before the crash. Foreign liabilities (largely made up of the deposits of Gulf Arabs and Lebanese working abroad) dropped from LL 1,160 million at the end of 1965 to LL 610 million in 1967, and only recovered to LL 1,170 million at the end of 1972. The position changed dramatically in 1973, with foreign liabilities reaching LL 1,520 million by the end of December, though part of this sudden jump can be attributed to a big expansion of local lending, which caused an increase in borrowing from banks abroad. Seen in perspective, the six-year stagnation in foreign liabilities suggests that the Intra affair destroyed Lebanon's role as the major channel of oil money from the Arabian Peninsula to Europe.

None of Beirut's present shortcomings seem to have prevented a stampede of foreign institutions seeking to establish a foothold in the city. During 1973 and 1974 new arrivals included three consortia investment banks – the Arab Finance Corporation, Banque d' Investissement et de Financement, and the Arab International Finance Company; a branch of Nikko Securities; the British insurance brokers Willis, Faber and Dumas, which entered a partnership with Middle East Airlines and the Intra Investment Company; a large number of banks' representative offices, including those of the Fuji Bank, the Bank of Montreal and Lloyds Bank International; and the exchange dealers Guy Butler International and P. Murray Jones. At the same time shareholdings in local banks have been bought by over a dozen foreign concerns, including the Chemical

Bank of New York, the United Bank of California, Toronto Dominion, the Libyan Arab Foreign Bank, and Crédit Suisse.

There would probably be a similar rush into Kuwait if the restrictions were lifted there – but meanwhile the enthusiasm of the foreign banks for Beirut, and the recent upsurge in business after the relative stagnation of the late 1960s, indicate that Beirut is building up a substantial lead over rival centres. The Lebanese believe that once the new banks have established themselves, and the financial community as a whole has gained a bit more experience in inter-regional lending, Beirut's development as a regional dollar market will gain a momentum of its own.

* * *

In both Beirut and Kuwait the emphasis in inter-regional banking operations to date has been on bond issues and syndicated loans. By the end of 1974 there had been rather over a dozen major transactions of this sort, with the biggest borrowers by far being the External Bank of Algeria and Algerian state industrial corporations.

Apart from the Kuwait Investment Company and the Kuwait Foreign Trading Contracting and Investment Company, there are already seven Arab or part-Arab institutions with considerable experience in underwriting and placing euro-dollar bonds. These banks and investment companies, whose names often appear in the lists on 'tombstone' advertisements, are the Alahli Bank of Kuwait, the Kuwait International Investment Company, the Arab Finance Corporation, the Intra Investment Company and three of the Arab European consortia – the Union des Banques Arabes et Françaises (UBAF) group, the Banque Franco-Arabe d'Investissements Internationaux (FRAB), and Banque Arabe et Internationale d'Investissement (BAII). Other institutions whose names normally appear only if the bond issue has an inter-regional flavour or is denominated in a Middle Eastern currency are: the National Bank of Kuwait, the Gulf Bank, the Commercial Bank of Kuwait, Banque Audi (in Beirut), the al Mashreq Bank, the Libyan Arab Foreign Bank, the Bank of Bahrain and Kuwait, and the Banque Européenne Arabe consortium. Only seven of these institutions, KIC, which manages the World Bank bond issues in Kuwait, the UBAF group, KFTCIC, KIIC, and, to a lesser extent, the Arab Finance Corporation, the Intra Investment Company and Banque Audi, have any major experience in the management of bond issues – and it is these banks that have led the way in setting up the inter-regional market.*

Other big loans and investments, which have not been the subject of tombstone advertisements, have been arranged by the American investment bank, Kidder Peabody.† As was explained in Chapter 9, Kidder Peabody was drawn into the Middle East in the wake of the Intra crisis, but since the beginning of the 1970s it has expanded its business in Beirut and Kuwait (where it maintains a representative office) into financial consultancy and the promotion of inter-regional finance.

Kidder Peabody's first major deal was concluded in January 1973, when it put together a group of Arab and European banks to provide Egypt Air with a $58 million loan facility for the purchase of four Boeing 707s, and an option on a further loan for a fifth Boeing if the airline required it. Later in 1973 Kidder Peabody was discussing similar schemes with Iraqi Airways and Iran Air, but the bank's most spectacular success came at the end of the year when it managed the finance for the long projected $400 million Sumed pipeline, linking the Gulf of Suez and the Mediterranean. On this occasion Kidder Peabody arranged for the governments of Kuwait, Saudi Arabia and Abu Dhabi to invest $60 million each, and for Qatar to contribute a further $20 million. The remaining $200 million was to be provided by the Egyptian government; and at the time the deal was announced it was thought that Kidder Peabody would be arranging credit for the Egyptian share.

*   *   *

Since 1971 there has been a steady build-up in the numbers of regional bond placements and syndicated loans announced each year – which shows that the idea of bond issues has now firmly established itself in the Arab world, and that the pioneering efforts of the Kuwait Investment Company and Kidder Peabody have met with considerable success.

*The managers of bond or equity issues are the half dozen or so banks which advise the borrower on the type of issue most appropriate for his requirements. This advice would cover such matters as the date, place and currency of issue, and, in the case of bonds, the interest rate and date of maturity. The managers also select the members of the much larger placing group, which finds buyers for the bonds, and the underwriting group, which guarantees to buy, at a discount, any bonds which remain unplaced. A bank may participate in all of these roles in the same issue.

†An investment bank differs from an ordinary commercial bank or a British merchant bank in that it may not take deposits or engage in most normal commercial banking transactions – the financing of trade for instance. The activities of an investment bank are concerned mainly with the underwriting of share or bond issues, financial advisory services, project appraisal and raising loans.

However, the movement of large blocks of funds in the $10–200 million range is only one aspect of the operations involved in the development of inter-regional finance. With a very few exceptions, such as Middle East Airlines, the institutions borrowing money by means of bond issues have been Arab governments and big government corporations – and although this activity suggests that the conventional aid funds are in part being *replaced* by the commercial capital markets as a source of development finance, it has not involved the work of the funds being *supplemented* by the movement of the smaller amounts of capital which may in the long run do most to stimulate the region's growth as an industrial society.

So during 1974 there was a growing interest in a new type of inter-regional finance. This involves promoting direct investment by Arabian companies and individuals in their own enterprises or joint-venture projects in other Arab states, and encouraging small and medium sized companies in the deficit Arab countries to come to the Gulf money markets to finance their expansion.

These ideas have led to the arrival in the Gulf of an entirely new type of consortium bank – which, unlike UBAF, FRAB and the other Arab/European consortia established in the late 1960s and early 1970s, will engage only in investment banking operations. The new banks are International Financial Advisers, a partnership of the London merchant bank, Robert Fleming, William Kent of New York, Banque Worms and a group of Kuwaiti merchants; Oryx Investments, a Dubian company owned by Arbuthnot Latham (another British merchant bank), Chartered Bank and seven of the most prominent businessmen in the Arabian Peninsula – including Abdel-Aziz Sulaiman and Adnan Khashoggi from Saudi Arabia; and the Arab Financial Consultants Company, a Kuwaiti based partnership of Arbuthnot Latham, and various Kuwaiti, 'other Arab' and international banking interests. In early 1975 it was announced that similar investment banking ventures were being established by Continental Illinois and a group of Bahraini investors in Manama, and by a partnership of the First Boston Corporation and the National Commercial Bank in Jeddah.*

The stated purpose of these banks (which are fulfilling a long-felt

*Other inter-regional investment institutions beginning operations in early 1975 were the Industrial Bank of Kuwait, established by the Kuwaiti government and commercial banks to lend to industrial companies in Kuwait and to companies having Kuwaiti participation in other Arab countries; and the Arab Investment Company, owned by the governments of Saudi Arabia, Kuwait, Abu Dhabi, Bahrain, Qatar, Egypt and Sudan, and based in Riyadh. Unlike IFA, Oryx and AFCC, the IBK and AIC will be lending their *own* funds. They will also be involved in rather larger projects than the investment banks.

need in the Arab world) is to provide consultancy and advisory services in identifying investment opportunities and analysing the economics of projects for both domestic and 'other Arab' clients; to help Western companies in the choice of partners and other matters involved in setting up business in the Middle East; and to arrange long-term finance – chiefly through equity share issues, which in times of inflation are probably a more profitable (if more complex) form of investment than bonds and other fixed interest securities. For large issues the investment banks might be joined in the management and underwriting work by Kidder Peabody, KIC, KFTCIC, KIIC, the UBAF group, Banque Audi and the Alahli Bank of Kuwait.

Over a period of several years this sort of work should have a gradual cumulative effect in building up a more sophisticated and enterprising attitude towards investment among the citizens of the Arabian Peninsula states. The wider public distribution of Arab equity shares should in itself encourage Kuwaitis and Saudis to think of making their own personal direct investments in the deficit states.

Oryx and the other banks would like to prove to the Arabs that equity investment, direct industrial investment and investment in developing countries with mixed state-controlled/private economies (all of which have traditionally scared the Arabs) *can* pay, if due attention is given not only to the availability of sufficient capital (which in the past has often been regarded as the sole requirement for a successful investment), but also to such crucial factors as marketing economics and the availability and quality of labour and management. Conversely it is hoped that small family businessmen, in both the deficit and the surplus countries, who have traditionally aspired to complete financial self-sufficiency and have looked upon borrowing as shameful will become more attuned to the Western business ideal of borrowing for the purpose of corporate growth.

The investment banks intend that this process of education should give additional impetus to the efforts now being made to establish a proper Arab stock exchange, trading both bonds and equity shares. This would not only facilitate the process of small companies in the deficit states drawing on Arabian capital, but also (in an indirect way discussed at the end of this chapter) encourage public companies in the surplus states to expand their operations into the rest of the Arab world.

The best position for a stock exchange would be in Dubai, Kuwait or Beirut – and ideally there should be a number of exchanges operating simultaneously, in the same way that there should be several major banking cities active in a regional dollar market. In the immediate future, however, the chances of there being more than two exchanges are small. In Bahrain and Qatar there are too few companies with shares to be traded, and in Saudi Arabia the financial community is too isolated. In Dubai a few years ago Shaikh Rashid asked a banking friend to examine the idea of having a really large stock exchange which would trade both local and Western securities, and accommodate the big British and American brokers (like Merrill Lynch) as well as Dubian partnerships. But it was eventually decided that until there was enough surplus capital in the United Arab Emirates to attract a significant number of foreign brokers, the establishment of a stock exchange would be premature.

In Beirut there is already a formal stock exchange, but it is almost completely dormant. During the 1964/66 period there was a short boom in some very speculative shares (including a Lebanese oil company), but this stopped with the general ebbing of confidence which followed the Intra diaster. Then in the later 1960s the Bourse Committee blamed the lack of recovery on the foreign firms – Delafield and Delafield, Paine Webber Jackson and Curtis, Bache and Co., Merrill Lynch, IOS, Gramco, and Consolidated Investors, – for diverting money from Beirut on to the New York stock exchange.

With the exception of Merrill Lynch and Bache and Co., all the foreign firms moved out (or collapsed) during the 1969/70 bear market, but the Beirut exchange has not become any more buoyant since. Very few securities are listed, and even fewer are actively traded. Most of the big Lebanese companies are nominally public, but in the majority of cases their shares are owned by the family, or friends of the family, which founded and manages the firm – and these people do not normally sell except to a buyer whom they know personally. The issue of new shares is likewise a semi-private deal among friends, and is not subject to the same stringent regulations that apply in London and New York.

In Kuwait the stock market is much more active, though the boom of 1973 and 1974 was caused mainly by the repatriations of capital which followed the dollar devaluations and the floating of sterling. The scale of recent activity is reflected in the index figures published by the Central Bank, which, starting from a base of 100 at the end of August 1970, show bank shares in March 1973 reaching 262, and industrials 212. Since that date some of the more popular stocks have climbed in an even more spectacular fashion, with Kuwait

Metal Pipes (issued in 1966 at KD 10) rising from KD 27 to KD 75 in December 1973, the Kuwait Cement Company rising from KD 23 to KD 50 in February 1974, and the Kuwait Shipping Company, over the same period, rising from KD 35 to KD 50. The boom has been equally apparent in subscriptions to new issues. The equity of the Kuwait Livestock Company, launched in 1973, was oversubscribed eight hundred times, and shares with a face value of KD 4 were traded at KD 15 in their first day on the market. Similarly, the stock of the Bank of Kuwait and the Middle East, floated in late 1971, was oversubscribed ninety-four times, and the increase in the capital of the Kuwait Foreign Trading Contracting and Investment Company was oversubscribed sixteen times.

At present Kuwaiti shares are traded through some half a dozen brokers, notably Abdel-Hamid Mansour Mazidi, Musaeed Ahmed Mahdou, and Khaled Ahmed al Yagout – who operate in much the same secretive manner as the exchange dealers. But this system is now to be changed.

In 1969 and 1970 the Planning Board decided that there ought to be a more formal stock market, and feeling that the British system would be more in tune with the Kuwaiti mentality than the American system with its mass of Securities and Exchange Commission regulations, they asked the Kuwait Investment Office in London to approach a well known British broker for advice. The broker and a colleague came out to Kuwait in May 1971 to make a study (which they did on a purely amateur basis without charging a fee), and submitted a report to the Planning Board recommending the development of a stock exchange in five stages.

The first phase envisaged opening a floor for the present brokers, with shares being traded on an open market by public auction, and not, as hitherto, by negotiation. No transactions done outside this formal stock exchange would be recognized as valid.

Of all the recommendations, this stage would involve the most fundamental change, because the idea of open dealing – spotlighting the price of every transaction and the number of shares sold – is alien to all the commercial instincts of the Kuwaitis, and, for that matter, of the Lebanese as well. The British brokers stressed that the open system would be very necessary if a Kuwaiti stock exchange was to enjoy international confidence, and suggested that some of the Kuwaiti brokers might come to London for training.

Phases two and three in the brokers' report would bring in dealings in Kuwait government bills and open the market to non-Kuwaiti buyers; and the final phases would see the expansion of the market to deal in foreign securities – both Western and Arab – and the admission of foreign firms of brokers.

Responsibility for putting this plan into effect was given to the Ministry of Commerce, and part of stage three has already been implemented through allowing the citizens of Saudi Arabia, Oman and the lower Gulf states to buy Kuwaiti stocks. In 1973 and 1974 the authorities, spurred by the fear that the current boom had got out of control, were in the process of setting up a formal stock exchange building with a view to implementing stage one.

The fear most often expressed in Kuwait for the future of the brokers' plan, is that in the early stages there will be too few shares being traded to give the new market enough initial momentum. At present there are only some fifty stocks quoted in Kuwait, but assuming that the part of the brokers' plan dealing with the introduction of foreign securities could itself be implemented in stages, there could soon be a lot more to be traded, even without bringing in Western shares or Kuwaiti treasury bills.

It may, for instance, be possible to arrange for the twenty or so Bahraini and Qatari public companies, and the similar number of Saudi concerns to have their shares quoted in Kuwait, though this might be awkward politically, because the governments concerned would probably fear Kuwaiti takeover bids. With rather less difficulty, the Kuwait government might issue bonds or shares in the Kuwait Airways Corporation (which is now entirely state owned), and increase the degree of public participation in Kuwait National Petroleum and Kuwait Petrochemicals Industries, which are by far the largest industrial concerns in the country. In the longer term there may be bonds issued by the Kuwait Fund, the Arab Fund and the Abu Dhabi Fund, which under the terms of their charters may ultimately be able to raise a combined total of almost $10 billion in this manner. Finally there are the existing World Bank bonds denominated in Kuwait dinars, and if an important regional capital market appears in future, there may be large quantities of bonds issued by other Arab governments and state-owned industrial corporations to be traded.

So far almost all the bond issues in the Middle East have been private placements, where the underwriters have kept the notes themselves as a long-term investment. And even those issues which have been open to public subscription, like the Kuwait dinar and Lebanese pound World Bank bonds, are mostly being kept by the banks and are seldom traded. Many of the bonds underwritten by KIC and KFTCIC are placed with the government and go into the

Kuwait state reserve. If, however, there were an Arab stock exchange, and an active secondary bond trading market, this in itself might cause more issues to be opened to public subscription.

*　　*　　*

Well before the stage of trading foreign and other Arab securities is reached in Kuwait, one of the benefits of having a more formal stock exchange in the state will be the education of the investing public. Most of the recent rises in the price of Kuwaiti shares have been quite out of proportion to the profits or prospects of the companies involved. The idea of a price/earnings ratio is unheard of, and if such a figure were calculated for almost any share it would be ludicrously high. Kuwaiti investors tend to buy purely on the basis of whether a share's market price looks high or low when compared with the shares of other companies in the same line of business.

So if the shares of the Commercial Bank, for instance, have a lower market price than the shares of the other four banks, there will be heavy demand for Commercial Bank stock – and this will continue until the market price has been pushed up to the level of the other banks' shares. This is turn may make the shares of the Gulf Bank look cheap, and cause heavy demand for this stock too – and so the process will continue in a leap-frogging pattern. Conversely, it was noticeable when the National, Commercial and Gulf banks once made a scrip issue at roughly the same time, causing the price of their shares to fall, that the price of Alahli shares dropped with them.

If the arrival of a formal stock market encouraged the Kuwaitis to abandon this style of buying and become more selective and more performance-conscious in their choice of shares, this would probably put pressure for greater efficiency on the managers of Kuwaiti companies, whose standards at present are not universally high. In particular, the demands of the stock exchange and shareholders for information might cause management to be more careful in its accounting procedures.

For the longer term it has been suggested that improved management may result in Kuwaiti and other Arab companies becoming more interested in expanding their activities into neighbouring countries and the world outside the Middle East. Although some companies (fewer than one would expect) have made enormous profits in Kuwait, there have in the past been a surprising number of bankruptcies, caused by the Kuwaitis' tendency to copy each others' successful investments and create a situation of over-intense competition, and in the long run the prospects for growth are probably better outside the state.

There are already several big public and private Lebanese companies with an international network of operations – for instance, Middle East Airlines; Trans-Mediterranean Airways, which is one of the world's biggest air-freight carriers; Albert Abela, the caterers, who have provided services for North Sea drilling rigs, and Frankfurt International Airport; and CAT (the Contracting and Trading Company), which operates an international engineering and construction business in association with the British company Motherwell Bridge. These companies grew up in the 1950s and 1960s, before the 'era' of inter-regional finance and the oil revenue explosion, and, like the state-owned companies in the republican Arab countries, they are beyond the scope of this book.

In the Arabian Peninsula the big companies have traditionally been much less interested than the Lebanese groups in international expansion, and much less able to undertake such operations. This is not surprising when one remembers that most of the big Lebanese companies were founded twenty years ago when Kuwait and Saudi Arabia had hardly emerged as modern states.

But in the past two or three years, several Kuwaiti and Saudi concerns have been thinking of overseas operations, and a few have already committed their money abroad. With the prospect of there being virtually unlimited capital and more sophisticated management available in future, it is now possible to speculate on whether the next decade might not see the beginnings of Arabian based international corporations.

M

12

ARAB COMPANIES OVERSEAS

Half a century ago Abdullah Juffali, a citizen of Onaizah, moved five hundred miles across the Arabian Peninsula to begin a new life as a farmer near Mecca. He had three sons, Ebrahim, Ali and Ahmed, and when he died Ebrahim, the eldest, was left alone to bring up his two brothers. The three of them continued to work on their father's farm, but at the same time they opened a small shop to sell hides, and then expanded the premises to stock motor-car tyres as well. For ten years or so they remained in these occupations until the early 1940s, when Ahmed, at the age of seventeen, began to play an active role in the family business, and pulled off a spectacular coup by winning the franchise for the Mecca electricity supply. From that moment on the story of E. A. Juffali and Brothers has been a classic example of the progress of many of the other big merchants houses in the Arabian Peninsula – including such names as the Sulaimans and Ghosaibis in Saudi Arabia, the Almoyyads and Kanoos in Bahrain, and the al Ghanims, al Sagars and al Bahars in Kuwait.

As a result of the Mecca contract the Juffalis became the Saudi representatives of General Electric; and, realizing the potential for selling electrical and mechanical equipment in a country where oil had just been discovered, they moved to Jeddah in 1950, and began collecting other agencies. The most valuable acquisition came quite early on, when they got the dealership for Mercedes.

Then in the early 1960s, when Prince Faisal was Prime Minister, the Juffalis made the crucial decision to send their best manager to Riyadh, which was just beginning to develop into a modern city under the impact of a government building programme. This decision, which was accompanied by the establishment of a major branch at Dammam in the Eastern Province, the brothers consider to have marked their point of breakthrough. Not only did Riyadh become their biggest single sales area, but the move also made them into a genuinely nation-wide group, and gave them a much sounder base than, for example, the 'Aramco merchants', whose operations are still confined largely to the Eastern Province, or the Ali Rezas, who never really broke out of the Hijaz.

Today Juffali Brothers is probably the biggest, richest and best managed of all the Saudi merchant houses. In addition to its various industrial holdings, and the General Electric and Mercedes dealerships, it now controls a list of agencies which includes: Volkswagen, Massey-Ferguson, Siemens, IBM, L. M. Erikson, Brown-Boverie, Michelin, York (the brand name for air conditioners made by Borg-Werner), and Michigan (the earth-moving machinery made by Clark Equipment). The company can also claim the distinction of having made Saudi Arabia the world's third biggest importer of Mercedes lorries after France and South Africa.

Ebrahim Juffali has now retired to the farm near Mecca, though he still buys odd bits of land and buildings as a hobby, and occupies a seat on the board of one of the country's most profitable industrial enterprises, the Saudi Arabian Cement Company, near Dammam. Ali is on the board of the electricity supply companies for Jeddah, Mecca and Taif; and Ahmed has become the managing director of the Saudi Arabian Cement Company, and has a position on the board of the electricity companies of Medina and Hofuf. Much of the family's work in these companies is done in close co-operation with Sulaiman Rajhi, the exchange dealer, who has major holdings in the Jeddah Electricity Company and in Saudi Arabian Cement.

The day to day running of the import business has been left mainly to Ahmed who, unlike many other Saudi merchants, and the Saudi government, is not afraid of employing Arab expatriates. He also has three full-time accountants on his staff – an unusual feature, shared by only a few other Arabian merchant houses, such as the al Ghanims of Kuwait and the Kanoos of Bahrain.

For all its past successes, by 1973 E. A. Juffali and Brothers felt that it had reached something of a watershed, and in the head office in King Abdel-Aziz Street, Jeddah, a good deal of soul-searching was going on. The management defined the problems roughly as follows: First, the company obviously could not be expected to maintain its previous phenomenal rate of growth. It was true that it could still hope for bigger sales of the more expensive consumer goods – York air-conditioners, for example – because future increases in government salaries would bring more citizens within range of affording this type of luxury. But many of Juffalis' capital goods – Mercedes lorries especially – had reached the ceiling of their market potential. If Juffalis (like any other large organization) stopped growing, there was a danger that inflation and rising costs would start to eat up its profits.

The second problem, as defined by the Juffali management, was that the company was extremely vulnerable to three external threats which lay beyond its control: (a) The exchange rate fluctuations in Europe and the continual revaluations of the Deutsche Mark might at some point have made Mercedes and Volkswagen uncompetitive (or less competitive) with their rivals in Saudi Arabia, notably Scania-Vabis lorries sold by Abdel-Aziz Sulaiman and Fiat motor cars sold by Adnan Khashoggi's Triad group. (b) There might have been periods when Juffali's massive demand for lorries could not be met, if Daimler Benz plants were overloaded or were closed down by strikes. And (c) there had already been times when the Syrian/Lebanese frontier had been closed (as from 8 May to 17 August 1973), preventing lorries landed in Beirut being driven down to Saudi Arabia. On these occasions the alternative route via the Syrian port of Latakia was inconvenient, because the lorries were unable to bring down a cargo of goods from Beirut on their delivery run; and the other possibility, sailing round the Cape, had the added disadvantage of being very expensive. If one or more of these dangers were to have materialized in the future, Juffali Brothers might have found the slow growth problem superseded by an even nastier rising costs/falling turnover situation.

Unless the company was prepared to sit back and go into a period of slow decline, its management had to think of some way of gaining greater control over the supply and price of the goods it sold, and of breaking out of the static turnover/rising costs circle by putting its operations on a completely new footing which would allow room for further growth. The answer seemed to be to go into the assembly business, either in Saudi Arabia, or somewhere else in the Middle East.

It was realised that assembling Mercedes lorries in Saudi Arabia would eliminate most of the Deutsche Mark revaluation problem (though currency fluctuations could still affect the price of parts); it would eliminate the Lebanese border problem, because the engine and body components would presumably be shipped to Jeddah via the Cape or (hopefully) the Suez Canal; and it would give Juffalis control over the rate of output. In theory, the establishment of an assembly plant would also enable Juffalis to market a cheaper and more profitable product, because wages in Saudi Arabia were well below German levels.

Set against these advantages was the fact that assembly would involve an enormous increase in the size of the Juffali organization and in the number of its employees, and this would call for a completely new style of management. Secondly, the fact that there was no protection for local industry in Saudi Arabia, which meant that a Juffali plant would be vulnerable to competition from, say, a Kuwaiti merchant who had a similar idea; and, thirdly, the Saudi labour force, although cheap, was not of very high quality.

If this labour problem was judged to be too serious, Juffali Brothers felt that they might go for the second option: building an assembly plant in some neighbouring Arab state. The company would have preferred to wait and see how other investors had fared under the new liberal economic regime before it committed its money to Egypt, and in the end it would probably have been faced with a choice between Lebanon and Bahrain, both of which have a labour force which was relatively skilled and not too expensive.

But again there were disadvantages. In Lebanon Juffalis would have come up against the old problem of Syrian/Lebanese and Syrian/Jordanian border closures; and in both Lebanon and Bahrain, where the company felt that its investment would be less secure politically than it would in Saudi Arabia, there had been recent waves of industrial unrest.

Meanwhile there was always the possibility that the Saudi government might one day forget its obsession with free enterprise, and institute some form of protection as a means of promoting local industrialization. There was some long-term uncertainty over the Saudi government's tariff policy, which is why Juffalis tended to assume the worst in this respect when considering both a Saudi assembly plant and an external assembly plant. But if tariffs were imposed, it was easy to see that with a plant in Lebanon or Bahrain, Juffalis would have found itself at a severe disadvantage in the event of a competitor, like Abdel-Aziz Sulaiman, putting up a plant for Scania-Vabis or some other type of lorry in Saudi Arabia.

By the end of 1973 the debate at Juffali Brothers had not yet been resolved[1], but one conclusion was definite: whether the company went into the assembly business or not, it had no intention in the foreseeable future of expanding its operations on an international scale outside the Middle East. In this respect Juffalis could be taken to represent almost all the big family businesses in Saudi Arabia and the Gulf, many of which, in the past few years, have been going through a similar process of soul-searching, and have run up against much the same problems as those being discussed in King Abdel-Aziz Street, Jeddah.

But there is one notable exception to this generalization, and that is the Triad group, which went international at a very early stage in its development, and has never had quite the same domestic base as the other Arabian family companies. Triad should not therefore be seen as a pointer to the future development of the merchant houses, because it is, and always has been, a different type of company. Its one point of similarity is that it is owned by a single family, the three Khashoggi brothers – and it is run by the eldest brother, Adnan, or 'AK' as he is known to the rest of the Saudi business community.

Khashoggi had a rather better start in life than the Juffali brothers. His father, who was the doctor to King Abdel-Aziz, sent him abroad to be educated at Victoria College, Alexandria, and Stamford University in California, where he took a course in business studies.

On his return to Saudi Arabia in 1954 Khashoggi foresaw the demand for building materials that the oil boom would bring, in the same way that the Juffalis foresaw the demand for electrical and mechanical equipment. So, to acquire the necessary technical expertise. he consulted the managing director of the gypsum (plaster of paris) industry in Egypt (who turned out to be a fellow Old Victorian) and he then obtained from King Saud the concession for the manufacture of gypsum in Saudi Arabia. At the same time he realized that Anglo-Saudi relations, which were then somewhat strained as a result of Britain's support for Abu Dhabi in the Buraimi Oasis dispute, would be bound to improve when the crisis subsided; and in preparation for this day he built up good relations with various prominent British companies, including Rolls Royce and Marconi, which he foresaw would eventually be needing a Saudi representative. These two groups of interests, the National Gypsum Company and the agencies, Khashoggi put together in 1955 in the al Nasr Trading and Industrial Corporation.

During the later 1950s al Nasr acquired a number of other defence and motor-car agencies; but in the past decade the group's expansion has taken place abroad, and Adnan Khashoggi now runs a commercial empire with a market value approaching $200 million. At the top of the pyramid al Nasr has been replaced by the Triad Holding Corporation, controlling several dozen companies spread all over the world. In Saudi Arabia itself the group still has a major interest in the National Gypsum Company, which has now gone public and is run by the second Khashoggi brother, Adil. There are two vehicle agencies, Triad Automotive for Fiat, also run by Adil, and National Auto Agencies for Chrysler, which does a thriving business in Dodge pick-up trucks. And biggest of all, there is Triad Marketing which is involved with defence equipment and aero-space companies, including Lockheed, the manufacturers of the Tristar, which has been bought by Saudia; Rolls-Royce, which has supplied gas and marine turbines and the engines for the Saudi air force Lightnings; and Raytheon, which has supplied laboratory equipment and Hawk ground-to-air missiles. On a more informal basis, Triad Marketing has also acted as an adviser to another aircraft manufacturer, Northrop. Because defence contracts are essentially inter-government deals, Triad Marketing should be thought of as the Saudi representative of these companies, rather than as a conventional sales agent in the Triad Automotive sense.

Overseas one of the biggest companies is Triad Leisure Holdings, run by the third and youngest Khashoggi brother, Essam. Among the interests owned by this subsidiary are restaurants in the United States; a share of Cedars Travel in Beirut; a film production company which shot the secret-agent movie *Embassy;* the Condas furniture factory in Beirut, which has provided custom-made furniture for such buildings as the Riyadh and Mecca conference centres; and Kenzo, a Paris fashion house which Khashoggi established for Kenzo Takada, who designed trendy clothes with the label of 'Jungle Jap'.

Other major Triad companies include: Triad Bancorp America, which owns the Bank of Contra Costa and the Security National Bank in Walnut Creek, California, and in November 1974 put in an unsuccessful bid for a share in a third institution, the First National Bank of San José; Uniao Triad in São Paulo, a trading and industrial concern with interests in meat canning; Triad Naft, which has acted as an agent for oil companies purchasing government crude in Abu Dhabi and Saudi Arabia, and which in 1974 acquired a concession to build an export refinery in Sudan; Triad Pacific which on the basis of a long-term charter agreement concluded with Pertamina (the Indonesian national oil company) has raised a major international loan to finance the construction of coastal tankers; various Triad real estate and trading companies in the United States, France and Belgium; and Uni-Triad Enterprises in London, which looks after various British investments, and liaises with the British companies represented by Triad in Saudi Arabia. (These companies no longer include Marconi.)

The most recent extension of operations has been in Sudan, where Triad Capital Management played a major role in arranging for the government a $200 million inter-regional syndicated loan guaranteed by the Saudi Arabian Monetary Agency. Apart from acquiring the Triad Naft refinery concession the group has established itself as a promoter of Sudanese agro-industrial enterprises. It is envisaged that these projects will be mainly government owned, but they will be managed by Arizona Land and Cattle, a United States company which Khashoggi bought in 1974.

Exactly how this vast and multifarious empire of trading and finance companies is organized is not easy to define. Officially the group's headquarters is the Triad Holding Corporation, with a management staff of some forty Arabs, Europeans and Americans operating out of the Gefinor Centre in Beirut. But in practice Triad revolves around the presence of its extraordinarily energetic founder, and, unofficially, it is said to be based in whichever of the world's capitals AK happens to be visiting.

*   *   *

Triad and Juffali Brothers, and the many other merchant houses like Juffalis, are family concerns. Apart from Triad, which is a rather exceptional company, they have all been formed in the traditional mould of Arab commercial enterprise, and as predominantly trading concerns they are inevitably tied to the home market unless, like the Dubian merchants, they are engaged in re-export or smuggling. But there is a second group of newer and mostly smaller, publicly owned industrial and service companies, and at first sight these would appear to have a much more appropriate base for international expansion, either in exporting or investing overseas. It is some of these companies which, it was suggested at the end of the last chapter, might gain a more inspired management as an indirect result of a proper stock exchange being set up in the Arab world.

The great majority of the new industrial companies have been established in Kuwait (from 1961 onwards), and one does not have to look far to understand the reason for this. The population of Kuwait is rather more sophisticated than that of its neighbours; there is more private wealth available, both to be invested in the new companies and to buy their products; and there has been some small measure of government tariff protection for domestic industries. Equally important, Kuwait's industrial growth has been stimulated by the existence of a developed infra-structure and a single concentrated market; whereas in Saudi Arabia progress has been hampered by the sheer size of the country and the dispersed population. In an industry where there is particularly large demand in Saudi Arabia it may be possible for a company to confine its marketing operations to just one province – as, for instance, the manufacture of cement is divided between the Arabian Cement Company near Jeddah supplying the Hijaz, the Yamama Cement Company in Riyadh supplying the central areas, and the Saudi Arabian Cement Company in Hofuf near Dammam supplying the Eastern Province. But with a product for which there is smaller demand, anyone thinking of setting up a factory has to consider that by the time his products have reached their more distant markets, they may be uncompetitive with imports.

In the long term as the population and the amount of wealth in private hands expands, and the 'development bottlenecks' preventing larger government expenditure are removed, there will probably be considerable growth of Saudi publicly owned industry, and because the potential market is quite large most companies will presumably be able to find ample outlets within the Kingdom. But in Kuwait a few companies are already beginning to discover that the domestic market cannot absorb any more of their product, and given that in future expansion schemes there may be economies in building on a larger scale, Kuwaiti companies should now, in theory, be thinking of exporting or investing overseas.

In practical terms, however, the situation in Kuwait is very different. Some (though not all) companies have a rather weak management, and although there is no corporation tax, a few companies have paid only small dividends or have actually made a loss. Until 1972 these included Kuwait National Petroleum and Kuwait Petrochemicals industries, though in both these concerns (which are mainly state-owned and fall rather outside the scope of this chapter) the failure was caused as much by bad luck as bad administration. Unfortunately, careers in industrial management do not appeal to the Kuwaitis who feel that, compared with trade, industry is somehow dirty and undignified, and the consequent shortage of local expertise can be made up only partially by attracting foreign staff with high salaries.

For any Kuwaiti company wishing specifically to export (rather than to invest overseas) there are a number of further difficulties. Although fuel is cheap, raw materials are expensive because they have to be imported. The only major exception here is the Kuwait Cement Company, which is hoping soon to replace the clinker it has been buying from Iraq with locally produced material. Labour, too, is more expensive than it is in neighbouring countries, and even with relatively high wages, skilled craftsmen are difficult to find because they are in short supply throughout the Arab world.

There are, however, a few Kuwaiti companies which have already begun to mount overseas sales campaigns as new plant comes on stream. These include Kuwait Flour Mills, Kuwait Metal Pipes, the National Industries Company, which turns out products ranging from lime powder and soap to car batteries, and Kuwait Asbestos Industries, which is owned by National Industries and is one of the best managed companies in the state. On a somewhat larger scale, at the beginning of 1974 tenders were being requested for the construction of a sheet steel mill which should find ready export markets in the dry docks being built in Bahrain, Dubai, Iraq and Iran; and at an earlier stage of planning there was a scheme for an aluminium smelter of the same size as Bahrain's Alba. But these projects will not make any impact on Kuwaiti exports until the later 1970s, and meanwhile in the 1972/3 financial year, only one Kuwaiti manufacturing company outside the petrochemicals industry (Kuwait Metal Pipes) exported goods worth more than one million dinars.

Corporate investment overseas in recent years has been equally limited. The companies lack the sophisticated organization and the large management staff, experienced in a multitude of fields from accountancy to public relations, which are necessary if they are going to mount a programme of expansion abroad. Many of the most successful companies in the Arab world have been something of a one-man band, and when the founder and driving force behind them has died suddenly they have suffered from a loss of momentum and have begun a gradual decline.

The classic example of this happening is seen in the Bin Laden company in Saudi Arabia. This construction firm was founded by a Hadramauti, Mohammed bin Laden, who began his career working as a bricklayer for Aramco on a daily wage of one riyal (about twelve pence). Every day (like most Hadramautis) he put some of his money into a little tin box, and eventually he saved enough to go into business on his own. At first his company did odd building jobs, but gradually bin Laden expanded into more ambitious work, building palaces for the al Saud princes in Riyadh; and in 1951 he made his breakthrough when he was awarded the contract for the Medina-Jeddah road, after a foreign contractor had withdrawn from the project.

From then on the company specialized in heavy construction, carrying out a series of massive road and airport projects, in Jordan and Ras al Khaimah as well as in Saudi Arabia. Shaikh Mohammed (as he was known in his later days) made a point of being on site as often as possible, and he used an aircraft for fast travel between projects. (On one occasion he had the unique experience of saying his morning prayers in Jerusalem, his midday prayers in Medina, and his evening prayers in Mecca, the three holiest places in the Moslem world.) By the time he died, by crashing his own aircraft in 1966, Shaikh Mohammed's company had become the biggest private contractors in the world, owning ninety of the largest excavators that Caterpillar produce. Unfortunately Shaikh Mohammed's tragic death occurred at a moment when the eldest of his fifty-two children was still in his early twenties, and there was no obvious successor. So, until such time as his sons proved themselves capable of taking over, King Faisal appointed the owner of another smaller construction firm to look after the company. This was no easy task. Shaikh Mohammed had left no senior management because to all intents and purposes he was the management, and without his knowledge and direction the company drifted. An abnormally high proportion of equipment was allowed to remain unproductive, and large bits of plant were reputed to have been lost in the desert.

In 1973 the company was working on two big projects – Jizzan airport and the Jizzan-Jeddah road, which as the crow flies is four hundred miles over very rough mountainous terrain. (To give some idea of the scale of road building operations in Saudi Arabia, this is roughly the same distance as from London to Aberdeen.) But when this contract, which the company was awarded without being asked to submit a tender, is finished, it is felt in Saudi Arabia that Bin Laden may have difficulty in bidding successfully for other large projects – and that its future will then rest on the goodwill of the King.

The case of the Bin Laden company is admittedly a rather extreme example of the 'one-man band' phenomenon, and this feature is anyway found more often in private organizations than in public companies. But there are other factors discouraging Arabian companies from investing overseas, and these lie in the complete difference between the business environment of Kuwait and Saudi Arabia and that of the industrialized countries. To begin with, in the West there is no friendly government at hand, as there is in Kuwait, to provide a cheap loan or extra capital should the company find itself in difficulties. The company is unlikely to be the monopoly supplier of its product, and competing with its rivals will mean entering the totally new realms of Western advertising and marketing campaigns. Then there are trade unions and a complex system of labour and commercial legislation to be dealt with. Finally, and worst of all, there is tax, which calls for completely new accounting procedures.

So it is not surprising that the Arabian public companies (other than Kuwait Shipping and Kuwait Tankers) with overseas interests have confined their operations to other Arab states, where conditions are not so different from those at home. Kuwait Flour Mills owns twenty per cent of Bahrain Flour Mills; Kuwait Insurance has branches in the lower Gulf, Saudi Arabia and Lebanon; the Kuwait Food Company (Americana), which has the local franchise for operating Wimpey bars, has set up restaurants in Bahrain, Dubai, Abu Dhabi and Saudi Arabia; and on a more ambitious scale Kuwait Hotels, which owns the Kuwait Hilton, has entered or is planning joint ventures in Khartoum, Agadir (Morocco) and Damascus.

Much larger operations are owned by United Fisheries of Kuwait and a company to which it is indirectly related, Gulf International. In the same way that Triad forms something of an exception in the ranks of the family merchant houses, so these organizations are untypical of the Kuwaiti industrial companies. Gulf International is a private concern with as many assets in the Sudan as in Kuwait, and although United Fisheries is publicly owned, it has its origins in one public and two private companies which merged in 1972.

The story of United Fisheries and Gulf International goes back to one day in 1959, when a prolific dairy cow belonging to Shaikh Sabah al Ahmed al Jaber, the present Kuwaiti Foreign Minister, fell ill. A Sudanese vet in Kuwait, Khalil Osman Mahmoud, was summoned to attend the animal, and in due course it recovered. Shaikh Sabah was delighted. He thanked Osman profusely, and during their conversation Osman was able to tell him that his real ambition was not to be a vet but to run a business. So Shaikh Sabah set up Gulf Fisheries, with his own capital plus a small contribution from a Kuwaiti merchant, Abdel-Aziz al Rashid, and Khalil Osman was appointed as manager.

Osman proved himself to be immensely energetic, a highly persuasive negotiator, and a great promoter of projects; and during the early years, when the company enjoyed a virtual monopoly of shrimping operations throughout the Gulf, everything went well. Profits grew steadily, until in the mid-1960s they were running at about KD 2 million a year.

By 1967 Gulf Fisheries owned fifty-six trawlers, as well as a number of tenders and factory ships used to carry out processing and packing at sea, and in the following year it placed an order for a further 104 vessels with the French company ACRP of La Rochelle. To bring the new boats on the rough passage round the Cape, Khalil Osman came up with the ingenious idea of buying the oil tanker *Borag*, and converting its deck to carry thirteen completed trawlers, and occasionally heavy bits of equipment for a desalination plant then being built on the industrial estate at Shuaiba. On its return voyages the tanker was later able to carry oil for British Petroleum, which made *Borag* itself into a profit-making venture.

The new trawlers enabled Gulf Fisheries to expand into waters outside the Gulf. In 1970 it began fishing in the Red Sea and off the coasts of Madagascar, Nigeria and New Guinea, while further operations were planned for Fernando Po, Senegal and Mauritania. But by this time the company was in serious difficulties.

Gulf Fisheries' initial profits had encouraged other Kuwaitis (with their passion for copying someone else's successful investments) to join the shrimping bonanza, and in the mid-1960s three rival companies were established. These were International Fisheries with twenty-three boats, Kuwait National Fisheries with ten boats and Mishari al Khaled al Zaid with six boats. As a result of the cut-throat competition which developed between these fleets, and the seventy-odd vessels belonging to Iran, Iraq, Saudi Arabia, Bahrain and Qatar, the Gulf became disastrously overfished. To make matters worse, while Saudi Arabia and the lower Gulf states charged a royalty of only sixteen per cent on sales of fish caught in their waters, the Iranians started demanding forty per cent, and from 1970 onwards the companies were forced to suspend operations in Iranian waters. (Khalil Osman comments that the Shah seemed not to distinguish between fishing rights and oil concessions.) Between 1968 and 1971 the catch of the four Kuwaiti companies dropped by two-thirds.

For Gulf Fisheries the problem was particularly acute, because at this time its development programme was only half complete. It already had the expense of running over 130 trawlers (many of which were found to have faulty engines), but its foreign operations were still too new to make up for a series of bad seasons in home waters. The two-million dinar profit which the company had been making a few years earlier turned into a loss of roughly the same amount. It seems that this situation had never been anticipated. In the rush to expand the company had not built up very large reserves, and by 1971 it was on the verge of bankruptcy.

None of the other companies was in a much better condition. In 1970 National Fisheries began to canvass the idea of a merger, and in due course Gulf Fisheries, International Fisheries and the government agreed to this scheme. The Kuwaiti court handling the merger appointed an 'expert' to assess 'the exact or correct value' of the three companies, and the expert called in Kidder Peabody, who pointed out to the court that although there were many ways of deciding the value of a company, none of them were normally described as 'exact'. Eventually Kidder Peabody carried out its assessment on the basis of the 'replacement value of a going concern'.

In May 1972 a new company, United Fisheries, was established with a capital of KD 10 million, of which forty-nine per cent was contributed by the government, thirty-five per cent by Gulf and sixteen per cent by public subscribers, who bought the shares of International Fisheries and National Fisheries. (Mishari al Khaled al Zaid remained independent, with its operations confined to areas outside Kuwaiti waters.) The Chairman of the new United Fisheries was Shaikh Sabah's highly talented twenty-four-year-old son, Shaikh Nasser al Sabah.

Despite the severe problems of reorganization involved in merging three former competitors, United Fisheries has staged a remarkably fast recovery from the depression of 1970/71. The catch in 1973 was estimated at a record twenty-two thousand tons, and sales at KD 29 million ($96 million), bringing more foreign exchange into Kuwait than any other product bar oil. (Because almost all the shrimps are caught outside Kuwaiti waters, and part of the revenues belong to the foreign partners in overseas joint ventures, the $96 million is not included in the export figures for Kuwaiti industry.)

The company's fleet now totals 157 trawlers (with plans for the purchase of fifty or sixty further vessels), ten factory ships and seven tenders – which makes United Fisheries the biggest shrimping concern in the world.

The main fishing areas are still the Gulf, the Red Sea and the coasts of Oman and Southern Yemen, but using the experience which its shareholders had built up before the merger United Fisheries has based its expansion policy on overseas joint ventures. In the Asian and African operations the company supplies the ships, the technical expertise, and, if necessary, a long-term loan at favourable rates of interest, while the foreign partner provides the crews, and at a later stage will probably take over the management. In early 1974 United Fisheries companies were operating off Mauritania, Senegal, Nigeria, Madagascar, New Guinea and Australia, and new ventures were being planned for Sudan, Somalia and Pakistan.

Khalil Osman has no seat on the board of the new company, but he has been retained as its official adviser, and he is still managing enormous sums of Shaikh Sabah's money in other operations. Well before the depression in the Kuwait fishing industry and the merger, Shaikh Sabah and Osman (who by this time had joined the Shaikh as a minority partner) had begun to invest in Sudanese industrial projects, which are now worth considerably more than the equity in United Fisheries. All the companies concerned are owned directly by Shaikh Sabah and his sons and Khalil Osman, but they are known collectively as the 'Gulf International group', after the name of the company which operates them.

Gulf International now runs well over twenty subsidiaries and associates. The largest of these is the Sudan Textile Industry, which the group bought in 1968 from the American government's Agency for International Development (AID) and a British construction consortium headed by Platt International and English Electric. Originally the factory had been owned by a Greek American, Mr Theodoracropoulos, but this gentleman had got into financial difficulties and AID and the British group, being his biggest creditors, had taken over. Under Gulf International's management the company has become the largest business in the Sudan, operating 150,000 spindles and 3,300 looms under one roof.

Other group subsidiaries in the Sudan are: the Modern Match Producing and Distributing Company; the Sudanese Glass Company, which manufactures the less specialized types of glass products like beer bottles; the National Agricultural Organization, a crop-spraying company owning some thirty aircraft; the Sudanese Kuwaiti Packaging Company; Sudanese Chemical Industries, which produces pharmaceuticals, disinfectants, medicines, insecticides and soap; Particle Board Industries; the Medical and Sanitary Products Company, making cotton wool and bandages from textile industry by-products; the Khartoum Publicity Company; Sudan Allware Industries, which makes cheap clothes; the African Plantation Company, which grows cotton and sorghum; two inactive natural resources companies, Digna Petroleum and Taroog Mining; and the Africa Palace Hotel in Khartoum. (In mid-1974 Gulf International was hoping to be able to run the Africa Palace as a Meridien hotel. Meridien is a new hotel chain owned and/or operated by Air France, in the same way that Trans World Airlines owns and/or operates Hilton hotels.)

Associates in the Sudan are United Insurance, and the Kenana sugar project – owned by the Sudan Government, the British mining, trading and plantation group, Lonrho, Nissho Iwai of Japan, Gulf International and the Riyadh based Arab Investment Company. Ultimately the output from Kenana is planned to rise to one million tons a year, which will make it the biggest sugar plantation in the world.

In Kuwait the Gulf International group owns large amounts of local stock and property, and substantial holdings in three associates, United Fisheries, the Kuwait Danish Dairy Company, and Hempels Marine Paints.

In other countries, subsidiaries are Meridien hotel companies in Beirut and Jeddah (making Gulf International the biggest hotel owners in the Middle East); the Star Match Company in Nigeria; and the Hamoor Tanker Corporation in Liberia – the owners of the *Borag*, which is still used to carry oil and heavy pieces of group equipment. In Lebanon the group also owns a share of Packfreeze, which used to be a significant buyer of Gulf Fisheries' shrimps.

The best known perhaps of all Gulf International's assets is its large shareholding in Lonrho, which in December 1974 was increased by an issue of new stock to some fourteen per cent – second only in size to that of Roland (Tiny) Rowland, the company's controversial chief executive.

The close association between the two groups began in 1971, when Khalil Osman, who had become an informal economic adviser to President Nimairy, set up the deal whereby Lonrho became the Sudanese government's overseas purchasing agent. Two years later during the Lonrho board-room row of 1973, Gulf International came up with a scheme to help Lonrho's liquidity problems with £8 million of additional capital. In the event this offer was rejected by the Lonrho board, and Gulf International's initial shareholding was acquired through the stock exchange in the normal way. In early 1974 the two companies also dropped a scheme for a jointly owned Sudanese textile factory. The only partnership to date therefore has been the Kenana sugar project, but as Gulf International's holding in Lonrho increases, it seems likely that there will be more joint ventures between the two companies.

The Gulf International/Lonrho association is significant, because it may be the first example of a new style of operations by Arabian companies, both private and public. It was suggested in an earlier chapter that if Arabs are to invest in overseas industry they like to have their hand held by a partner taking an equal risk – and Rowland has already seen the potential for this sort of co-operation. As he said in 1973: 'The combination of Western technology, African resources and Arab money will be unbeatable – that is where the future of Lonrho lies.'

Rowland's views are not necessarily representative of the British (or for that matter the American or European) business community as a whole, but in the foreseeable future it is only through this sort of partnership with Western corporations that Arabian companies, other than such exceptions as Triad, United Fisheries and Gulf International, are likely to invest overseas on any significant scale.

---

[1]In 1974 Juffalis opted for Saudi Arabia as the site of their truck plant. An application for its construction was being considered by the Saudi authorities in October that year.

13

THE STATE RESERVES

In most of the last seven chapters the money under discussion has been privately owned – and whether it has been invested in bank deposits, apartment blocks, Arab bonds or shrimping boats, the amounts involved have been relatively small. But it is now time to turn to government money, and to move from the millions of private dollars to the billions and hundreds of billions of dollars that are now beginning to pile up in the oil states' reserves.

On the trends visible at the end of 1974 it was established that in the current year the OPEC states as a whole would have generated a revenue surplus of $65/75 billion. These figures were worked out by adding oil revenues paid and due for 1974 production ($105 billion), income from non-oil exports ($7 billion) and investment income ($8 billion); and deducting merchandise imports ($32/36 billion), net service transactions ($10/16 billion) and private current transfers ($3 billion). Depending on what calculations were made on the price of oil, the volume of production, the rate of interest received on the surpluses, and the rate of growth in expenditure, the position in the year 1980 in constant 1974 dollar terms could be projected at anything between a deficit of $4 billion and a surplus of $54 billion – with a middle of the road consensus estimate being $30 billion.

This consensus estimate is based on total OPEC revenues in constant dollars being $140 billion in 1980 (as suggested at the beginning of Chapter 4), and it makes two major assumptions on the patterns of expenditure and surplus revenues investment. First it assumes that the expenditure of OPEC states will grow much faster than was expected soon after the price rises of 1973. This is partly because the spending performance of the producers in 1974 showed that their revenue-absorbing capacity had originally been seriously under-estimated; and partly because it is assumed that there will be a steady removal of 'development bottlenecks' and that the industrial con-sumers will help accelerate the development of OPEC states through concluding the bilateral package deals discussed in Chapter 5.

Secondly, it is assumed that substantial sums will simply be given away, and that much more money will be pumped into inter-Arab or Third World development banks – like the Kuwait Fund and the Islamic Bank; and that a big block of funds will be recycled via bodies such as the International Monetary Fund, which will be lending to finance balance of payments deficits. All the surplus put into development banks and recycling funds will be earning con-siderably less than a commercial rate of interest, and part of it may receive no interest at all.

On these two assumptions – that OPEC expenditure in 1980 will be running at over $100 billion, and that about a quarter of each year's surplus will be earning a negative real rate of interest in various funds – the cumulative surplus of OPEC by 1980 is unlikely to amount to more than $300 billion.

This $300 billion can be thought of loosely as being the OPEC governments' future reserves, though, strictly speaking, the calcu-lations above have been aimed at working out a current account surplus. Although the bulk of this surplus is bound to be in the hands of governments, in the non-socialist states a large part will also belong to the private sector.

The concept of reserves here can include money invested in any-thing from property to bank deposits at call, but the chronic surplus Arabian Peninsula states generally make a distinction between 'reserves' – meaning all assets held overseas – and 'The Reserve' – meaning money invested as a sort of national pension fund, which will provide for expenditure when the oil runs out. The capital in The Reserves of the Arabian OPEC states is, and always has been, invested long term. The popular belief in 1974 that almost all of the OPEC surpluses were being held short term as a matter of policy can be accounted for partly by the fact that the non-surplus states were indeed holding their (temporary) surpluses in cash form, and partly by the fact that the Arabian Peninsula states earmarked a great part of their surplus in the early part of the year for purposes other than allocation to The Reserves. The funds committed by the Arabian countries to their budgets, the capital of new or expanded develop-ment banks, gifts to the front line Arab states, bilateral current account aid and loans to both underdeveloped and developed countries, and loans to the International Monetary Fund and the World Bank had to be held short term before being disbursed. When it is also borne in mind that even money (from new revenue cheques and maturing investments) allocated to The Reserves could not be put into long term investments immediately, and that increased domestic spending by Arabian countries involved an increase in the amount of money in circulation internally and an increase in the amount of exchange invested short term overseas to back the local currencies, it becomes obvious that short term holdings were bound to account for a very large proportion of the total 1974 surplus.

However, this huge increase in the amount of cash held abroad by the Arabian Peninsula states was more or less a once and for all phenomenon. The cash will, so to speak, be spent once a year, and the amounts required to be held in this form will in future increase more slowly. In contrast the sums in The Reserves will grow bigger each year and will eventually make short term holdings as a proportion of total reserves look insignificant. This effect was already becoming apparent in the second half of 1974, and this prompted many commentators in the West to speak of a move by the oil producers towards longer term investment, implying, wrongly, that there had been a change in the Arabian Peninsula governments' investment policies.

It follows from this view of reserves as pension funds that the Arabs are much more concerned than Western governments to earn as high a rate of interest as possible, and to avoid inflation and devaluations eating away the real purchasing power of their holdings.

At different times all the main surplus states have lost considerable sums through devaluations, with the biggest loss being the $250/300 million which the Saudis incurred in February 1973. For that part of their reserves in dollars the producers have no redress in the event of a devaluation, but, in the case of money held in sterling, those Arab countries which were formerly British mandated or protected territories – including Kuwait, Abu Dhabi and Qatar – used to have a measure of protection under the Sterling Area Agreements of 1968.

The Agreements of 1968 were signed by all sterling area countries, with the exception of Kuwait, which felt unable for political reasons to conclude a written agreement, but reached an almost identical 'understanding' with the British government. The Agreements came about as a result of a series of currency crises which Britain had undergone in 1961, 1963, 1964, 1966, 1967 and 1968. The immediate cause of each crisis was a run on sterling triggered off by bad trade figures or the expectation of a devaluation, but underlying the trouble was the fact that although the sterling area countries had kept their official sterling balances relatively stable since 1960, the increase in their reserves had been put into other currencies, mainly dollars. To make the situation worse, after the devaluation of November 1967 some of the sterling area countries began actively to move their money out of sterling.

During each crisis the European central bankers, who meet every month at the Bank of International Settlements (BIS) in Basle, mounted short-term rescue operations, but in early 1968 the British government and the central bankers began discussions on more permanent agreements. The outcome was that the bankers agreed to provide Britain with a ten-year loan facility (the Basle Facility) on which the Bank of England could draw to offset fluctuations in both private and official sterling balances. But before finally concluding the deal the bankers suggested that the sterling area countries should themselves make a contribution, partly by depositing some of their non-sterling reserves with the BIS to help finance the United Kingdom's drawings, and partly by promising to keep a fixed proportion of their official reserves in sterling.

Accordingly, in autumn 1966 an exchange of letters took place, under which the sterling area countries agreed not to allow the proportion of sterling in their reserves to drop below the level of mid-1968, and the British government in return guaranteed the value of that proportion of each country's official sterling reserves (other than equity shares) which exceeded ten per cent of its total reserves. Under this formula if a country had total reserves of, say, £100 million, and £50 million was in sterling, the guarantee would cover £40 million. The guarantee level was fixed at $2.35, which meant that if the pound sank below this parity, the sterling balances of those countries covered by the Agreements would be written up at the expense of the Bank of England's Exchange Equalization Account.

The weakness of these Agreements was that the guarantee was expressed in terms of dollars, and there was no provision for a sterling devaluation or downwards float following a devaluation of the dollar itself. This defect become important in 1972. In July that year, seven months after the Smithsonian Agreement (the general realignment of currencies against the dollar negotiated at the Smithsonian Institute in Washington in December 1971), it was decided that sterling should be floated; and although the pound soon sank from about $2.60 to $2.40, it was not until the autumn that it dipped below $2.35.

In September 1973, when the original Agreements expired, the guarantee level was pegged again for six months at $2.42; and in March 1974 the British government announced a further agreement, better suited to a regime of floating currencies, under which the guarantee was related to sterling's movement against a weighted average of all the major trading currencies.

During the middle and the latter half of 1974 the changes in the world economy created by the oil price rises made even these modified arrangements irrelevant. In part this was because in circumstances where a huge British trade deficit was unavoidable, the parity of sterling would be determined not by factors over which the British government had any control, but by the Arabs themselves – and, given their desire to diversify part of their reserves out of the dollar, and the prospect of the British economy being strengthened later in the decade by oil from the North Sea, the Arabs regarded sterling as quite an attractive investment. At the same time the exclusion of such long-term investments as property and equity shares from the Agreements meant that an increasingly large and important part of the sterling reserves of Kuwait, Qatar and Abu Dhabi was falling outside the terms of the guarantee. Accordingly, the British government, with the tacit consent of the Arabs, who by this time were more concerned with the threat of inflation than with devaluations, decided that at the end of 1974 the Agreements should be cancelled.

In all the Bank of England paid out some £140 million under the Sterling Area Agreements. In early 1973, at the original $2.35 level, the Bank disbursed £60 million (of which about £25 million is thought to have gone to Kuwait), and in early 1974, at the $2.42 level, it paid out a further £80 million. In general the Kuwaitis and Qataris expressed themselves to be fairly satisfied with the working of the Agreements, but the Abu Dhabi Finance Ministry, whose sterling investments were largely in equities at the time of the first pay-out, received little benefit.

The Arabs' other main anxiety in the management of their reserves – earning as high a rate of interest as possible – is illustrated by the oil states' reluctance to join the International Monetary Fund's Special Drawing Account. Because the workings of the IMF and this Account are fundamental to the discussion of the recycling problem in the next chapter, they are worth examining here in some detail.

The International Monetary Fund was one of three institutions (the others being the United Nations and the World Bank) which were established at the end of the Second World War to ensure that the world's affairs should in future be conducted with a greater degree of international co-operation than had been seen in the 1920s and 1930s. Whereas the UN's role was largely political, and the World Bank was given the job of lending capital for reconstruction projects in Europe and development projects in newly independent countries, the IMF was charged with improving the payments mechanism in international trade as a means of preventing the 'transmission' of depressions which had led to the massive slump in the early 1930s. In the main this involved discouraging countries with payments deficits from adopting 'beggar my neighbour' tactics (excessive unilateral action like big devaluations) which would be likely to transfer their own problems on to their trading partners, causing a reduction of output and unemployment. To help such countries the Fund was given a store of liquidity in its 'General Account' out of which debtor nations could finance their deficits while they worked to improve their trading position by domestic means.

The store of liquidity in the IMF was provided by each member's quota, which can be thought of as its subscription, paid one quarter in gold and three-quarters in its own currency. If a state wishes to draw money to finance imports it may sell the Fund more of its own currency in exchange for foreign currency up to an amount not exceeding 125 per cent of its quota. These drawings are done in five separate tranches, each of twenty-five per cent of quota. The first is known as the 'gold tranche' and can be drawn as of right, but thereafter drawings of the four 'credit tranches' become conditional on the drawing state agreeing to implement increasingly severe instructions, which the IMF will lay down to force it to remedy the cause of its drawings – in other words, its trade deficit. If a state has not drawn anybody else's currency, but has had its own currency drawn it is said to have a 'super gold tranche' position in which it may draw as of right not only its gold tranche but an amount equal to the sum of its own currency that has been drawn. No interest is paid by the IMF on quota, and no interest is payable by a state on its gold tranche drawing. The Fund, however, will pay interest of one and a half per cent on a country's super gold tranche position, and will charge interest rising from one to five per cent on a state drawing the credit tranches.

During the later 1940s and the 1950s the mechanism of the General Account worked very effectively, but by the early 1960s it had become clear that there was a need for additional international liquidity, and so it was decided in 1964 that the General Account should be supplemented by a Special Drawing Account.

The units in which the new Account deals are Special Drawing Rights (SDRs) which were simply 'created' in four issues – at the beginning of 1970, 1971, 1972 and 1973 – and allocated to those states joining the Account in proportion to their quota. The SDRs have no backing (except the members' obligation to provide currency against them at the IMF's request) but until the end of 1974 their value was defined in terms of monetary gold. Because monetary gold is linked to the dollar (except in the dollar devaluations), and other trading currencies now float up and down against the dollar, SDRs have undergone an effective depreciation against the stronger currencies, and their real purchasing power is, of course, being continually eaten away by the inflation which affects all currencies.

All SDRs are kept in the IMF, and when a state wishes to use part of its allocation, the Fund will designate a second country which will accept some of the first state's SDRs, and provide in exchange some convertible currency which the first state can use to pay for its imports. The IMF will pay the country providing the foreign exchange an interest rate of one and a half per cent on its 'extra' holding of SDRs. So if an oil state were to provide, say, $100 million of convertible currency earning ten per cent in its reserves, and were to receive in exchange an equivalent sum of another state's SDRs, it would suffer a net loss of interest of eight and a half per cent.

In the form in which the scheme was introduced, a country was only obliged to accept SDRs to an amount equal to three times its SDR allocation, but the Americans in the early 1970s were pressing for an expansion of the system, involving the SDR becoming the world's major reserve asset. It was this thought that frightened the Arab oil producers. Although the loss of interest on a maximum sum of three times what would have been their very small SDR allocations would not have been serious, the prospect of a day coming when they would (indirectly) be selling most of their oil for SDRs was extremely unattractive. The Arabs rightly decided that the SDR scheme was designed for the needs of industrial countries with 'normal' reserves, and not for oil states with 'pension fund' reserves: and consequently Kuwait, Saudi Arabia, Qatar, Abu Dhabi (or, strictly speaking, the United Arab Emirates) and Libya declined to participate in the Account. (Other states which did not participate were Lebanon, Singapore, Portugal and Ethiopia. Significantly, the oil producers which were not building up big reserves when the Account was introduced did participate.)

* * *

Bearing in mind the purpose of the Arab oil states' reserves and the way in which the necessity of earning maximum interest affects their investment policy, it is now possible to examine in detail the composition of each of the big surplus countries' reserves as they stood in the middle of 1974.

KUWAIT

As a result of the sudden surge in revenues which accompanied the fifty-fifty profit split and the shut-down of Iranian production at the beginning of the 1950s, Kuwait began to generate a significant surplus long before any of the other Middle Eastern oil producers. To manage its reserves, in 1952 the government opened a dollar portfolio of equities and convertibles with the First National City Bank in New York, and at the same time it set up the Kuwait Investment Board (KIB), composed of five English financiers headed by Claude Loombe, who was than in charge of the Middle East department in the Bank of England. The Secretary of the Board was Mr H. T. Kemp, the ruler's representative in Petroleum Affairs, who ran the Kuwait Agency, which was the pre-independence equivalent of the present Kuwait Embassy in London.

The KIB continued to invest the largest block of the Kuwait reserve until 1964, when it was replaced by the Kuwait Investment Office, the London arm of the Ministry of Finance and Oil. Three years before this the KIB's work of advising Kuwait on the broad outlines of its investment strategy had been taken over by an international advisory committee, composed of Eugene Black, the President of the World Bank, Hermann Abs, the Chairman of the Deutsche Bank, Lord Piercy, who had followed Claude Loombe as Chairman of the KIB, Samuel Schweizer, the Chairman of the Swiss Bank Corporation, and Marcus Wallenberg, the Chairman of the Enskelda Bank.

Two of the lasting principles of government investment evolved by the committee were that Kuwait should support the pound sterling, and that it should not switch money between portfolios to profit from parity changes or differences in interest rates. This second principle is also part of the investment philosophy of all the other Arabian oil producers – although interest rate and parity factors are obviously taken into account in decisions on which portfolios should receive the largest amounts of the surplus in each revenue cheque. The only minor departures from the normal management of government funds have come at the time of Arab-

Israeli wars, when some producers have felt obliged to make a gesture against United States policy by avoiding the use of their normal American banks in certain current transactions, or by liquidating part of their longer-term dollar investments to make current payments which would normally have come out of the funds invested in short-term deposits. An example of this procedure was Kuwait's decision in the autumn of 1967 to make the first of its subsidy payments to Egypt and Jordan out of one of its dollar portfolios, rather than out of the sterling current account held by the Kuwait Investment Office (KIO).

The international committee of advisers presided over a considerable diversification of the Kuwait reserve – including the opening of two portfolios (one equities and convertibles and the other property) with Chase Manhattan in 1964, and the first direct purchases of overseas property by the Finance Ministry – but since 1969 the committee has not held any formal meetings. Kuwaiti investment policy is now in the hands of the Prime Minister, Shaikh Jaber al Ahmed, the Minister of Finance and Oil, Abdel-Rahman Atiqi, and the Director of Investment, Khaled Abu Saud – though these men periodically ask the advice of former committee members, and of such prominent Kuwaiti figures as Hamza Abbas Hussein, the Deputy Governor of the Central Bank, Ahmed Duaji, the Director General of the Planning Board, and Abdlatif al Hamad of the Kuwait Fund.

During 1974 Kuwaiti oil revenue cheques, paid quarterly, took the states' total holdings of gold, foreign currencies and investments from about $3 billion at the beginning of January, to rather over $5 billion at the end of March, and a bit under $8 billion at the end of June. These figures, and most of the figures in the following paragraphs, are unofficial.

Of the $8 billion certain investments, including property and assets denominated in Kuwait dinars, would not usually be defined as reserves by the IMF, while the Kuwait government itself would normally exclude from its definition all investments held by the Central Bank, liquid assets such as cash and short-term deposits held by the Kuwait Investment Office, and, on some occasions, the Kuwait dinar assets. In fact the government's definition of its reserves varies – to the confusion of outsiders it often refers to all its investments in bonds, equities and convertibles under the heading of 'equities', but in general 'The Reserve' can be taken to mean: foreign currency holdings of equities and convertibles, and various other long-term investments managed by the KIO (about $2 billion at the end of June 1974), bonds ($0.5 billion), and property ($0.4 billion). In mid-1974 these investments of some $3 billion were earning a very satisfactory return of eleven per cent, which works out at an annual rate of income of $330 million.

The items which compose both 'The Reserve' and the balance of the Kuwait government's total assets can be discussed under six headings, as follows:

(1) Central Bank Assets: At the end of June 1974 the Kuwait Central Bank held $959 million, which was composed of gold, cash and foreign government securities backing the currency issue, and automatic interest-free drawing facilities in respect of the state's gold tranche and super gold tranche position in the IMF.

(2) Cash: Most of the oil cheque received for the second quarter of 1974 was allocated to the government's budget. Because it receives no internal tax revenues, the Finance Ministry draws on its oil income to finance not only capital and current foreign-exchange expenditure, but also domestic expenditure in dinars. Between the time of payment and its remittance to Kuwait this money is kept on short-term deposit in sterling by the Kuwait Investment Office in the City of London. When money from matured bonds and long-term deposits awaiting reinvestment was included, the amount held short-term by the KIO at the end of June 1974 was just under $2 billion.

(3) Equities and Convertibles: The largest single block of 'The Reserve' is held by the KIO, which is run by Shaikh Fahad al Mohammed al Sabah, with a team of Kuwaiti, English and Scottish investment managers, operating in accordance with general guidelines laid down by Abdel-Rahman Atiqi and Khaled Abu Saud in the Finance Ministry. The KIO portfolio is composed mainly of British equity shares and convertibles, but it also contains a certain amount of long-term sterling and euro-dollar deposits, and sterling debentures and gilt-edged stock.

Apart from a few investments such as the shareholding in the Intra Investment Company, which are held direct by the Finance Ministry, the rest of Kuwait's equities and convertibles are in two dollar portfolios managed by the First National City Bank and Chase Manhattan, two international portfolios run by the Swiss Bank Corporation and the Union Bank of Switzerland, a French franc portfolio managed by Crédit Lyonnais and three deutsche mark portfolios run by the Deutsche Bank, the Commerzbank and the Dresdner Bank. It was the Dresdner Bank in November 1974 which managed Kuwait's purchase from the Quandt family of a large shareholding in Daimler-Benz, thought to be up to fifteen per cent of the company's capital, worth about one billion deutsche marks. In early 1974 the Finance Ministry decided to diversify its assets further by opening a yen portfolio – though by the autumn no decision had yet been taken on which Japanese bank should be asked to manage it.

In general, the companies which have attracted most Kuwaiti buying are those which the government feels will help its own programme of industrial development – such as chemical companies. The sort of relationship envisaged as the Kuwaiti shareholding increases would be one in which the foreign company will provide technical and management expertise, and Kuwait will provide finance and a guaranteed supply of raw materials – which for a chemical concern would involve various petroleum products and natural gas. These ideas are very much the same as those which prompted Iran to buy twenty-five per cent of the Krupp steel subsidiary – though in Kuwait's case there is the additional major consideration of buying a real asset which will retain its value for twenty or thirty years.

It was mainly in the larger British industrial companies in the autumn of 1974 that Kuwait was building up stakes approaching ten per cent – at which level it would have been obliged to declare its holding. With the London stock market at an extremely low ebb, the acquisition of significant shareholdings was unavoidable. At the beginning of September the thirty companies in *The Financial Times* Ordinary Share Index (which includes such names as Distillers, ICI and Courtaulds) could have been bought for only $11 billion, while British Leyland could have been acquired for less than a third of the price paid for the shareholding in Daimler-Benz.

Fearful that substantial purchases of important companies' stock might provoke an unfavourable public reaction, in the summer of 1974 Kuwait sought and received an endorsement of its policy from the British government. If they felt that the investment would be advantageous, the Kuwaitis were then prepared to buy fifty per cent or more of a major industrial company – though their official policy was not to intervene in the management, unless this would have been clearly in the company's own interests. At this time Kuwait was not exercising its voting rights in any British company, and it did not take up the two seats to which it was entitled on the board of Daimler-Benz.

(4) Bonds: In mid-1974 Kuwait's holdings of bonds were worth some $500 million, about fifteen per cent of the reserve. Most of the bonds were issued by governments or government agencies, and

they were bought on the primary market – principally from the Kuwait Investment Company, the Kuwait Foreign Trading Contracting and Investment Company, and such banks as Crédit Lyonnais, Société Générale, Morgan Guaranty and Algemene Bank Nederland. These institutions act as custodians for the bonds, holding them until they mature, but they are not portfolio managers. Decisions on which issues the government should subscribe to, and the amount of bonds to be bought, are made exclusively by the Finance Ministry.

(5) Property: During 1974 there was a big expansion in the Kuwait government's holdings of overseas property. Although the Finance Ministry had begun buying property in the early 1960s – partly through the Chase Manhattan portfolio established in 1964, and partly through direct investments in such assets as long leases on Kuwaiti embassies – it had previously kept its total investment fairly small. This policy ran contrary to much of the advice given by members of the international advisory committee – but the Ministry's reasoning was that although it could buy management for individual properties, the work of supervising a major property-buying operation would impose too great a strain on its manpower resources.

About one-third of the government's foreign property in mid-1974 was in the portfolio run by Chase Manhattan. Most of the investments in this portfolio were situated on the east coast of the United States, and in order to expand and diversify its American holdings, in September the Finance Ministry was in the process of setting up a second portfolio to be managed by the Bank of America, whose operations are centred in California. These arrangements were being made through the Kuwait Real Estate Bank, a new Kuwaiti public company. The initial amount to be allocated to the second portfolio was $50 million – compared with about $150 million with Chase Manhattan at this time.

All the rest of the property in the Kuwait reserve has been bought direct by the Finance Ministry. In September 1974 there was a further $150 million-odd invested in United States' property purchased from various American real estate companies. In Britain Kuwait government holdings totalled about $100 million and the Ministry was in the process of negotiating a big purchase in Liverpool, a £107 million ($250 million) takeover of the St Martins Property Corporation, which owns such buildings in the City of London as Winchester House and a block at St Martin's-le-Grand and Gresham Street, and, on the south bank of the Thames, a long lease on Tintagel House, which among other Metropolitan Police offices contains the headquarters of the Serious Crimes Squad. Although the negotiations for this takeover were handled by the Kuwait Investment Office, it was not intended that the property company should become part of the KIO's portfolio. (It is interesting that the St Martins deal marked the beginnings of a major change in the attitude of the British financial community towards Arab investment. The *Sunday Telegraph* commented that the depressed property business began to see the Arabs 'not as an enemy stealing cheap assets from under its nose, but as the most powerful ally it could acquire'.)

The Finance Ministry calculated in 1974 that it was getting a yield of about five per cent on its British property, but no capital appreciation – while the blocks of US property were yielding about eight per cent and appreciating at ten per cent a year. Given the very long period over which Kuwait intends to hold its assets, the temporarily poor appreciation in Britain did not unduly worry the Ministry – but the lower yield, which was felt to be a more permanent feature, meant that, despite the St Martins takeover, the main emphasis in Kuwaiti policy was on expanding operations in America.

In Europe the most important asset held in 1974 was the share in the land on the Champs Elysées – which Kuwait, together with the governments of Qatar and Lebanon, had bought from the Intra Investment Company – but in September that year negotiations were under way for the purchase of two big buildings in Paris (one of which, the Tour Manhattan, the Kuwaitis agreed to buy in February 1975) and a further property in Switzerland. In the Arab world at the same time, the Finance Ministry was investing through the Kuwait Hotels Company in the construction of a hotel in Morocco, and through the Kuwait Airways Corporation in a Beirut Sheraton to be built in the Coral Beach area.

(6) Kuwait Dinar Assets: The Finance Ministry's investments in its own currency in the third quarter of 1974 totalled KD 540 million, about $1,800 million. This figure was composed of: government shareholdings in Kuwaiti public companies – KD 50 million ($165 million); low-interest loans to Kuwaiti companies – KD 120 million ($400 million); the paid up capital of four government establishments – the Kuwait Airways Corporation, the Central Bank, the Savings and Credit Bank,* and the Kuwait Fund for Arab Economic

*The Savings and Credit Bank is a small government institution established in 1965 to extend low-interest loans to Kuwaiti industrial projects and housing. In practice, almost all of its loans have gone to finance the building of personal accommodation by low-income Kuwaitis.

Development – KD 160 million ($530 million); loans to other Arab countries, including over KD 100 million of outstanding low-interest or interest-free special reserve loans made between 1961 and 1965 – KD 140 million ($470 million); and subscriptions to international organizations – the IMF, the World Bank and the Arab Fund, for instance – plus dinar bonds bought from KIC and KFTCIC – KD 70 million ($235 million). This last item did not include commitments to the IMF's new oil facility or special loans to the World Bank (both discussed in the next chapter) which in September 1974 had not yet been disbursed.

The KD 100 million odd of outstanding special reserve loans in the domestic currency account have been more or less written off as grants by the Finance Ministry; and on a number of occasions the amount of new income being channelled into government assets has been considerably reduced by outright gifts. These have included a total of $1,000 million voted for Egypt and Syria by the National Assembly during and after the Fourth War of October 1974 (though in September 1974 only part of this money had actually been paid over); $33 million voted to subsidize Syria's defence bill in June 1973; $83 million paid to Egypt, Syria, Jordan and Iraq in July 1967 to offset war losses; and the annual subsidy of $185 million to Egypt and Jordan agreed at the Arab summit conference in Khartoum in August 1967. It was also decided at this conference that Saudi Arabia should pay $170 million and Libya $100 million a year, making a total of $455 million, which was divided into $320 million for Egypt and $135 million for Jordan. The Kuwaiti payments to Jordan have been suspended on several occasions as a result of King Hussein's policy towards the Palestinians – but, when Kuwait has felt able to resume its aid, Jordan has received back-payments to cover the amounts outstanding.

SAUDI ARABIA

In 1958 Anwar Ali, a Pakistani official with the IMF, was invited to move to Jeddah to take the job of running the central bank, the Saudi Arabian Monetary Agency (SAMA). At that time the riyal had just been devalued by forty per cent, the government owed $400 million to international creditors, and Prince Faisal, who had issued the invitation to Anwar Ali, had been called in as Minister of Finance to restore the nation's fortunes. Over a period of two years Prince Faisal and Anwar Ali succeeded in their task, and from 1960 onwards SAMA began to build up a monetary reserve, which now seems destined to become the biggest block of capital under one institution's ownership that the world has ever known.

For ten years or so the reserve grew very slowly, staying in the $600–700 million range from 1965 to 1970, and apart from the payments made under the Khartoum Agreement, the Saudis were not able to extend the same enormous inter-Arab loans and gifts that the Kuwaitis could afford. Only recently has it become possible for the Saudis to be more generous. In 1973 they set aside a billion dollars to pay Arab costs in the Fourth War.

The Saudi reserve is managed from a distance by SAMA and its foreign advisers, who in 1973 were two bankers seconded from Morgan Guaranty and one from Union Bank of Switzerland. Traditionally, the eighty per cent of Aramco revenues paid in dollars were split exactly fifty-fifty and credited to SAMA accounts with Morgan Guaranty and Chase Manhattan in New York; and were then transferred to branches of the same banks in London to be invested in accordance with SAMA instructions. The remainder of the revenues, in sterling, were again split fifty-fifty and placed with the Midland Bank and Chase Manhattan in London. These sterling payments ceased in December 1974, causing some panic on the exchange markets.

The Monetary Agency's investment policy has been extremely conservative. For twelve years after a surplus began to accumulate the reserve was held almost entirely in dollars (with a very small amount of sterling and even fewer deutsche marks) and was invested in government or government guaranteed bonds and in deposits with just nine banks – Morgan Guaranty, Chase Manhattan, First National City, Bank of America, Bankers Trust, Midland, Lloyds, National Westminster and the Algemene Bank Nederland.

But in 1972 two major policy decisions were taken by the Council of Ministers. First it was decided that with the surplus piling up at $90 million a month, the approved list of banks should be expanded, and SAMA chose twenty-five more institutions by a method not unlike drawing names out of a hat. Although this list is semi-secret there are a number of unofficial outside 'advisers' who are prepared to take the credit for having drawn it up, or for having drawn up a very similar list. The explanation for the many claimants to author-ship lies in the habit the Saudis (and other Arab governments) have of asking the same advice, in secret, of a number of different visitors whom they have grown to know and trust. Because these visitors often tend to give the same advice, it is generally difficult to establish on whose instigation a new policy may be based. But in the case of the approved list there is no doubt that the banks were finally picked by SAMA itself.

Secondly, in response to years of advice from foreign bankers associated with SAMA, and a loss of $150 million in the Smithsonian parity realignment, SAMA was authorized to diversify the reserve into other currencies. At this time however dollars were earning a good rate of interest, and nothing was done to implement the Council of Ministers' decision until SAMA lost a further $250/300 million, in the second devaluation of February 1973. Then diversifi-cation started within a week. Using new income (rather than liquidating existing dollar assets) the Saudis began buying a much larger amount of sterling, and deutsche marks, French francs, guilders and yen – until the reserve reached its mid-1974 proportions of about seventy-five per cent dollars and twenty-five per cent other currencies.

As of the middle of 1974 the bulk of the reserve, about eighty-five per cent, was still in the form of certificates of deposit or fixed de-posits, mostly with a duration of three to five years. All of this money was with banks on the approved list, which contained, in America: Morgan Guaranty, Chase Manhattan, First National City, Bank of America, Bankers Trust, Manufacturers Hanover, Continental Illinois and First National Bank of Boston; in Canada: Bank of Nova Scotia, Canadian Imperial and Toronto Dominion; in Japan: Mitsubishi Bank and Bank of Tokyo; in Britain: Midland, Lloyds, National Westminster, Chartered and Barclays (which had very little money, because there had been some doubt in SAMA about whether or not Barclays was on the Arab blacklist); in France: Banque de Paris et des Pays Bas, Banque Nationale de Paris, Crédit Commerciale, Banque Française du Commerce Extérieur and Crédit Lyonnais; in Germany: Deutsche Bank, Dresdner Bank and Com-

merzbank; in Belgium: Société Générale de Banque; in the Netherlands: Algemene Bank Nederland; in Italy: Credito Italiano and
Banca Commerciale Italiano; in Spain: Banco Centrale; and in
Switzerland: Union Bank and the Swiss Bank Corporation. At various
times the Saudi government has done a small amount of business
(unconnected with the reserve) with other banks – including the
British Bank of the Middle East, and Kleinwort Benson, which has
been retained as an adviser on a very small government pension fund
scheme.

The approved list should not be thought of as an official document
circulated among all the banks which have been included in it. It
was drawn up simply as instructions for SAMA staff, and many of
the banks concerned have no idea of its existence. For eighteen
months after the list was expanded by far the largest deposits remained with Morgan Guaranty, Chase Manhattan, First National
City and Algemene Bank Nederland, while several banks on the list
received no money at all. In this category were the two Swiss banks
– the Swiss Bank Corporation (which was included with the original
nine before the 1972 extension) and Union Bank – both of which
were offered funds, but felt unable to meet the Saudis' request for a
higher interest rate to offset the withholding tax. The Swiss banks
only began to receive SAMA deposits during the Fourth War in
October 1973, when the Saudis, wishing if possible to avoid investing
money with American institutions, placed with them several hundred
million dollars of new reserves and recently matured time deposits.
This money was in the form of ordinary dollar deposits, not fiduciary
deposits.

Apart from a very small amount of gold (which, together with a
different block of bonds and deposits, is earmarked each week for
backing the Saudi currency) the rest of the reserve in mid-1974 was
invested in various fixed interest securities. Most of these were bonds,
which under SAMA regulations may only be bought if they are
issued or guaranteed by governments of proven financial standing;
or official institutions – such as the World Bank; or agencies or
instrumentalities of governments – like the European Investment
Bank (which the EEC governments set up to finance state projects)
and Eurofima (a finance company for rolling stock on European
railways). All these bonds are bought on the primary market – the
secondary market is simply too small for the sums SMA likes to deal
in – and are kept until maturity. As a slight diversification, in
November 1972, SAMA made its first purchase of British government gilt-edged stock, and after December 1973 it entered the

o

market on a really large scale. It seems that it must have been largely responsible for the ten per cent rise in the value of UK government securities between the beginning of April and early June 1974.

In the months since the October 1973 oil price rise it has become obvious that further changes are needed in the deployment of the Saudi reserve. From $3,570 million at the end of October, reserves including cash grew to $3,860 million in January, $5,510 million in April, $7,090 million in June, and $9,480 million at the end of August – and with this rate of increase, in the autumn of 1974 SAMA was already running into several very fundamental difficulties.

It was becoming impossible for SAMA to continue diversifying out of the dollar, because the European currencies and the yen were not available in large enough quantities, and there were signs of a shortage of 'acceptable' government bonds. But most serious was that some of the banks which had traditionally taken the greatest part of SAMA money were turning away new deposits by offering very unattractive interest rates. Apart from their desire not to become over-dependent on a single client, and to avoid creating difficulties in their capital structures, the banks' problem was that they were unable to find borrowers. The last of these considerations applied not so much to the Saudi long-term deposits as to the huge amounts of money (including Kuwait's $2 billion cash account) being held by all the OPEC states at call or seven days' notice prior to being remitted for current expenditure or allocated to aid and long-term investments, and to the short-term deposits of Libya and those 'non-surplus' countries, like Iran, which were likely to be able to spend their reserves within a few years, and did not regard their assets as a 'pension fund'.

It is not SAMA's custom to make announcements about its reserves, but in 1974 there were signs that a change in direction was being contemplated. This was clearly not going to take the form of a further expansion of the approved list. Throughout the summer there was a spectacular stampede of foreign bankers to Jeddah – which at one point reached such proportions that Anwar Ali is said to have resorted to interviewing the visitors in groups – but the most that any of the bankers gained was a promise that SAMA would bear their names in mind, and would consider using their services in future.

In the second half of the year substantial quantities of money were being assigned to loans for developing countries and to various oil surplus recycling funds, and in 1975 a large block of capital will presumably go into the Islamic Bank and Saudi Arabia's own proposed development bank. At the same time the Saudis were planning to set up an overseas investment corporation, with offices in London, New York and Zurich, which would channel money into such assets as equities and property. The implementation of this scheme was inevitably delayed by the change in the governorship of SAMA – which after the death of Anwar Ali on 5 November was taken over by Abdel-Aziz Quaraishi.

For the longer term it is thought that Saudi Arabia, together with Kuwait and the other producers with a large chronic surplus, will invest a major part of its funds in big government-to-government loans – such as the $1,000 million semi-official borrowing from SAMA announced by the Bank of Tokyo in September 1974, or Iran's commitments of $1,200 million to Britain and $1,000 to France. At some stage these direct loans may involve the issue of indexed bonds or other new securities, like the $3,500 million issue of special non-marketable US government bills being bought by SAMA during the autumn of 1974. As a supplement to these arrangements it has been suggested, both in the Middle East and in the West, that the producer and consumer governments might also combine to form one or more huge consortium banks, which would invest in anything from certificates of deposit to new industrial enterprises.

ABU DHABI

At the beginning of 1967, a few months after Shaikh Zaid had replaced his elder brother Shaikh Shakbut as ruler, the Abu Dhabi reserve stood at $25 million – which was broken down into $16 million of deposits and other paper investments, $7 million of loans to other governments, and $2 million of real assets – namely a stock of rice and weighing machines for resale. This very modest sum (which gives the lie to the common belief that Shaikh Shakbut was a miser who piled up a vast hoard of gold and paper notes) grew to $43 million by the end of 1967; but in the next two years Abu Dhabi spent more money than it received, and by the end of 1967 the reserve had been reduced to zero.

The present reserves, therefore, have been accumulated since 1970. By the end of 1972 they had reached $230 million – of which $140 million was invested and $90 million was in short-term deposits; and by the end of 1974 they were $1,900 million. This figure was made up of $1,350 million invested long term, $400 million in cash, and $150 million allocated to the World Bank and the IMF. It did not include loans to Arab governments and contributions to the capital of development banks – like the Abu Dhabi Fund – and other international institutions.

The relatively small size of the Abu Dhabi reserve can be attributed to Shaikh Zaid's extreme generosity (which involved the allocation of several hundreds of millions of dollars towards the cost of the Fourth War), the demands of the United Arab Emirates' budget, and the cost of participation in Abu Dhabi's oil concessionnaires – which because of the relative newness of operations was proportionately much higher than in the other Gulf states. Had it not been for the large price increases of October and December, by the end of 1973 Abu Dhabi's reserves would have shrunk again to $140 million – even without the unexpected cost of the Fourth War. And as it was the extra revenues came too late for the state to avoid borrowing $180 million on the London market in October that year.

Responsibility for the reserve is in the hands of the Abu Dhabi Investment Board, which was set up in 1967, and is composed of Sir John Hogg of Williams Glyn (as Chairman); Longstreet Hinton of Morgan Guaranty; John Tyndall of Bankers Trust; Jean de Sailly of Banque Indochine; Nadim Pachachi, the OPEC Secretary General from 1970 to 1972 and Abu Dhabi's petroleum adviser; Mohammed al Mullah, a member of one of the big Dubian merchant families; Ahmed Soweidi, the federal Foreign Minister; Mohammed Habroush, the Abu Dhabi Minister of Finance; and John Butter, the Abu Dhabi Director of Finance. In 1972 John Morrell of Robert Fleming also became a member.

The Board meets once every three or four months to decide on investment strategy – including the division of funds between different portfolios and currencies, the type of securities to be bought, and the amount of money to be kept on deposit in sterling. The Ministry of Finance then orders transfers from the Abu Dhabi government's account with the National Westminster Bank in London (which receives the oil revenue cheques) to the Investment Board account at the Bank of England, and to the two portfolio managers (the Union Bank of Switzerland and the Crown Agents) which are not represented on the Board.

At the end of 1974 the $1,350 million of long-term investments in the Abu Dhabi reserve was divided into eight blocks. Five of these blocks, accounting for some $650 million, came under the control of the Investment Board, which supervised one property portfolio and four portfolios of mixed composition – which may at times be a hundred per cent equities, but in 1974 contained a very large amount of fixed interest stocks and convertibles. These mixed portfolios were managed by Banque Indochine in Europe, Morgan Guaranty in North America, and Robert Fleming in Britain and Japan (Fleming began the Japanese portfolio in March 1972, and took over the sterling portfolio from Bankers Trust in 1973). The property portfolio was managed by Joseph Tyndall – acting in a personal capacity rather than as a representative of Bankers Trust – and at the end of 1974 its biggest single asset saw a forty-four per cent stake, worth £36 million ($84 million), in the Commercial Union building in the City of London.

Two more blocks of the reserve, worth about $550 million, were in bond portfolios (opened in 1971 after two years in which Abu Dhabi's equities had performed rather badly) and were managed by the Crown Agents and Union Bank of Switzerland. The remaining block, worth some $150 million and coming under the Finance Ministry control, was in the form of dirham loans to governments or government authorities in France, Ireland, Austria, Finland, Spain and South Korea.

QATAR

When Shaikh Khalifa assumed power in February 1972 the Qatar reserve stood at $280 million, and by mid-1974 it was thought to have reached some $700/800 million – excluding short-term deposits, capital participation in local companies and contributions to development funds and other international institutions.

Considering that Qatar has a very much smaller income than Abu Dhabi, and that there has been a big increase in development spending under the new regime, the state's reserve has grown very fast. Apart from the rise in oil prices, much of this growth can be attributed to the dramatic cuts that the new ruler has made in his own salary and in the stipends of the al Thani family. Unlike Shaikh Zaid, Shaikh Khalifa has further refrained from making large international gifts. With Qatar's oil resources limited, and production nearing its ceiling, he is known to be more anxious than the rulers of the other major producers for his country's reserves to be expanded.

Qatar's reserves are managed in much the same style as those of Abu Dhabi. The overall direction is in the hands of the Qatar Investment Board – composed of Lord James Criehton-Stuart of Coutts; the Minister of Finance, Shaikh Abdel-Aziz bin Khalifa; the Director of the Ruler's Office; and the Director of Finance, Abdel-Khader Khadi.

One or two assets, such as the land on the Champs Elysées, are held direct by the Finance Ministry, but most of Qatar's investments in mid-1974 were divided into five blocks. The exact proportion of the reserve in each block varied from month to month, but in rough order of size the portfolios were: a very successful sterling fund managed by Baring Brothers; a rather less profitable dollar fund managed by Hambros; a deutsche mark fund, which was built up from 1969 to 1973 with new income which would otherwise have gone into the dollar portfolio; and two small Swiss franc funds.

LIBYA

The Libyan reserve grew faster in the years before the oil revenue explosion than any of the reserves in the Arabian Peninsula. From a modest $96 million at the end of 1962 it reached $1,590 million at the end of 1970, and has since increased to $2,350 million in October 1973, $2,550 million in April 1974, and $3,350 million at the end of July.

The payment of revenues is managed by a rather complex system under which the oil companies transfer dollars to Tripoli, buy dinars from the Central Bank, and then instruct the commercial banks holding their accounts in Libya to pay the dinars to the National Oil Corporation, which is duly taxed by the Treasury. In this respect Libya is unique, being the only Arab oil-producing state where it is possible to speak quite literally of the surplus revenues doing the famous 'U-turn'.

The Libyan reserve is under the direct management of the Central Bank (in the same way that the Saudi reserve is controlled directly by SAMA); and whatever Libya's reputation in Arab politics, the Bank has earned a name for being extremely pragmatic and commercially minded in its investment policies.

From Tripoli the Central Bank transfers the surplus to the London or New York offices of Bankers Trust (who act as the Libyans' main correspondents) and from here in early 1974 most of the money (about seventy-five per cent) was placed in short term deposits, of an average six months' duration, with some twenty or thirty of the biggest banks in America, Britain and Europe. The rest of the reserve was divided between long-term deposits, government securities, bonds and a minor amount of equities. The bulk of these holdings remained in dollars but there were also small amounts of all the other main trading currencies. Up to late 1971 a much larger proportion of the reserve was in sterling; but when Libya left the sterling area in December that year, it pulled much of its money out of the pound, and since then very little has returned. (Libya's departure from the sterling area, and its simultaneous nationalisation of British Petroleum's assets on its territory, were intended as protest gestures over what the government regarded as British connivance in the Iranian invasion of the Tumbs Islands, formerly held by Ras al Khaimah, which preceded Britain's official withdrawal from the Gulf by some twenty-four hours.)

At various times a great deal of money, drawn either from the reserves or from current revenues, has been given away – partly through subsidies to the front-line Arab states, such as the $100 million a year which Libya agreed to pay to Egypt and Jordan at the Khartoum Conference in 1967, and partly through miscellaneous gifts to non-Arab governments, and political organizations like the Palestinian guerrilla groups. Part of the government's surplus (which is not included in the official figures given above) has also been diverted into long-term regional lending through the Libyan Arab Foreign Bank, which the Central Bank established in 1971 for the purpose of carrying out foreign business which would normally fall outside the scope of central banking operations.

In most respects the Libyan Arab Foreign Bank resembles a government-owned commercial bank. Its capital has been subscribed entirely by the Central Bank, but it takes non-government deposits, and the bonds it underwrites are kept in its own balance sheet and are not placed in the official reserve. Apart from arranging for it to hold certain state investments, such as the participation in Union des Banques Arabes et Françaises and UBAF Limited, the government has used the Foreign Bank to establish development bank subsidiaries in Uganda and Mauritania. In these cases the capital of the subsidiaries and some of the deposits at their disposal have been provided by the Foreign Bank; but much of the money channelled to Uganda and Mauritania through these banks has come direct from the Libyan government, either as aid for specific projects, or in the form of politically motivated loans for the more general purpose of financing gaps in budgets or balance of payments deficits.

14

THE RECYCLING PROBLEM

One of the most striking conclusions to be drawn from the analysis of the oil states' monetary reserves is that in effect their surplus does a U-turn and comes straight back to be invested in the major industrial countries, and, on a smaller scale, in the developing world. In fact most of the money never leaves the consumer states at all. It is simply transferred from the accounts of the oil companies in London and New York to the accounts of the producers in the same centres – and is then spread among the other European states, Canada and Japan.

In this way those consumers with a current deficit – which in 1974 meant almost all the industrial countries bar Germany and Sweden – can 'borrow' from the producers in one month to pay for the next month's oil imports. So while their balance of trade may be in deficit, their balance of payments may be in equilibrium, or may even show a slight surplus. Britain, for instance, ran a trade deficit of $6,460 million during the first nine months of 1974, and yet its reserves increased by $590 million.

Given that the Arabs have to invest their surplus somewhere, and that only the supply of dollars and sterling and only the Western capital markets are big enough to accommodate such vast volumes of funds, this recycling process is inevitable. But the problem for the consumers is that the recycling may not necessarily take place in the most appropriate possible way.

The first problem is that the surplus might be channelled into the 'wrong' types of asset. The worst of these would be short-term deposits, which in addition to creating problems in the banks' capital structures, cannot be lent long-term to finance new productive investment, stimulating growth in the consumer economies. In effect short-term deposits are dead money.

Only slightly less serious, if it were to occur on a large scale, would be investment in existing property, which might set off a socially undesirable boom in values. This would be liable to stimulate consumption out of capital, and quite apart from the bad economics involved in the consumers borrowing for spending rather than for new investment, as Anthony Harris remarked in *The Financial Times*: 'the idea that the rich should live richly off the country's capital, while the rest suffer the inflation caused by higher oil prices is hardly acceptable politics.'

Depending on the mood of the market the same problems might apply with Arab purchases of equity shares – though here there is the alternative possibility that big Arab buying would regenerate the confidence of investors, and so enable companies to raise more money on the stock exchanges for the purpose of financing new plant and equipment.

In this case the consumer governments would prefer the Arabs to avoid buying into companies whose operations have a bearing on national security. It was these considerations that caused the US government to block plans for Arab and Iranian investment in Lockheed and Grumman, and which drew from Dr Arthur Burns, the Chairman of the Federal Reserve Board, the comment that while he would welcome the investment of petro-dollars in 'companies like Quaker Oats', foreign capital in 'some of our strategic enterprises would concern me'.

Ideally the consumer countries would like the OPEC governments to finance their own new ventures in the West, and to lend direct to established companies through buying new bonds and shares or entering joint ventures. Both of these routes would involve creating productive capacity to match the build-up of debt. To some extent the consumer governments will be able to stimulate this type of investment themselves, partly by encouraging their own companies to resort to international markets when raising new capital, and partly by making fiscal adjustments, involving investment grants and tax concessions, which will make certain investments more attractive than others.

The second, and much more serious, problem is that the OPEC surpluses might not be recycled in accordance with each consumer country's balance of payments needs. In early 1974 it was thought that this would probably mean that little money went into the developing countries, and that there would be an unbalanced distribution even among the industrialized nations. The United States having the richest economy and the biggest stock market, and Britain, having a similarly large capital market, might receive more than their share of Arab investment – and in Britain's case this would become more pronounced as the North Sea came on stream in the later 1970s, and its trade deficit disappeared. In short, the consumer countries with the strongest economies, the least dependence on imported oil, the smallest trade deficits, and the least need to import capital would be liable to get the biggest slice of Arab funds.

In this case the poorer countries would be tempted to dismantle all barriers to inflows of capital, and raise interest rates in an attempt to attract Arab funds for themselves. Inevitably the stronger countries would then be forced to do the same, and as a result there would be a free-for-all scramble for Arab capital, a competitive bidding up of interest rates, and enormous movements of hot money. In the end the weakest countries would simply be unable to compete – having a low credit rating and little chance of ever being able to pay back a large amount of high-interest borrowing.

This situation, quite apart from being undesirable in itself, would have even more disastrous consequences. Finding themselves with a continuing balance of payments deficit, and seeing their reserves dropping towards zero, the weaker countries (both industrial and underdeveloped) would wish to correct the position by boosting their exports and reducing their imports, and so improving their balance of trade with the stronger countries. This they might try to do through such devices as devaluations, multiple exchange rates, tariffs, import quotas and the introduction of demand restraint policies at home. Presumably the rich nations would again retaliate.

Thus a free-for-all in the capital account sector would be liable to lead to beggar-my-neighbour policies in the current-account sector – and there would follow a period of contracting world trade, depression, unemployment and political instability – everything in fact that the world's economic establishment has been trying to avoid since the monetary system was reconstructed at the end of the Second World War.

Although the thought of a depression was very much in the minds of governments in 1974, on the rather limited evidence available it seems that in practice during the first eight months of the year the private capital markets coped reasonable well with the recycling of petro-dollars. According to some very rough estimates released by the US Treasury, the OPEC surplus of some $25–28 billion in the January-August period was divided between: the United States $7 billion, Britain $3 billion, Europe $2 billion, the Third World $3 billion, and the euro-markets (through which the money could be channelled to countries which were not getting sufficient OPEC investment direct) $10–13 billion. The developing countries' receipts contained a certain amount of money channelled through multi-national government-backed institutions such as the World Bank, but even so the figure of $3 billion was felt to be encouraging. At the beginning of the year it had been widely predicted that without massive assistance from the industrial world, the developing countries' reserves would be exhausted within six months.

Later in the year, on still hazier evidence, it appeared that there had been a further improvement in the situation. The OPEC states were themselves spending more than had originally been anticipated, and they were investing an even greater amount of their petro-dollars in the developing countries, which spent this money as they received it. The Western industrial powers, therefore, were able to finance more of their oil deficit through exports, which meant that the recycling problem was not only being somewhat reduced in scale, but was being supplemented sooner than expected by a problem of a real transfer of wealth (discussed in the Conclusion of this book).

This implied that the governments' thinking, which throughout the year had put the main emphasis on means of improving the recycling mechanism and supplementing the work of the private capital markets, was lagging slightly behind events – though, given that some of the European countries receiving less direct OPEC investment, such as Italy, were beginning to reach the limit of their credit-worthiness on the euro-dollar market, it did not mean that the officially sponsored recycling schemes set up in 1974, and the larger schemes planned for 1975, were in any way being made redundant.

Right from the time of the oil price rises in October and December 1973 it had been apparent that the existing official arrangements, which had been used to help recycle the surpluses of the more prosperous industrial countries during the 1960s, could not easily be adapted to recycle petro-dollars. They were not geared to handling surpluses and deficits of anything like the size either of those which were anticipated or those which materialized in 1974; they worked on the basis of nominal interest rates which did not suit nations which regarded their reserves as long-term investment capital rather than as current assets, and in some cases they were provided and used by industrial countries only.

For all practical purposes the OPEC states had been outside the established network of official monetary arrangements. The main surplus oil producers had not participated in the IMF's Special Drawing Account; they did not have international trading currencies; their IMF quotas were miniscule in proportion to their reserves, and on only one occasion had any of their currency been used by the Fund (this being a drawing of under two million Kuwait dinars in 1971); they had not been involved in any of the inter-central bank swap facilities, which were used to recycle flows of private hot money between industrial states; and they were not party to the General Arrangements to Borrow (GAB), which had been instituted to meet rather bigger deficits than could be provided for by normal IMF drawing, but were confined to the use of the Group of Ten.*

Given the lack of scope for adopting these arrangements, in early 1974 the industrial countries set about constructing new mechanisms. At an IMF meeting in Rome in the middle of January the Fund's Managing Director, Dr Johannes Witteveen, proposed the establishment of a new borrowing facility, which would be funded with petrodollars provided either by the producers or by consumers which were receiving more than their share of OPEC capital, and would charge a near-commercial interest rate of seven per cent. During the summer Witteveen went on a fund-raising tour of the oil states, but by the autumn contributions totalled only some $3.5 billion – subscribed by most of the richer OPEC countries (including Saudi Arabia which promised the largest contribution, of $1.2 billion) and Canada, Norway and the Netherlands. In anticipation of this somewhat disappointing result, when the IMF met again in Washington in June the industrial states, whose weaker members had originally been thought of as the main borrowers, decided that the facility should be reserved primarily for the use of developing countries.

At the same meeting it was agreed that Special Drawing Rights (SDRs) should in future be valued not in gold terms (which involved them floating up and down with the dollar) but in terms of a group of major trading currencies. Although this meant that SDRs still depreciated with inflation, it at least showed that changes were possible, and held out the possibility of SDRs eventually becoming a 'constant money asset' based on a basket of commodities. Combined

*The General Arrangements to Borrow were established in 1961, when the world's ten richest industrial nations agreed that in the event of one of their number needing to make a massive drawing, they would lend extra funds to the IMF. The nations concerned were the United States, Britain, Germany, France, Italy, Japan, the Netherlands, Canada, Belgium and Sweden. These countries became known as the Group of Ten – and although they were later joined by a non-IMF member, Switzerland, and by Luxembourg, Denmark and Ireland, the name has not changed. When the GAB was originally constituted it was envisaged that it would be used by the United States, but in practice, during the 1960s it was used only by Britain and France.

with the Fund's earlier decision to raise SDR interest rates, the redefining of the SDR prompted several of the biggest surplus states to make known their intention of joining the Account at the time of the next allocation.

While the IMF was putting together its oil facility and working on various other monetary reforms (one of which was the new valuation of the SDR) two other official recycling schemes were being promoted – one by the United Nations, which raised only $150 million, and was eventually forced to 'redefine' its role so that it could treat bilateral aid to the Third World as a contribution to its own account; and the other by the World Bank, which by the autumn had raised some $2 billion in special OPEC government loans, and was hoping to double this total in 1975.*

As with the IMF facility the producers' response to these schemes was felt to be disappointing, and although towards the end of the year it began to be realized that considerable sums of petro-dollars had been lent to the developing countries on a bilateral basis, and that recycling among the industrial nations had been more even than expected, the problems of countries like Italy showed that the situation might become a lot worse in 1975 and 1976. The feeling among the Western governments, therefore, was that it would be wise to have some much bigger recycling arrangements standing by.

In early October at the IMF meeting in Washington (the Fund's third in 1974) the German Finance Minister, Herr Hans Apel, proposed the formation of two linked institutions grouping both the producer and the industrial consumer states: an international bank which would lend money long-term to governments and companies, and an investment fund which would buy industrial holdings for the OPEC governments and finance new enterprises, particularly in those countries which were less able to attract oil producer investment direct. At the same time the British Chancellor of the Exchequer, Mr Denis Healey, outlined a plan for a Mark II IMF facility, carrying a higher interest rate than its predecessor, which would be geared mainly to the needs of the industrial world, and would handle about $30 billion a year when fully operational. It

*These loans were entirely separate from the normal World Bank bond issues. By the end of March 1974 there had been ten issues in Arab countries – six in Kuwait dinars for $441 million, two in Libyan dinars for $135 million, one in Lebanese pounds for $31 million, and one $15 million private placement made with SAMA in 1968. In all the amount raised was $622 million, and the amount outstanding $606 million. This represented six per cent of total World Bank bonds outstanding.

was Mr Healey's idea, rather than the German scheme (which was a somewhat longer-term suggestion, and may be revived in future) which attracted most attention among the other finance ministers; and accordingly the IMF staff was instructed to draw up a study of the Mark II facility which could be discussed in more detail at the Fund's next meeting in January 1975.

One month after the idea for the new IMF facility had been launched, the US Secretary of State, Dr Henry Kissinger, proposed in Chicago that the major oil consumers should agree on a 'common loan and guarantee facility', not dissimilar to the General Arrangements to Borrow, which would recycle up to $25 billion a year. This scheme did not involve the creation of any special fund. It was suggested that the operation could be carried out by government-to-government loans among the consumer states, or by the surplus consumer countries agreeing to underwrite borrowings on the private market by the deficit countries – managed either directly, or indirectly through an institution such as the Bank of International Settlements in Basle.

As such the Kissinger plan was a 'secondary' or 'last ditch' recycling operation, which would come into play only if the private capital markets and the new IMF facility failed to achieve even recycling in the first instance through borrowing from the producers.

*   *   *

Towards the end of 1974 the emphasis in government thinking, reflected in the Healey and Kissinger plans, was on removing the recycling problems of the West – where an economic collapse in one country would be most likely to prove infectious and to drag the world down into a major depression. But during this time it was the developing countries which were stirring the consciences of people in the industrial states, and which were attracting most public sympathy.

The attitude of the developing countries themselves towards the oil price rises was somewhat ambivalent. As Anthony Harris observed in *The Financial Times*, on one hand they saw the increases as intolerable (in the sense that they could not afford them) and on the other as welcome (in the sense that they were one in the eye for the industrial nations) – and so they were in the strange position of congratulating OPEC on its achievement, while asking for easier terms for themselves. In view of the oil producers' 'thinking' on the need for a redressing of the balance between rich and poor countries, and on their own role in bringing about this change, OPEC's reaction to this situation in the long term will be of considerable significance.

Compared with the big industrial consumers the oil import bills faced by the developing countries were fairly small, rising from roughly $4 billion in 1973 to $12–15 billion in 1974. But it appeared that these countries would be able to meet only $8 billion of the new bill through their export earnings and drawing on their reserves, IMF credit tranches and SDR allocations – and, if they were to avoid bankruptcy, a gap of some $4–7 billion had to be financed directly or indirectly by OPEC.

The burden was not spread evenly across all the developing states. At one extreme there were several countries – Syria, Egypt, Tunisia, Gabon, Malaysia, Argentina, Mexico, Colombia, Brazil, Bolivia, Peru and Trinidad – which were (or soon would be) self-sufficient in oil, and in some cases were already small exporters. These states actually profited from the oil price rise.

Then there were two further groups of countries in which the extra cost of oil was partially offset by higher receipts from exports, or an increased flow of gifts and aid. These included Brazil, Malaysia, Zaire, Zambia and Morocco, which were already benefiting from a big rise in the price of the commodities they produced; and the deficit Arab states and the Moslem nations of Africa and Asia – with whom the Arab oil exporters, Iran and Nigeria, felt a special solidarity.

At the other extreme there were a number of non-Moslem countries with big populations, ambitious development plans and small commodity exports, for whom the oil price rise was potentially disastrous. These were Kenya, Tanzania, Malagasy, Ethiopia, Sri Lanka, Thailand, the Philippines, Taiwan, South Korea and Uruguay.

During the early months of 1974 the direct response of the oil producers as a group to the problems of these hardest hit countries (and of the mass of countries which fell between the two extremes) seemed to be just as disappointing as their international response through the IMF, the United Nations and the World Bank. A large number of new development banks (mentioned in Chapter 10) were announced during the first half of the year, but these were intended to give project aid, in relatively small amounts, and were not likely to become operational until mid-1975 at the earliest. At a time when their reserves were in danger of exhaustion, the developing countries were very much more interested in receiving long-term current credits, in larger amounts and within a matter of a few weeks or months.

What producer-sponsored current recycling schemes were discussed during 1974 turned out to be unsuccessful. An OPEC fund, which would have been administered by the Secretariat in Vienna, received strong backing from Iran and Venezuela, but little from the other members, and after being steadily watered down for nine months, it was finally abandoned at the Organization's conference in September. An Iranian recycling bank, which would have grouped representatives from OPEC, the industrial world and the developing nations, suffered a similar fate. Both these failures can be attributed to the Arab's reluctance to enter any arrangements which might be dominated by non-Arab states – and in Saudi Arabia's case there was the further consideration that while there remained a possibility of persuading the other OPEC members to cancel part of the December 1973 price rise, the establishment of long-term recycling mechanisms would not only have been premature, but would also have been likely to endorse the increase.

The only scheme which got as far as having any capital allocated to it was a small $200 million Arab-African Oil Assistance Fund set up in January under the auspices of the Arab League and the Organization of African Unity. And throughout the summer this was beset by difficulties concerning the method of payment, and inter-African disputes over which countries should have priority in drawing on the money.

Later in the year there appeared to be a big improvement in the oil producers' aid programme. There was a steadily growing gap between the calculated OPEC surpluses, and the placements which could be traced to markets under the surveillance of the industrial world's financial institutions. This tended to confirm the earlier belief of the US Treasury that although the producers had channelled only some $3 billion to the developing countries during the January-August period, an additional $12 billion had been promised for disbursement (directly or indirectly) later that year or in 1975. Overall it seemed that the flow of aid and investment from the OPEC members to the developing countries in 1974 was going to amount to some $10–12 billion – which was slightly more than enough to cover the anticipated additional oil deficit, and represented a rather larger share of the total aid burden than that borne by the traditional donors of the industrial world.

The bulk of the producers' assistance was channelled on a direct bilateral basis – though at the end of the World Food Conference in

Rome in November the OPEC states announced that they were going to set up an agricultural aid collecting agency, which would raise money from their members and hand it over to established international bodies like the World Bank and the UN's Food and Agriculture Organization. At the same time there was a growing suspicion (based only on circumstantial evidence) that the OPEC members as a group might have been financing producer cartels in other raw materials.

This upsurge in OPEC assistance suggests that the small initial flow stemmed mainly from the members' desire to take stock of the situation in which their vast new wealth had placed them, before coming to major decisions on their aid and investment policies.

But even towards the end of 1974 there still appeared to be a certain OPEC hesitancy with regard to Third World recycling. This showed up in the members' continuing reluctance to initiate any permanent and formal assistance programmes for current credits (on either a bilateral or a group basis), which meant that in the long term there was liable to be no close relationship between the amount of aid each developing country needed and the amount it received.

The type of assistance the producers would have liked to be giving in larger quantities would have involved creating new real (inflation-proof) assets – industrial or agricultural – where the OPEC government would provide, say, forty-nine per cent of the equity, and would give a loan to cover that part of the Third World partner's capital needed to finance the foreign-exchange cost of the project. An example of this sort of scheme in operation was provided in December by Saudi Arabia's involvement in a deal between British Leyland and Egypt for the construction of a Land Rover assembly plant in one of the new Egyptian free zones. Under this agreement British Leyland was to put in a nominal amount of capital in return for a management contract and a disproportionately larger dividend, while the bulk of the $130 million capital was to come from the Saudi Arabian government.

The problem for the producers in promoting a large number of these deals on a strictly bilateral basis (involving only themselves, the developing country and an independent foreign contractor) is that they require more manpower than they have at their disposal – and so the OPEC countries would like the ideas for individual schemes to be put to them by big Western corporations or by the recipient countries with the backing of industrial governments or companies. There would be advantages for all parties in arrangements of this type. For the Europeans, Americans and Japanese they

P

would provide an opportunity for earning more petro-dollars through exports, which would reduce the scale of the uneven recycling problem; and for the developing countries they would not only provide new industries, but would also have an indirect effect in promoting a guaranteed and regular flow of current credits from the producers. Once the OPEC states see that at least part of their surplus being recycled to the Third World is inflation-proof, they have let it be known that they will feel a lot easier about making a formal 'sacrifice' of a large part of their reserves through institutional-izing a programme of current credits at concessionary rates of interest.

*   *   *

Taking the year as a whole co-operation between the producers and the consumers on recycling in 1974 was not as close as it might have been. Right from the start the problem got mixed up with the oil price issue.

The Americans took the line that the prices announced in December 1973 were 'impossible'. They were reluctant to take monetary measures to adapt to the situation on the grounds that these would 'legitimize' the new levels; and they were particularly concerned about proposals such as those put forward by the Germans in September, which would give the producers risk-free investment opportunities, and might actively encourage OPEC to keep the price high. Indeed, Washington's opposition to formal recycling schemes may have been based on the assumption that the greater the uneven-ness of capital flows, the stronger would be the support of the other consumers for its campaign for a price reduction.

So for the first nine months of the year the Americans resolutely maintained that the private money markets could look after recycling on their own. These views were only modified in November, when Dr Kissinger announced his plan for the consumers' 'common loan and guarantee' facility – and even this was essentially a 'last ditch' scheme, to be put into operation only if the price campaign had failed (as already seemed to be the case), and the money markets and all other recycling mechanisms had proved inadequate.

The OPEC countries meanwhile were afraid of being exploited by the proposed recycling schemes. In the past they believed that the West had seen them as a limitless source of cheap energy, disregarding their interest in conserving their resources; and in 1974 they began to fear that the West might begin to regard them as a limitless source of cheap credit, disregarding their interest in their own development. They were somewhat suspicious of institutions like the IMF, which they felt worked mainly to the benefit of the industrial powers; and they saw a double motive in Western appeals for them to increase their aid to the Third World – such as that made by Dr Kissinger at the World Food Conference in Rome. Apart from their belief that these appeals were designed to foster the illusion that they were being thoroughly selfish with their money, and so muster Third-World support for the American campaign to lower the oil price, they felt that the West was hoping to reduce the size of the ultimate transfer of wealth it would have to make by ensuring that as much as possible of the petro-dollar surplus was whittled away by inflation.

Accordingly the producers' response was normally to suggest that the West should share the aid burden with OPEC on the basis of gross national product and average per capita income. At Rome Algeria, Venezuela and Nigeria all took strong objection to Dr Kissinger using food as a means of political pressure, claiming that the Third World's problems stemmed not just from the oil price rises, but from a long established imbalance and unfairness in international trade manipulated by the financial centres of the industrial powers. Iran told the Conference bluntly that it had already committed nearly six per cent of its GNP to assistance over the 1974/1978 period, and that in 1973 the aid given by the industrial countries had amounted to no more than two-thirds of one per cent of their GNP.

In many respects the OPEC members' statements on recycling and Third World aid during 1974 added up to a diplomatic initiative of the same sort as that launched in 1973 in support of their thinking on 'oil for industry'. As with their earlier initiative they used a 'stick and carrot' procedure. In response to some extremely bellicose speeches by American leaders they gave equally tough replies, but at the same time they stressed their willingness to enter an 'objective dialogue' with the consuming countries.

To fulfil their 'thinking' on using their money to create a new world economic order, involving a sharing of Western wealth both by themselves and by other members of the Third World community, they wanted to be sure that their support was given only to an official recycling mechanism which would promote the industrialization of the developing countries, give OPEC members a bigger say in the running of institutions like the IMF, and take account of the pension fund character of their reserves – possibly through incorporating issues of indexed bonds (bearing a small real rate of interest), or channelling money into new or existing real assets in the industrial countries. The responsibility for making detailed proposals along these lines was placed on the industrial world, as it had been with the 'oil for industry' initiative.

Whether the Western countries felt that it was in their interests to respond to this initiative or ignore it depended on the whole complex equation of their assumptions on the level of future oil demand and domestic supply, and, consequently, on OPEC's bargaining power and ability to maintain high prices. In general the Europeans and Japanese favoured a response, while the Americans favoured rejection – and although higher interest rates were incorporated in the new SDRs and in the Mark II IMF facility, in 1974 no decisive move was made in either direction.

However the producers made it known that if the industrial countries' appraisal of the supply and demand situation eventually led them to drop the idea of confrontation, and if a response was made which was found to reflect OPEC ideas, they would be prepared to take part in a multi-national conference. According to the formula suggested by Saudi Arabia at the United Nations in February, the conference would be composed of representatives of OPEC, the industrial powers and the developing countries; its agenda would include not only aid and recycling, but also the acceleration of the producers' own industrial development (in general terms), and the price of oil.

Conclusion

THE TRANSFER PROBLEM

It remains finally to look in very simple and theoretical terms at what the higher cost of oil will mean to ordinary men and women in the industrialized countries of the West. This can most easily be understood if the analysis is begun by presenting two purely hypothetical cases, representing two extreme (and impossible) patterns of producer spending behaviour. The argument in both cases rests on the distinction between a 'financial transfer' which takes place when the producers receive paper currencies for their oil, and a 'real transfer' which represents the ultimate payment in goods and services diverted from domestic consumption in the oil importing states. In both cases it is assumed that in real terms the rise in oil prices in 1973 and 1974 was a once and for all phenomenon, and that in future the dollar price will do no more than keep pace with inflation.*

Case 1: The producers spend all their additional revenues: If it is assumed that following the oil price rise the producers are able to spend all of their extra revenues as fast as the money is paid to them, then the relatively painless financial transfer, represented by the payment of paper dollars by the industrial countries to the OPEC members, will be followed by an equivalent and more painful real transfer of goods and services. Both transfers will continue to be made as long as the producers continue to export oil.

A greater proportion of ordinary citizens' personal income will be going to pay for the higher cost of oil (both directly through pur-

---

* Part of the material in the following paragraphs has been drawn from an article in the *Sunday Times* of 3 February 1974. The article was headlined: 'How the West can pay the new Arab oil bill', and was written by Jan Tumlir, Director of Research of the GATT Secretariat, the body which administers the General Agreement for Tariffs and Trade.

chases of petrol and heating fuels, and indirectly through purchases of all goods and services affected by higher manufacturing, transport and running costs), while the additional income of the producers will be being used to import the goods and services which would have been bought (directly and indirectly) by ordinary citizens had they not been paying more for oil.

The expansion of gross national product in the consumer countries will not (in theory) be affected, because the demand formerly provided by Western citizens will be replaced by an equally large demand from the OPEC countries; but there will be a slowing down or cessation of the growth of real personal incomes, which will last for as long as it takes the oil producers to re-gear their development plans and to work up to their full spending capacity. After this period of stagnation, real income growth will resume as normal, and the fact that the real transfer is still being made will not be noticeable. But real personal incomes, in theory, will remain a few per cent below what they would have been had there been no oil price rise.

Case 2 : The producers invest all their additional revenues: Going now to the opposite extreme, and assuming that for some extraordinary reason the producers will be able to spend none of their extra revenues until such time as their oil wells run dry, then the financial transfer in respect of oil exports will continue on the same scale and for the same length of time as in Case 1, but the real transfer (or that part of it which results from the 1973 price rise) will not begin until the producers start to liquidate their assets.

In the period between the price rise and the end of oil exports the producers will be investing their extra revenues in the industrialized countries – either in paper assets, ranging from certificates of deposit to euro-bonds, or in real assets, like property and factories. At the same time the individual consumers will be finding that more of their personal incomes will be going to pay for oil (as in Case 1); but instead of reducing their purchases of other goods by an equivalent amount, they will be financing their extra expenditure by drawing directly or indirectly on the money invested by the producers. This they will do either through selling to the producers their bonds, shares and properties, and withdrawing their bank deposits (which will be replaced by petro-dollars); or, if the producers' investment policy turns out to favour building new assets, through spending the income which they would otherwise have saved. (In theory, if the producers invest in new assets, the consumers will also have the option of cutting their spending, continuing their saving, and in effect allowing the producers to build the 'extra' productive capacity which will provide the output for the eventual real transfer.)

In effect, the consumers will be amassing a burden of future debt, and when, twenty years hence, the producers start to liquidate their assets, the consumers will suffer a period of reduced real income growth, as part of the money which they would normally spend on buying goods and services is diverted into buying back the assets which they have earlier sold to the producers.

The picture will be complicated slightly if the producers receive a real rate of interest on their investments. This will represent an additional financial transfer – being made in increasing amounts during the period of oil exports, and in slowly diminishing amounts after oil exports have ceased – and it will mean that ultimately the real transfer made by the consumers will be bigger than it would be in Case 1.

*   *   *

If it is now assumed that each of the two hypothetical cases is half correct, there will emerge a very simplified picture of what really will happen to the oil consumers following the price rise of 1973.

While the OPEC states are still producing oil the annual real transfer will be equivalent to, say, half the annual financial transfer, and the real transfer will continue to be made until such time as the producers' assets have been liquidated. Consequently the reduction of real income growth will, in theory, be split into two periods. Some Western countries may suffer much more in one period than they will in the other – depending on how much OPEC investment they have received, and how much of their larger oil bill they have been able to pay for by increasing their exports to OPEC states – but taking the industrial world as a whole, neither of the slow income growth periods should see as severe a reduction as would occur in Case 1 or Case 2 alone. If it happened that the producers got to the point of earning so much interest that they never needed to liquidate any of their assets, the consumers would continue to make equal real and financial transfers indefinitely, but they would not suffer a second period of reduced real personal income growth.

*   *   *

To some extent the consumers will be able to determine how much of their real transfer is made during the period of oil exports, and how much is deferred - but which policy it will be in their own best interests to adopt will depend on what assumptions are made on the nature of the producers' investments, and the future rate of inflation in the industrial countries. If it is assumed that the Arabs are going to be happy to keep their reserves in paper assets earning a money rate of interest, and if inflation is going to run at a rate of over twenty per cent, it will obviously be better for the consumers to delay paying their debts, because by the time the assets bought in 1974 are liquidated they will be practically worthless.

However these are perhaps rash assumptions – not so much because inflation will necessarily be brought under control, but because if the OPEC members (and particularly the Arabs) are going to produce the oil that the industrial countries require, they will insist on putting a large part of their reserves into investments of more permanent worth. They will buy real assets – holdings in industrial plant, land and buildings which will maintain their value in real terms; and they may persuade the consumer governments to sell them indexed bonds which would pay a small real rate of interest. In this case it would appear to make no difference to the consumers whether they defer paying their debt or not, because the expansion of their own gross national product will keep pace with the appreciation of the Arabs' investments, and although a delayed real transfer would be greater in absolute terms, in proportional terms it would not be any bigger than a transfer made in the 1970s.

But leaving aside all calculations on the transfer problem, there are two quite different considerations which would make it convenient for the consumers if the producers were to spend as much of their extra revenues as possible. These are the dangers of uneven capital recycling, and the possibility of petro-dollars going into the 'wrong' type of investment.

To bring about the desired increase in OPEC expenditure the consumers might co-operate with the members' wish to have their development accelerated through 'oil for industry' packages, and they might also encourage the producers to invest as much of their surplus as possible in new real industrial and agricultural assets in the Third World. From the producers' point of view the funds employed here would constitute part of their invested reserves, but for the industrial countries OPEC investment in the Third World would amount to the same thing as greater OPEC expenditure.

Part of the money available to be invested in the developing countries might be given as aid by development banks or recycling funds; but part of the money (coming from official and private sources) might be committed on a purely commercial basis by interested companies such as Gulf International, and the Kuwait Foreign Trading Contracting and Investment Company. So, if the West wants to promote the maximum flow of OPEC funds into the developing world, it will have to create conditions which will make this sort of commercial investment profitable.

This will mean accepting that in future the Third World's industrial capacity will have to be built up within the framework of a more open world economy, where the new factories of Africa, Asia and South America will be able to export part of their output to the affluent markets of the West. If this does not happen the new industries are likely to be less profitable, and the OPEC states (comparing the return on these assets with the return available on investments elsewhere) will reduce the amounts being pumped into the Third World, and will revert to a policy of investing more in the industrialized countries. If, on the other hand, a more liberal regime of international trade is allowed to evolve, the West may find that the redistribution of income caused by the producers investing in the developing countries will put the world's economy on an altogether sounder footing, and that the real income growth of all nations will accelerate faster than ever before.

*   *   *

At the end of 1974, when only a matter of months had elapsed since the massive oil price rises of October and December 1973, it was still unknown how much of their extra revenues the producers would eventually be able to spend on their own development, and how much they would invest in the Third World. It was therefore impossible to work out accurately how big a proportion of the financial transfers from the industrialized countries would be followed by an immediate real transfer, or to estimate how severe would be the reduction of real income growth in the Western economies.

In practice there will be any number of factors exaggerating or disguising this reduction. In most countries the measures being taken to combat inflation during 1974 were producing an additional decline in personal spending power, and in all countries the regearing of production for export rather than internal consumption will itself have a mild recessionary effect. Whatever forces may be working in the opposite direction (disguising the real transfer being made) the decline in real incomes will be big enough to be noticed by ordinary citizens. They will find themselves postponing their foreign holidays, and buying smaller cars and fewer household durables – cutting back in particular on the more expensive electrical goods, like washing machines.

As to the time span of the period of reduced income growth, this again will be unknown until it is seen how quickly the OPEC countries will be able to work up to a new level of spending. In 1974 it was assumed that this process would take about three years (or rather longer for the biggest surplus states), while it was thought that if the producers decided to recycle more of their revenues to the Third World **tha**n would be needed to offset the region's additional deficit, the developing countries would be able to attain a new level of spending almost immediately.

These estimates may turn out to underestimate the OPEC members' capacity for rapid change, but rather than try to give a more precise prediction of when normal income growth in the industrial world will be resumed, it may be best to sum up the situation in the bald statement of a *Financial Times* headline which appeared during the crisis of the winter of 1973:

'The Future Will be Subject to Delay'

Index